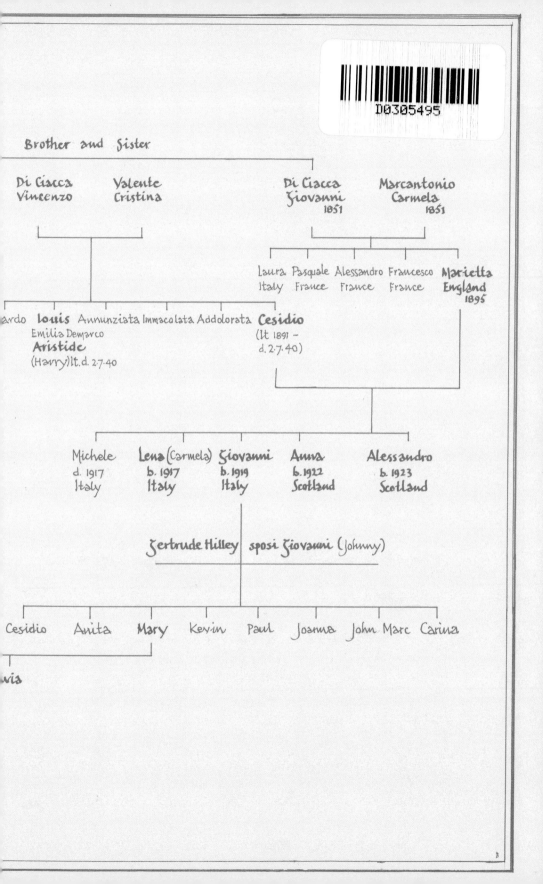

Brother and Sister

Di Ciacca Vincenzo — Valente Cristina

Di Ciacca Giovanni 1851 — Marcantonio Carmela 1851

Laura Italy | Pasquale France | Alessandro France | Francesco France | Marietta England 1895

...ardo | louis | Annunziata | Immacolata | Addolorata | Cesidio (It 1891 – d. 2.7.40)

Emilia Demarco
Aristide
(Harry) It. d. 2.7.40

Michele d. 1917 Italy | Lena (Carmela) b. 1917 Italy | Giovanni b. 1919 Italy | Anna b. 1922 Scotland | Alessandro b. 1923 Scotland

Gertrude Hilley   sposi Giovanni (Johnny)

Cesidio | Anita | Mary | Kevin | Paul | Joanna | John | Marc | Carina

...wis

Dear Olivia

An Italian Journey of Love and Courage

MARY CONTINI

CANONGATE

Edinburgh · New York · Melbourne

Dear Olivia

Mary Costin

This edition first published in 2006 by
Canongate Books Ltd, 14 High Street,
Edinburgh EH1 1TE

1

British Library Cataloguing-in-Publication Data
A catalogue record for this book is available on
request from the British Library

Typeset in Sabon by
Palimpsest Book Production Limited, Grangemouth, Stirlingshire
Printed and bound in Italy by Legoprint S.p.a.

1 84195 844 1 (10-digit ISBN)
978 1 84195 844 6 (13-digit ISBN)

www.canongate.co.uk

This book is dedicated to
Vittorio Fortunato Crolla (1915–2005)
who lived his journey
in love, courage and hope

Dear Olivia

I have often told you about your ancestors who were poor shepherds from the south of Italy. They emigrated in the early 1900s and chose to make Edinburgh their new home.

Your father's grandfather, Alfonso Crolla, opened a shop in 1934, when his own daughter, Olivia, was eleven years old, the age you are now.

Over the years I have heard many stories about their experiences, what kind of life they left behind, why they were forced to leave Italy and how they chose to settle and raise their families in Scotland.

I have heard stories of courage, faith and love; of prejudice, disaster and loss. Moving and inspiring stories of hardship and determination, success and failure, tears and laughter. Now that so many of your ancestors have gone, I have recorded the stories in the words that they told me, to pass them on to you. So that you can get to know them and understand the sacrifices they made for your future, I have pieced together their experiences and have tried to imagine what it must have felt like and how life would have been.

We have inherited an ethos of work, a glorious heritage of family and food, and most important a faith in God. This is the final piece of the jigsaw, the untold part of your heritage that illuminates the past.

Their example will help you to be strong and honest and to realise that you must never judge a person by religion, race or appearance. You must resist prejudice and always search for the truth.

I hope their story will inspire you to be optimistic and hard-working, and to reach for great things. I want you to learn to love and respect them and be as proud of them as I am.

All my love
Mummy

1

It was pandemonium. The pig was running crazily around the piazza. Women were running behind it grabbing at its tail. Children screamed with delight as it snorted and barged at their aunts. The women, skirts tucked into their aprons, squealed as the pig charged towards them. Ass, cockerel, hens and goats all joined in the cacophony of excitement.

Maria stood decisively, rope in hand, and assessed the situation. Without a hint of doubt she yelled at the pig.

'Aaaiiihh!'

She threw down a handful of acorns. The pig stopped in its tracks. Then it immediately buried its face greedily in the nuts. In a split second Maria stepped forward and with a flick of her wrist expertly slung the rope over its head. Before the pig could react, Maria tightened the noose and pulled the rope round its snout; the pig was caught.

The children cheered.

'Zia Maria is the winner! Zia Maria is the winner!'

'*Brava! Brava! Bellezza* Zia Maria. *Bellezza!*'

Zia Maria had guaranteed their feast tonight.

It was the middle of January, just after dawn, seven days since the full moon. It was a good omen. On the mountains all around, the snow glistened gloriously in the early light. The rays bounced off the ice creating the illusion that the whole valley was on fire. It was bitterly cold. The last stars waning in the sky promised a clear day: a perfect day for slaughtering the pig.

A huge, blackened, cast-iron pot of boiling water was securely balanced on the fire. The women had prepared the bonfire before dawn so that the water would be ready on time. Maria told the older

3

children to drag the protesting pig to the post and tether it. She tied its snout and mouth shut, muffling its squeals. The pig was not happy. Powerful and fat, black and glossy, at well over a hundred kilos, it preferred not to be manhandled by a woman and a bunch of kids.

Maria was apprehensive. The men had not yet come down from La Meta. They were needed to despatch the beast. Tadon Michele could manage but he was not as strong as his son Alfonso. She moved away from the scuffle and went to look for Alfonso.

She was a handsome woman: tall, with strong, broad shoulders, a round face with dark, sultry eyes, and glowing, olive skin. Her thick, dark hair was parted at the side and bundled high on her head, covered with a red kerchief. She was heavy with her first child. At twenty-four she was resilient and resolute. Maria would make a good mother.

The rope round the pig's snout broke. The children scattered, terrified. The pig squealed, its shriek echoing around the mountains, ricocheting from hillside to hillside. In this the pig made a mistake. Its clamour alerted its executioners.

Maria Crolla c. 1913

4

Alfonso Crolla c. 1913

The three brothers, Alfonso, Pietro and Emidio, were already on their way down from the mountain when they heard it. They had spent the last few nights on the meadow half-way up the mountain, *il Prato di Mezzo*. They laughed and called back to the pig in fun, projecting their voices to make them echo down to Fontitune.

'*Non ti preoccupare, porchetta bella! Andiamo!*'

The men quickened their pace. Taking the lead, Alfonso strode out quickly and came round the bend ahead of his brothers.

Alfonso was tall and striking: a fine-looking man. He walked straight-backed, his head held proudly with an air of authority. His jet black hair flopped over his broad forehead. He had a long, aquiline nose with a glorious dark moustache that decorated his soft, sweet lips. His deep, smoky brown eyes appeared to brim with emotion as if tears would well up and spill over at any moment.

He was dressed in shepherd's garb, with a roomy brown smock belted in at the waist over loose-fitting trousers. His legs were covered with white linen rags, tied criss-cross with leather straps

5

that secured goat-skin soles under his feet. The footwear, *le ciocie*, was the same as that worn by shepherds in these parts for centuries. A thick sheepskin was draped over his back, with his bagpipes, *zampogne*, slung over his shoulder.

As she caught sight of him, Maria's heart leapt. She was always disconcerted by her reaction to him. She sighed. Wasn't he handsome? Of the three brothers, Alfonso was the strongest, the leader.

'*Che bello*,' she thought to herself. She raised her arm to attract his attention. 'Alfons'! Alfons'! *Vieni ca! Vieni ca!* Come on! The pig's ready! *Forza! Forza!* Hurry up!' she called up the hill, her hand cupped at the side of her mouth.

Catching sight of her, Alfonso smiled. He loved her very much, this new bride of his. He walked towards her. As she called again, he slowed down and halted. He was in no hurry. He wanted her to come to him. He wanted to watch her move towards him. He just wanted her.

Maria reached him, exasperated that he had stopped. Her brows furrowed. 'Alfons! What are you playing at? The pig's ready. Can you not hear its screams?'

Alfonso wasn't thinking about the pig. He put his hand over her mouth to quieten her and drew her towards him. She pulled her head back, embarrassed at his actions. Anyone might see. Ignoring her protests he kissed her strong and hard with all the passion of a young man insanely besotted. Unable to resist, she relented and kissed him back.

Immediately he felt her submit, he pushed her away playfully. He just needed to know that she wanted him, that she felt the same fire in her soul that he did. He needed to know that he was in charge. She could wait. He put his arm round her waist and turned towards the village.

Further back up the road his brothers had seen everything. They had lingered behind laughingly, allowing the lovers some privacy.

Alfonso called again, his voice echoing around the hillsides. The small crowd struggling with the pig heard him and cheered and clapped.

Finalmente! Finally Alfonso was coming. Now the fun would start.

As soon as he arrived, Alfonso set to work. He threw off his sheepskin and pipes and grabbed the large cloth his sister-in-law handed him. He tied it securely round his body, high under his arms. The women threw some fresh straw under the pig and positioned a flat skillet at the ready. Taking the knife from his father, Alfonso stood astride the pig, held it down with his legs, pulled its head back with the rope and, without giving another thought, slit its throat.

The pig shrieked in protestation. Its blood spurted out over the cloth and splashed down over Alfonso's sandals. The pig writhed in fury, but soon, weakened by the shock and loss of blood, it fell to the ground. The climax was over.

Emidio secured the pig's hind legs. '*Tira! Tira!* Pull!' Together with the other men, he pulled it up by the rope and tied it to the post. They dragged the skillet under the twitching carcass as the blood dripped from its throat.

Tadon Michele nodded his head. '*Bravo*, Alfonso, *figlio mio*. Not a bad job.'

The children had stood transfixed, terrified to watch, too fascinated not to. Now they erupted with glee, shouting and dancing around, they cheered and clapped, relieved that the job was done. As the sun warmed them from the early morning chill they sang with delight.

Once all the blood had drained from the victim the women worked quickly and scrubbed the pig clean. With buckets of boiling water and stiff brushes they scoured at the bristles on its black back, removing as many of its coarse prickly hairs as possible. A red-hot poker from the fire was used to singe off stray hairs in its snout and ears.

Two trestle tables had been set up in the piazza. The pig was laid out on its back. With his sharpest knife Tadon Michele slit its belly from the cut in its throat right down its flank to reveal its steaming, pungent innards.

'*Mannàggia! Che puzza!*' The children held their noses and ran away screaming, chased by their mothers attempting to clip them across their ears for swearing.

Emidio pulled the innards out into a ready pot: intestines, bowels, bladder, heart, lungs and spleen. Maria and Filomena, her mother-in-law, took them to the well and rinsed them again and again in a tub with constant changes of freezing cold water. When the intestines were clean they rubbed them with some vinegar then dusted them with ground corn flour, hung on a string like washing to dry out.

Maria sorted everything else out, cleaned it and laid it on the table: the kidneys, liver and heart, the spleen, lungs, stomach and bladder. Every part would be used. Nothing would be wasted.

Emidio hacked off the trotters and gave them to Filomena and his mother to scrub, the nails to be manicured clean. They would be stuffed with minced pork flavoured with ground pepper, cinnamon, cloves, nutmeg, mace, bay and thyme. The four trotters would be hung to cure for several weeks, making delicious *zampogne*. All the while, as everyone was working, the odd cuts of meat, fat and skin were chopped up roughly and ritually tossed into another huge wooden tub; this mixture would be made into sausages later in the afternoon.

By now the sun was high in the sky. It was still intensely cold but no one noticed; they were all working attentively, finishing their jobs. It would soon be time for *pranzo*.

The pots and skillets were balanced on a brazier on the smouldering embers of the fire and the cooking began. In no time the air was filled with the appetising aroma of grilling and crackling, of spices and herbs. The noise and smells and bustle gave the piazza an air of festivities, a feeling of tradition.

The pig needed to be butchered. First the head and tail were severed and placed in a bucket of brine to soak before being cooked the next day. The carcass was turned over and, with an axe and hammer, Tadon Michele cut the animal in two.

He separated the cuts with the patience and precision of a surgeon. The front legs and haunches were set aside to make the prosciutto: deep-pink firm flesh covered with a thick white layer of fat. A room at the back of one of the houses had been prepared to dry the hams. The chimney had been blocked so that some of the smoke from the fire would linger, adding flavour to the prosciutto. The dry, cold mountain air circulating from the narrow slits in the stone wall created the perfect ambience for the hams to dry.

Over the next few weeks Pietro would frequently massage the pig's legs with salt as the hams slowly dried and cured. When they were ready he would wash them in warm water and mould them with his strong muscular hands to shape the *prosciutto* into its familiar form. To protect the top of the ham at the bone, he would seal off the flesh with a plug of suet mixed with salt, the *sugna*. Pietro followed the age-old rituals with passion.

Next, Tadon Michele cut the ribs, the shoulder and the fatty underbelly to make *pancetta* and bacon. All the extra fat was to be rendered down to make lard, rubbed with salt and herbs: exquisite cooking fat for the coming months.

Maria and Filomena carried the skillet with the solidified blood over to the fire. Maria watched as her mother-in-law mixed in herbs and spices and added the mixture to onions that had been cooking on the brazier. They were preparing Alfonso's favourite, *sanguinaccio*, the blood pudding.

Alfonso came over to keep an eye on the proceedings. 'Now, Maria, *cara*, you need to learn how to make this just like my mother.'

He put his arm round his mother and kissed her cheek lovingly. 'You teach her well, Mamma, otherwise there'll be trouble for you both.'

Just as Maria was going to answer him, without warning the canon boomed out across the valley. It was fired every day from the Castello in nearby Picinisco to call the field workers all over the valley to eat. Today the inhabitants of Fontitune would all eat together in the piazza. Already some scraps of pork were sizzling on sticks on the fire. The appetising smell mingled with those of the garlic frying, the fat rendering and the blood pudding cooking. The stench of the pig's guts and the odours of a farmyard were masked by the intoxicating aroma.

The children fought and squabbled over *i ciccioli,* the scraps of skin and crackling that were fried in flat skillets on the fire. They were flavoured with orange peel, garlic and chilli, and when they were chewed these crunchy morsels burst with flavour, deliciously filling the mouth with sweet, juicy pork, salt and garlic. This was an annual treat experienced only on the day they killed the pig. It was a taste and sensation so intense that in leaner times, when food was scarce, it returned to haunt them in dreams, waking them in the night, salivating, filling their nostrils with that imaginary, evocative smell.

The men were exhausted. They sat on the wall by the edge of the

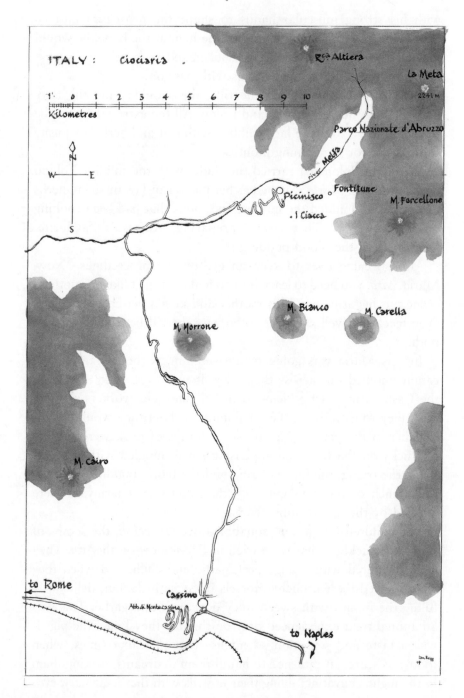

Map of the Fontitune/Picinisco area

piazza and shared a bottle of wine. They ate thick slabs of polenta that had been grilled on the fire, and the remaining sausages from last year. They ate hungrily, rubbing their mouths with the backs of their hands, tearing off pieces of tough, dark bread to soak up the juices on the tin plates. The children hovered round, certain of being offered the juiciest morsels from their fathers and uncles. The women ate as they worked, sharing the cooking, passing the prepared food round to the men and the children. Everyone ate well. Today there was plenty.

After eating their fill, the men gradually fell silent, one by one falling asleep against the stone wall, oblivious of the rough edges digging into their backs. The children settled down beside them, exhausted after such an eventful morning.

Maria looked over and laughed. Her husband looked very content.

'*Guarda*, Mamma,' she shared her amusement with Filomena.

Alfonso had fallen asleep with the bottle of wine in his hand, his white apron still tied under his armpits, smeared with grease, red stains of the pig's blood and black soot from the fire. His mouth had settled into a gentle smile.

'*Brava*, Maria. My son is happy.'

'So am I.'

After a rest, they all had to get back to work. Tadon Michele took charge.

'Come on boys, wake up. We've still got work to do!'

During the morning any scraps and odd pieces of pork had been chopped and tossed into a big wooden tub. They were mixed with dried fennel, coriander seeds, crushed *peperoncino,* ground black pepper and coarse sea salt. From time to time the women mixed it with their hands, adding red wine to encourage the pork and fat to absorb the flavour of the spices. After leaving it in the cold air it was eventually ready to be made into the spicy sausage, *salsiccie.*

Alfonso lifted the huge wooden tub onto the table. The dried intestines were cut and checked to see that there were no tears and blemishes.

The men set to work. Skilfully and easily they tied knots into the ends of the casings, then stuffed handfuls of the flavoured meat mixture, rhythmically caressing the *salsiccie* so that the meat was

11

packed in tightly, massaging them to expel any air, twisting the ends and tying them with string, weaving sausage after sausage, stringing ten or twelve at a time. Once each string was made, the younger boys who watched and learned took the *salsiccie* to the back smoky room and hung them up beside the prosciutto from the rafters to dry.

Pietro, Alfonso's older brother, had a passion for the seasoning in the sausage. All spring he collected herbs and spices from La Montana, dried them and mixed them ready for the day of the pig. His *salsiccie* were stuffed into one long casing, about a foot in length and bent over like a hook, dried hanging from a wooden pole. Over the years Pietro's *salsiccie* had built up a reputation for being the tastiest. They were chewy and moist, quite spicy, not too hot, with hints of flavour from fennel seed and cumin.

Sometimes he rendered down some fat and stored the sausages buried deep in the pure white lard. These were moist and juicy, creamy and mouth-watering.

As the men finished making the last sausages the women called to the children to help with the tidying up. Each child had a task, rewarded by the absence of a slap across the head. They worked as hard as the adults, scrubbing down the table, pulling water from the well, carrying the pots to the wash tub in the piazza and scrubbing them clean with cold water and a wooden brush. Finally the piazza was swept with a bundle of twigs made into a broom.

This pig was not the only one to meet its fate that day. Pigs and hogs had been slaughtered in villages all over the valley. From the valley below, the bells of the two churches in Picinisco started to ring out. The evening celebrations were about to begin.

2

Fontitune was a tiny hamlet of a dozen or so houses. They were strung along a dirt path leading to the summit of Monte La Meta, the highest mountain on the Abruzzo/Lazio border, north of Monte Cassino. The centuries-old houses were simple: two thick-walled stone rooms stacked one on top of the other. A narrow door allowed access; thin slits in the walls provided scant light and air. Each dwelling butted against the next, slightly higher than the previous, as they snaked their way single file up the side of the hill.

There was a small piazza edged by a low stone wall. A steep dirt-track, passable only on foot or by ass, led down to the village of Picinisco, about an hour's walk away. An ancient stone well provided plenty of clean, fresh water, each bucket-load pulled heavily up by a makeshift crank at the side.

The Crollas had lived in Fontitune for generations. Working as self-sufficient shepherds, their lives were exceedingly hard. In the winter, often cut off by snow for weeks on end, they survived with cunning and resilience. Bitterly cold nights gave way to bright clear days. With only wood for fuel, a fire in the single large grate in the ground-floor room of each house provided the only heat. At night the animals shared this room, their dirt and stench tolerated for the welcome warmth generated by their body heat. The families slept huddled together on rough corn sheaves piled on the earthen floor of the room above.

The stony earth with sparse topsoil produced meagre crops of vines, olives, tomatoes, corn and wheat. Some houses had side rooms, used to store their preserved foods to last through the winter. Tomatoes, cooked and bottled in the late summer, took pride of place beside flagons of olive oil. Staples of dried beans and chick peas were essential; sacks of dried corn and wheat stood ready to be ground into polenta and flour to make bread and pasta. Herbs and spices collected from the hills hung drying from the beams.

Fontitune c. 1890

Barrels of home-made wine were stacked high at the back, furthest from the entrance. Precious stores of salt and coffee were kept hidden in locked chests.

Shelves were planks of wood wedged between the walls. Hand-made pecorino was preserved in wicker baskets. Fresh goat's milk ricotta dripped its whey into a bucket below. The hams and sausages from the pig would be hung from the rafters, preserved to last until the following year.

While the men had been making the sausages and the children cleaning up, the women of the village had started to prepare *La Maialata*, the feast of the pig. Every part of the animal that could be, had been preserved and cured, salted and dried. The fresh pork that was left would be eaten in the next few days. Soon the forty days' fasting for Lent would begin, so they would all make the most of this opportunity.

By six o'clock it was almost dark. The women were nearly ready. The dishes were made to recipes and rituals handed down from mother to daughter. The ingredients never changed, the dishes

14

cooked with respect: *la noglia, l'jumacche Fellate di Sant'Antonio, i piedi di porco* – food that sounded like magic potions and tasted of nostalgia.

The women cooked together: mothers and daughters-in-law, sisters and cousins, all gossiping and laughing. They had all heard by now that Alfonso had kissed Maria then pushed her away, and the afternoon was spent deliciously analysing what he might be up to.

The men often spent large periods of time away from their families, either up on the pastures with the sheep or, in the winter, down on the plains at the coast, wintering their flocks away from the snows. This made the women fiercely independent and over-protective of their families, especially their sons. They endured the hardships and danger of survival in the mountains with great courage.

Recently and more ominously, the men had been absent because of war. Alfonso and his brothers had already completed two years of National Service, and in the previous year they had fought in the Italian war against Libya.

Tadon Michele and many of the older men also left the village to look for work away from the mountains. When they came back they talked of cities and trains and opportunity. When he was younger, Tadon Michele had walked from city to city ending up in Paris, London then Manchester and finally, Edinburgh. Playing his pipes and singing shepherds' songs he had slept rough in doorways and parks. He had saved every penny and had come back with more money than they had ever seen.

He told them that there were itinerant Abruzzesi everywhere. In any town or city you just had to ask a few questions and before long you'd find small groups of peasants selling chestnuts, sharpening knives, working on farms, anything that they did at home. He used to laugh when he told the women how much money the people in cities had and how easily they gave it away. For people like them, who had so little money and bartered their produce to survive, this was a complete mystery.

Thank God, every time Tadon Michele had gone, he had come back safely. Some of the men didn't come back. Some men got into trouble and ended up in prisons. Some men went further and took

15

huge ships and travelled to America, journeys that took weeks on the ocean. One of the boys from Picinisco, Angelo Conetta, had gone to America with his wife, one of the Di Ciacca girls. Her mother hadn't seen her daughter in ten years.

Tonight was not the time to worry about such things. The older children had started to lay out jugs of water and flagons of wine on the tables. The wood-fired bread oven at the side of the third house had been lit in the morning and the women placed the large dark crusty loaves they had baked on the table. A huge round *pastone*, pie with egg, ricotta, cured ham and sausage, had been baked slowly in the oven as it cooled. It was placed ceremoniously in the centre of the table.

A huge tin pan was full of bubbling golden corn polenta; young Carmella, Maria's niece, was stirring it constantly with a long wooden stick. Bitter winter greens collected from the side of the hill were fried with garlic, spicy *peperoncino* and thick green olive oil, pressed just weeks earlier.

The pork ribs were rubbed liberally with crushed fennel seeds, salt and olive oil and some of the fresh sausages were skewered on sticks. They were laid in the embers of the fire to grill slowly, the fat browning as the flesh near the bones stayed juicy, the appetising smells of spice and chilli filling the air. As fat melted it spat into the flames, creating mouth-watering aromas of sweet pork and rosemary, bay and wild thyme. Maria had slowly cooked some fine sliced onions with chopped garlic and *peperoncino* in warmed green olive oil. She stirred it with a wooden spoon so the onions melted down and didn't singe or burn. She had collected the pieces of pork that she needed, the tail and the ears, *la coda e le orecchie* Once they had seared in the heat she covered them with a thick red blanket of tomatoes that had been cooked and bottled in the late summer. She crumbled in some basil that had been hanging to dry and covered the pot with the lid balanced on the spoon. She cooked her *sugo* slowly and let it bubble and splutter till it reduced perfectly.

Alfonso came over and pulled her to him as she bent over the pot: 'Will it be good?'

She tilted her head to one side, and shrugged her shoulders. Alfonso always wanted to tease her. She was annoyed with him now. She was tired. She just wanted him to be sweet.

'*Certo!* Of course!' She snapped at him.

She loved him but they'd not had much time on their own. She was still getting to know him. She pushed him away. This just encouraged him and he laughed and kissed her on the lips. She blushed. She felt embarrassed in front of her mother-in-law and Tadon Michele, but as she stood up they clapped and laughed. The children, sensing the mood, shouted to anyone who would listen as they danced around the fire,

'*Zia Maria è innamorata di Alfonso! Bacio! Bacio!*'

This gave Alfonso every excuse to kiss her again, this time holding her so close she couldn't breathe. When he let her go she stumbled backwards and had to hang on to him to stop herself falling. Everyone let out a roar of approval and cheered. She blushed again and then burst out laughing.

Since Christmas hundreds of long reeds had been collected and tied together with vine branches and piled 50 feet high. These bundles, *fascie*, were put in place at the entrance and the exit of the hamlet, a traditional symbol of safety and defence of the community.

As soon as the sun set, the men lit the *fascie*, waiting till it blazed, burning wildly in the night breeze and illuminating the dark that had descended so quickly. As they looked out across the valley they saw bonfires being lit at all the other villages and hamlets. The valley looked breathtaking, as if the stars and angels had fallen from the sky and were hovering, protecting every group of houses.

The food was all ready, set on the table. As she had done every year, as her mother had done before her, Filomena brought a huge steaming bowl of pasta and beans, *sannie e fagioli*, held high above her head, in honour of Sant'Antonio Abate. In ancient, pagan times, borlotti beans, the *fagioli*, were the symbol of death. Religion was cooked up with superstition. The scraps of thick pasta were mixed with pancetta and soft, juicy beans swimming in rich tomato soup. Everyone cheered as it was brought to the table, and they all made the sign of the cross.

'*In nome del Padre, del Figlio e dello Spirito Santo . . .*'

Then the feasting began.

After they had eaten the pasta, Maria's *sugo* with pasta, ribs, *costelette*, and the sausages, and they had all drunk plenty of wine,

17

the older boys took up their pipes and began to sing the ancient laments they had learned from their grandfathers. They took little notice of the underlying meaning that warned of the continual battle of good and evil, of life and death. After a while they made their way with the single men down to Picinisco to play their pipes in the streets throughout the night. They would frighten the inhabitants with stories of the struggle Sant'Antonio had with the Devil and with luck earn some money or food as a reward.

The children sat beside the old grandmothers while they terrified them with the ancient stories of Sant'Antonio Abate. He was the patron saint of the pig, although, to be frank, he had abandoned the poor pig today. They told the children how the holy man fought with the Devil and resisted his remorseless temptations. Tomorrow was his feast day and they would all go down to Picinisco for the annual blessing of the animals.

As if to make sure the Devil knew not to come near them, the women all began to chant the evening prayer of thanksgiving. The children knelt and joined in the rosary:

'*Santa Maria, Madre di Dio, prega per noi, peccatori, adesso e nell'ora della nostra morte, Amen.*'

Every time the children had to chant the final words 'at the hour of our death' they shivered with terror in the dark. The fire of the *fascie* blazed mysteriously and the animals wailed out as if in sympathy for the unfortunate pig.

Once the women had tidied and the *fascie* had been made safe, they all drifted off to bed. Husband, wife, children and paternal grandparents slept together on the mats in the top room of their houses.

Alfonso, accustomed to sleeping in the open, pulled Maria aside and laid her down on a makeshift bed beside the smouldering embers of the reeds. He wrapped his dark cloak and sheepskin round them and they lay awake under the stars, whispering. The moonlight cast strange shadows. The air was freezing cold; their breath lingered like mist. The mountains loomed darkly all around them.

'Maria, this will be our last *Maialata* in Fontitune. This will be the last winter you will have to struggle. Our baby, *se Dio vuole*, will not have to endure this life.'

Maria shivered. She was afraid of Alfonso's plans for them to leave Fontitune as soon as the baby was born and go to live in Scotland. He had been away so many times before: for National Service, then to the war. That was bad enough. She had been terrified he would be killed. Terrified he would lose a limb or come back blinded like the boy in Picinisco.

Alfonso and a lot of the young men were full of talk about emigrating, about leaving to live in another country, leaving their homes and their families.

'You know, *cuore mio*,' he continued, sensing her body stiffen, 'we have no choice. Do you understand? We can't live here. It's impossible. You know Tadon Michele has only a little land. He has to divide it among four sons. All with wives and families to feed – *e impossibile!* The pig today, between eight families! So we raise two pigs . . . but nothing will change. It is impossible to continue here.'

'Alfonso, I know all the boys are talking like this. But I am afraid. I don't want to leave here. I am strong; our children will be strong. We'll survive, as our grandparents and great-grandparents survived before us. Why do you want to throw away all we have? Risk all we have here?'

Alfonso held her closer and kissed her cheek. He stroked her hair. They had talked about this many times. He knew she didn't want to go.

'*Cara*, you must trust me. It's a greater risk not to go. Remember, I'll be with you all the time. I'll look after you.'

'But I can't speak English. I can't read. I can't write. I know nothing of Scotland.'

'You are young. You are clever. You'll learn everything. You must trust in God.

He will look after us. He always protects us. And I promise you, Maria, *carissima*, I'll be with you all the time. I promise you, *avanti a Dio*, I'll never leave you.'

Maria fell silent. She couldn't argue with him any more. His mind was made up. Gradually he fell asleep. His young wife lay awake beside him, thoughts racing through her mind. She was terrified of leaving her home, terrified of what lay ahead. He was right. She had no choice. He was her husband and she would have to follow him anywhere.

19

She would trust in God: she started to say her prayers, '*Santa Maria, Madre di Dio*', imploring the Madonna to protect them and guide them; invoking the Blessed Heart of Jesus to shield them from harm; beseeching Sant'Antonio to pray for them, '*Sant'Antonio, prega per noi.*'

She thought about the faith that her parents had: an unconditional faith in the Will of God. She would believe too. She would abandon herself to the Will of God. God would protect them and guide them. *Dio vede e provede.* God sees and provides. All would be well. Fortified by prayer, she fell into a deep sleep.

Having scented the blood of the pig, a pack of wolves circled the houses. The burning *fascie* kept them at bay but they howled in frustration. Clouds had descended between the mountains, obscuring any light from the fading moon. The sky was pitch black. The wolves howled again, even louder.

Maria awoke with a start. A cold wave of fear gripped her heart. In her nightmare she had seen Sant'Antonio fighting with a fierce wolf, a wolf with the face of the Devil. She was overcome with an overwhelming premonition of danger. She turned to Alfonso and held him close. What did this mean? What terrible evil lay ahead of them?

3

Picinisco, Italy
17 January 1913

The whole village of Fontitune was up well before dawn. Before
they could leave for Picinisco they had to carry out all the daily
chores. Maria and Serafina, her sister, built up the fire, lit it again
and refilled the pot with water from the well. They called young
Carmella to help and within half an hour the water was starting to
warm up. The remains of the evening's festivities had all been tidied
away. Alfonso and Pietro gathered the ashes from the previous
night's bonfires and spread it in the area where the sheep would be
milked in the spring. They believed this would protect their sheep
from the evil eye, *malocchio*.

Tadon Michele went into the back room to make sure the sausages
and hams were in good order. He was not yet fifty years old but
he had the appearance of a grandfather. Years of sleeping out in
the cold winter months had left him weather-beaten and wrinkled.
He was shorter than Alfonso, barely five feet and three inches tall.

He was dressed ready for the day: dark trousers and his only
grey jacket, a clean white shirt, crumpled and frayed at the collar,
and a dark grey waistcoat. Although his hair was white, his moustache was still dark and bushy, giving him the air of authority that
he deserved.

The women had started to wash the children. The pot was taken
off the fire before the water became too hot. Each child was rubbed
and scrubbed just as the pig had been the day before, almost as
harshly. Their hair was washed and their teeth rubbed clean with
soft wood. They were lifted out, squealing with shock at the cold
air, then rubbed dry in big sheets before being whisked home in a
bundle to be dressed.

The older children had been occupied since dawn, dressing the

21

animals which were to be presented to the priest for the Holy Blessing of Sant'Antonio. Pietro had already chosen the plumpest young piglet from the last litter. He washed it, tied ribbons round its neck and bows on its tight curly tail. It squealed in protest. Until next January this fortunate animal would be cosseted, fattened and treated like a prince. Then it would meet the same fate as its relative had yesterday. It would become good sausages.

The ass had been brushed, its hooves checked and its pathetic, scraggy mane teased into pigtails, a proud feather tied ludicrously between its ears. A goat and sheep had been decorated with makeshift garlands of early flowers: wild violet narcissus, gold-centred green hellebore and rose-coloured Alpine cyclamens. The delicate winter aroma of the flowers mingled with the pungent smell of sweat.

The married women in the village wore their one special outfit. Long coloured skirts, red or blue, green or yellow, the bottoms decorated with strips of coloured ribbon and embroidery. These were covered with long white aprons and white or coloured lace waistcoats over full-sleeved lacy blouses. Around their waists they tied coloured cords and, on their heads, hair piled high and fixed with long bone combs, they arranged long white or black lace mantillas. They wound the straps of their *cioce* round and round their legs, the flat leather soles providing protection from the stones on the path.

As the sun rose behind La Meta, the church bells began to peel across the valley, calling the motley group to attention. Tadon Michele led his flock of family and animals down the hillside. The animals, attached to strings pleated with brightly coloured ribbons, were held in turns by the children, who pulled and pushed, nudged and yanked, to make them move.

In Picinisco, Don Dioniso had also been up before dawn. The priest in fact had been up all night. He had succumbed once again to temptation. Aptly named after the Greek God of Wine, Don Dioniso was well aware of his weakness. He struggled with it daily. Don Dioniso's sin was the sin of over-indulgence: the sin of greed.

The previous day had been a regretful one. It had been a day of intolerable temptation. It had been a day in which he had fought with the Devil and, worse than that, a day when the Devil had won.

He had risen earlier than normal, even before the field-workers had left the piazza. He had lain prostrate in the sacristy of the church of San Lorenzo and had contemplated the life of Sant'Antonio Abate, the saint who, like him, had struggled with temptation.

He had decided to dedicate himself to the Saint for the whole day. Instead of feasting and indulging like his parishioners he would stand apart from their traditions and rituals, their greed and gluttony. He would not join the crowd. On the eve of the Saint's feast day, a day of abundance, he would set an example. He would fast.

Don Dioniso struggled constantly with his insatiable appetite. He was not, however, aware of his other imperfection. He could not see, although his long-suffering parishioners could, that he was also guilty of the sin of pride. It would in fact be many years before Don Dioniso recognised and forgave himself for this flaw in his character.

His day had started, therefore, with the very best of intentions. Don Dioniso had said Mass to a congregation inflated with those who appear at church only on Holy Days and Obligations. The doors were pushed open, allowing a dreadful draught to annoy his left ear, as the men of the village, who always stood protectively at the rear of the church, spilled out into the piazza.

Picinisco c. 1900

At least today the piazza was fairly quiet. Tomorrow, on the feast day itself, there would be even more hangers-on, even more opportunists. Tomorrow the piazza would be full to bursting with musicians and beggars, animals and officials, nuns and Neapolitans! Today was bearable; tomorrow would be Hell!

After Mass, Don Dioniso had counted the takings, and felt gratified. His sermon had made them dig deeper than usual into their pockets and the fund for the restoration of the church of Sant'Antonio Abate in St Eusebio in Rome would be nearer its target. Don Dioniso had smiled to himself. His longed-for promotion to the safety and sanity of Rome was surely a day closer.

He hated his exile. How could he survive another year in this God-forsaken outpost of Catholicism? The people here believed in a cocktail of religion and superstition; they were ignorant but trusting, argumentative but biddable. And yet he had never known a people who had such a sure faith in God. They believed unconditionally. He had to give them that.

He had decided the best way to handle his fast would be to remain alone, to pray, to keep out of the way of temptation; to keep out of the way of food. So, although many parishioners and officials had searched him out, no one had been able to find the priest. They had checked all his usual haunts, the kitchen, the dining room, the baker's shop, but he was nowhere to be seen.

He had in fact been hiding in the ancient bell tower. This was not entirely comfortable, as the sacristan, as was the custom, pulled the bell-cord every fifteen minutes, so that the villagers knew what the time was. Only at twelve, when the cannon boomed out over the valley and the chimes bellowed twelve times, had he given in and descended.

In the afternoon he had thought he would faint with hunger, but his anguish had strengthened his resolve. He had succeeded so far. He would not give in. In fact he had felt rather pleased with himself. Tomorrow he would shame his weak parishioners. In his sermon he would tell them how he had overcome his temptation.

And so Don Dioniso's second weakness, the sin of pride, the sin that he had not yet recognised, tripped him up. Sins are like that. Like a precariously balanced stack of cards, one falls and they all tumble.

As the day had shortened and the fires of the *fascie* had been lit, he had fallen foul of the aroma of *i ciccioli*. His head had spun with the onslaught of the enticing smell, his stomach had groaned and his mouth had filled with saliva. He had inhaled deeply, indulging his senses in the exquisite aroma, and sighed with pleasure.

He had stopped short! Oh no! What had he just done? Had he enjoyed the pleasure of the smell of the food too much? Weakened by starvation and lack of nutrients, by smelling the food, had he, in fact, succumbed to temptation and broken his fast?

Is a fast a fast if one smells the food, inhales the aroma and imagines the sensation of the garlic and pork, the toasted orange rind and the fat? Is a sin a sin if it is enjoyed in the mind instead of the flesh? Now that he had succumbed to his senses, had his fast ever been a fast at all?

It is a sad reflection on the man that he, inevitably, decided that he had in fact broken his fast. And, it followed that, as he had not eaten at all that day, he would be neglecting himself and his parishioners if he did not join in the feasting with them. He had argued, with authority, that the Madonna herself, who loved all her children on this Earth, would not ask anyone to continue to suffer if they had tried their best but had failed.

So, later than they had expected him, Don Dioniso had visited his parishioners, called on his friends, paid his respects to his official colleagues and had eaten his fill. He had then spent the rest of that night of the eve of the Holy Feast of Sant'Antonio walking around his sparsely furnished bedroom riddled with indigestion and guilt, wishing he were dead!

Now he stood on a makeshift platform in the middle of La Montana, the piazza at the top of the village. He looked resplendent in the priestly vestments of the feast day, his loose cassock a relief over his distended belly, his head bursting, his indigestion burning his gut. He steeled himself for the onslaught. The statue of Sant'Antonio Abate stood beside him, together with the official reception committee, a selection of altar boys, acolytes, the Sindaco, officials and police officers.

Standing on the platform, elevated above the crowd, he could see further over the valley than usual. How beautiful the mountains stood, one rising above the next, higher and higher. The trees created a lush, luxurious carpet of deep green. Higher still his eye searched, seeing, in the pale violet morning light, ominous clouds at the top of La Meta. The mountain was covered with snow. The sky in the distance looked heavy.

'Please God we will be lucky and get rid of the influx of peasants by tonight before the snow arrives and the roads are blocked.'

As he put his hand over his eye to cut the dazzle of light, he saw the procession approaching from Fontitune. And as they made their way down the mountain, groups and families joined them from other trails to form a motley crew of *nonne* and fathers, babes and piglets in arms, asses and donkeys on leads, children and aunties in tow, all bringing their livestock to be blessed.

Don Dioniso watched the approaching maelstrom with foreboding. To start the proceedings the Sindaco signalled to the chief police officer, who signalled to the band leader, who promptly started up the band. As the very first peasant arrived with a spectacularly decorated ass, Don Dioniso dipped his aspergillum into the Holy Water, lifted his right arm and with a flick of his wrist and a flourishing Sign of the Cross began showering his flock with his blessing.

He blessed sheep, goats, the odd cow, cockerels, dogs, donkeys, horses and plenty of pigs, all scrubbed and cleaned, barking and screeching, defecating and farting! The music, adding to the excitement, was overpowering for some of the animals who decided to take their chances with the Devil and bolt back up the mountain or, worse still, up the animal in front!

'*Madonna Mia! Sant'Antonio, Aiutami!*'

By the time the Crollas arrived in the queue, the place was mayhem.

Don Dioniso felt he would collapse.

'*Grazie a Dio.*' The church bell sounded a quarter to ten. The exhausted priest stepped down

Picinisco piazza and feast day procession

26

with a final over-enthusiastic flourish of all the remaining Holy Water, relieved that the first part of his duties was over.

How he managed to get through the crowds, down the Via Montana, packed twelve abreast from wall to wall, and not be crushed to death he would never know. However, professional to the last, puffed and pink, sweating and ever so slightly dishevelled, he arrived at the altar just on time, two steps behind Sant'Antonio who had been carried ceremoniously through the crowds aloft on the shoulders of the officials.

The church was already full to bursting; the doors, wedged wide open, were jammed with men, and outside he could see the crowds arriving from Ponte Melfa and Atina.

Just as he lifted his hand to start Mass, the music started out in the piazza with a well-practised rendition of the new Italian National Anthem, Marcia Reale, *Viva il Re!*, 'The Royal March, Long Live the King!'. What that had to do with the beginning of Mass or the celebration of Sant'Antonio Abate, Don Dioniso did not know, but he would not be deterred. Noise or not, animals or not, Mass would begin.

'*In Nome del Padre, del Figlio, e dello Spirito Santo . . .*'

By the time he was about to deliver his sermon, he was furious. The band was still playing; it was about half-way through the overture of La Traviata. Then the street vendors, who had set up stall earlier, started to call out their wares. Even though it was January and the fields were fallow, the street traders still had plenty to sell.

'*Pistacchi di Sicilia!*'

'*Baccalà! Stoccafisso!*'

'*Limoni e Aranci d'Amalfi!*'

The congregation was restless, women looking round, nudging each other, reporting which neighbours they had spotted, and passing the latest gossip along the pews while simultaneously whacking the children across the ears to stop them talking in church!

'My dear brothers and sisters in Christ,' Don Dioniso began, 'My *dear* brothers and sisters in Christ. Why are you here? Do you believe? Do you have faith? Do you have the strength to resist temptation like Sant'Antonio Abate? When you struggle with the temptations of the Devil, who wins?'

As the subject of the sermon dawned on the congregation, they sat to attention. This would be worth listening to. Sensing their change in mood, Don Dioniso thought smugly to himself, 'It always works a treat. Mention the Devil and they always pay attention.'

And so the priest's sin of pride caught him out again. The congregation sat to attention, not because they thought he could teach them something, or because he might save their souls. No, they sat to attention, ears strained to hear every word, because they all knew, each and every one of them, of Don Dioniso's spectacular struggle with the Devil the day before. They all knew of his indisputable failure.

The priest had not imagined that, as he moved from house to house last night, later than his parishioners had expected him, anyone could have seen him. The streets had been deserted. In his haste to scuttle from house to house he had been completely unaware of the boys from Fontitune. They were also moving from house to house, singing songs and playing their *zampogne*, and as they did they carried the news that Don Dioniso was succumbing to his well-known sin of gluttony and was on his way.

Some householders hid their food, some doused the lamps and pretended to be asleep, some drank up the last of the wine, but, even so, the boys were able to report that in the closing hours of the day they had seen the short, round priest with his long black soutan and wide-brimmed black hat trip over, inebriated, at the top of the Via Montana and roll all the way down the hill to the back door of his church.

Unaware of their betrayal, Don Dioniso carried on with his sermon regardless. If he had known what they were thinking he would have been mortified. However, despite his weakness, he was rewarded for his good intentions. He managed to deliver three sentences that cut at the consciences of his smirking parishioners.

'You want to leave,' he addressed the young men, 'you want to seek your fortunes. *Tu vuo' fa'L'Americano?* You want to live in America! You want to have a better life than your fathers and your fathers' fathers before them? Be aware of temptation. Be aware of the Devil! What will be your Devil? What will destroy you and your families?'

He yelled at the top of his voice. He banged his fist on the pulpit. He dropped his voice spectacularly so that they had to strain their ears to hear his words.

He whispered slowly, as if the Devil himself were talking.

'*La Bestia trionfante!* The monstrous apparition of materialism! Money. Money and greed! *Soldi e avidita di ricchezze!* That will be your temptation! That will be your downfall!'

The congregation sat stunned, their smug thoughts banished in a new awareness of self-doubt and guilt. The priest, without realising it, had done his job. He had made them think and had alerted their consciences.

After Mass everyone spilled out into the piazza, relieved to escape from the mad priest's ranting.

'What does he know? How can he understand? He doesn't have to feed a family. He just feeds his own fat belly!'

Nevertheless, the priest had struck a raw nerve, one that would remain with them for years to come.

In the sacristy, Don Dioniso slumped in the bishop's chair, exhausted to the point of collapse. He tried to work out whether or not he had done well. Had they listened to him? Had they at least been cautioned in their ambitions?

In his past five years in the parish he had seen an ever-increasing stream of young men and their families leaving the villages, a stream that was in danger of becoming a flood. Deep down he was concerned for those left behind. Would they feel neglected and abandoned? Would those who left become materialistic and god-forsaken? He had done all he could for the moment. He would pray for them tonight.

He heard a cry from a Neapolitan street vendor in the piazza. Exhausted, he took five lire from the collection and called the sacristan to go and buy a dozen *bombolone*. He deserved a treat.

4

Picinisco
17 January 1913

The beggars had positioned themselves strategically at the door of the church. The band was playing *Fratelli d'Italia*, 'Brothers of Italy', the popular rousing tune by Novaro. The street traders raised their voices even louder to call out their wares. The winter sun was shining, the air sharp and clear. The children were despatched up to La Montana to feed and water the animals, leaving the men free to talk and the women to wander towards the stalls.

The piazza was very jolly, crowded with peasants in traditional costume, coloured skirts and head-dresses, adding an exotic air. The beggars pushed between the people, nudging them with grubby hands, moaning to attract attention. A hermit in rags yelled out unexpectedly every few minutes, repeating his constant conversation with Satan. Filthy gypsies with long hooped earrings and gold coins dangling round their foreheads stared menacingly at the women and whispered threats under their breath. Some sat in groups with Tarot cards and taunted people that they could see their future.

Maria had brought three small cheeses balanced on a roped cloth on her head. She had given one to Don Dioniso as an offering at the blessing of the animals. By the end of the day he'd collected enough food to tempt him for a further six weeks, all through Lent. Now she looked to the stalls to see what she could find that might be needed through the rest of the winter. It would snow tonight. They might be cut off until spring.

The stalwart stall-holders made their way up to Picinisco, struggling on the zig-zag road from the bottom of the mountain, carrying their wares. They knew what the *paesani* needed. They would argue and barter with price, trading their produce for pecorino, sheeps' skins, wild herbs and rare seeds.

Some stalls had pots and pans, cheap aluminium cups, tin plates and cutlery. One stall had piles of salt cod, *baccalà*, that had been imported from Norway and Scotland; the cod was soaked, rinsed and cooked during the fast days of Lent. From the baker's shop in Atina, the nearest town in the valley below, there were boys with long poles threaded with *bombolone*, Don Dioniso's favourite giant doughnuts. There was a stall with nails and string, all sizes, and hammers and bric-à-brac, and many stalls with piles of clothes: shirts and trousers, boots and hats, jackets and waistcoats, all second-hand or older. One stall-holder from Naples sold nuts and *pistacchi, torrone* and sweatmeats. Another stall was piled high with Amalfi oranges and lemons.

A man played a barrel organ. The shepherd boys played their pipes, holding out a can to collect lire; asking for coins for music was not regarded as begging. A crippled boy sat brandishing a picture of La Madonna di Canetto. He was abandoned. Society, fearful of disease and disability, shunned the disabled. Within the family it was hidden and denied. A black man, tall and sinewy with many hoops around his long neck, held eight monkeys, each on a thin red lead tied to a collar dangling with noisy bells. The monkeys crawled over his shoulders and his back; the children swarmed around him, fascinated.

Maria traded a cheese for a pungent, salty side of *baccalà*. She had dried plums in the summer, which she would cook with the cod to add sweetness. She rummaged among the clothes and chose a thick black cloak which she would give to Alfonso as a gift when their new baby was born. The stall-holder parcelled the *baccalà* in some brown paper for her and she tied it together with the cloak, rolled up into a parcel to carry home.

At the next big market in the spring she and the women from Fontitune would set up a stall of their own to sell pecorino and fresh ricotta.

Her business done, Maria looked for the youngsters, who were all congregated at *la fontana*. This ancient fountain provided a constant stream of ice-cold mountain water to the houses around the piazza. It was a natural meeting place, under the naked canopy of the ancient oak tree that acted as a giant sunshade in the height of summer.

Maria sat on the shallow wall that overlooked the valley below. The dirt road winding up and up to the heights of Picinsico could be seen snaking its way across the valley, miles away in the distance and then up and up to the mountain at the other side. Corner hairpin bends, one after the other, so steep that the twice-weekly bus that brought visitors, news and provisions swung out precariously over the edge at every turn. Donkeys and horses attempting the climb laden with parcels struggled to prevent themselves sliding and tumbling over the edge. This town had been built in a strategic position, so that enemies could not approach unnoticed. At night the lights from the villages of the surrounding mountains created a stunning panorama for miles around.

The company of families opened parcels of bread and sausage, some cheese and a few pears and settled down to eat. Some of their Piciniscani cousins joined them to catch up with news. As always, the men broke away and went to find a free space to eat and talk in peace! Maria was sitting with her mother, Arcangela, who had come with her cousin Marietta. They lived in I Ciacca, a small hamlet of farm buildings down the hill below Picinisco. Though they lived barely five miles apart, they saw each other rarely in winter as visits to Picinsico were few and far between.

Marietta had been born in London, her father one of the earlier opportunists. He had walked north with his family and lived in Paris for some years, then had moved on to London. Things were almost worse in London than here. The dreadful overcrowding in Clerkenwell, London's Little Italy of the late 1890s, was intolerable. Disease and infection were rife. Her father had played a barrel organ with a monkey just like the ones in the piazza, holding out a cup to collect pennies. Eventually he progressed to selling ice cream off horse-drawn wagons in the parks of London along with scores of other immigrant Italians.

But life in London proved to be too difficult and, when Marietta was still young, seven or eight, they came back to Picinisco, although Laura, her eldest sister, had married and stayed behind in London. Her mother's health never recovered from the cold and damp of the city and, sadly, she died. Marietta, now aged sixteen, lived with her ageing father and her brothers.

'How is Compare Giovanni?' Maria asked.

'Not bad. He's getting older you know, he's a bit slower than he was. Alessandro is doing fine. It's amazing how he manages.' Alessandro, six years her senior, had lost a leg in a road accident with a speeding horse and carriage in Paris when he was a young boy, a thing that had distressed his mother terribly.

Marietta c. 1915

Marietta went quiet, thinking about her mother. She looked out over the valley and thought how beautiful it was; how calm and peaceful. Marietta was in love with Picinisco.

Maria wanted to talk to her young cousin. She pulled her over to sit on the wall beside her.

'Marietta, have you heard that Alfonso wants to go to Scotland? He wants me to follow him after the baby is born. I'm worried sick. How on earth can I manage to live in a country where I can't speak the language? I can't read. I can't write!'

Marietta was concerned for her friend but tried not to show it. She had seen how her own mother had struggled and found it very difficult to cope away from home. She tried to reassure Maria. 'It will be fine, Maria. It will be fine. Scotland sounds like a nicer place than London, a much nicer country. I imagine it's not unlike here, with mountains and hills and lovely lakes.'

'But I cannot speak English like you!'

Marietta was lucky. She could speak English and Italian perfectly. She could read and write. She had gone diligently to the Italian Sunday school and, unlike most Italians, her mother had let her go to the local school as well. She missed some things about London.

'Maria, *cara*, the only thing I can say is give it a try. You'll be able to learn English, and your lovely baby when it's born will learn to speak both languages, like me. It will learn to read and write. And you can always come back again like my mamma.' They both fell silent at this. Marietta's mother had come home to die.

The men had moved towards the General Store, which enterprisingly had kept its doors open and placed a couple of wooden tables and some chairs outside. Giovanni Di Ciacca, Marietta's father, was talking to Maria's cousins, Cesidio, Gerardo, Vito and Louis. Cesidio was in uniform, home on leave during his National Service. The boys were tall and similar in looks; they formed a powerful image. A litre flask of wine lay half-empty in front of them. A game of *scopa*, the Neapolitan card game, lay abandoned as the boys talked animatedly together.

They all stood up to greet their uncle, Tadon Michele, and Alfonso, Pietro and Emidio. They greeted each other with genuine affection, kissing on both cheeks and embracing each other. The young men were all in their early twenties, some newly married, some single. They were cousins and second cousins, their families inter-marrying for many generations. Cesidio poured some wine for the newcomers and they toasted each other.

'Sant'Antonio!' They toasted the Saint: hands raised, glasses chinked, wine knocked back.

'*Viva l'Italia!*' Glasses chinked, wine knocked back. The glasses were all refilled, generously.

They loved this game and, in turn, called out a toast:

Cesidio Di Ciacca c. 1915

34

'Don Dioniso!' With a roar of laughter the last of the wine was despatched. They all sat down, pulling chairs and boxes out from the shop.

'Well, Alfonso,' began Cesidio, '*come stai?*'

'Good. Good. *Grazie a Dio*, the war is over. Why we had to fight those poor people I'll never know, but it's done now. Looks like it's successful and things will settle down. How long do you have to serve, Compare?'

The boys' parents were godparents to each other's children. They called the older men *compare* as a mark of respect. The relationships between them all were very close, not least because they all lived close to Picinisco: the Crollas up in Fontitune, the Di Ciaccas in a string of rough farmhouses below the village on the other side of the hill.

'We should be home by the spring, *Grazie a Dio*. Who would have thought that we would be called up? I don't know what they are training us for. We should be fighting here, for our families. I am not interested in war, for God's sake. We have enough to do here, staying alive!'

Tadon Michele spoke up.

'*Ragazzi, attenzione!* Do what you have to do but keep your heads down. We don't need any heroes here. The world is dangerous. Things are changing so fast. God knows what the future will bring.'

Alfonso put his hand into his back pocket and brought out a crumpled folded envelope. It was addressed to him with a strange blue stamp, unfamiliar to the younger boys in the group. The postmark was Edinburgh. Alfonso opened it and pulled out a photograph. He passed it to Cesidio.

'Zio Benedetto Crolla and his wife and three children. They're standing outside their shop. It's near the port, not a stone's throw from where he landed in Scotland when he got off the ship from Antwerp. Can you believe it? He has his own shop! And here's a picture of Giovanni. He looks pretty good, don't you think?'

Giovanni, Alfonso's older brother, and his cousin Benny had left for Edinburgh four years ago, working for the De Marco family, some of whom had emigrated ten years previously.

The boys pored over the photograph, intrigued. The two arched windows of the shop were full of boxes of glasses of ice creams,

Cesidio (far left) and his brothers in the piazza at Picinisco c. 1913

displays of packets of cigarettes and boxes of chocolates. Signs embedded in the glass read 'Cadbury's' and 'Fry's'.

Gerardo had the least English. 'Fry? Has he got a fish and chip shop?'

Tadon Michele laughed. 'No, it's a brand of chocolate.'

They laughed, and when Tadon read out the name scripted above the door in bold Roman letters, 'Crolla Newhaven', they applauded and cheered.

'Crolla Newhaven!'

They spontaneously stood up and raised their glasses again and good-humouredly saluted their relative.

'Benedetto Crolla Newhaven!'

Everyone in the piazza looked over to see what the commotion was about. Those young men! They were always excited about something!

They all sat down again. Tadon Michele looked at his son. 'Alfonso, what does the letter say? How is Giovanni? What does he say?'

Alfonso lowered his voice. 'Papà, Giovanni says there is work for Emidio and me and whoever else wants to come. He says life is easier. The people there don't want to work in ice cream shops. There are plenty of places to open, with no competition. He says people there are happy to buy chocolates and cigarettes and ice cream from Italians. There are even one or two cafés. Zio Benny says he'll give me a job, show me how to do the work and then I can rent a shop of my own.'

'It's all very well to talk about it, Alfonso, but you know I tried. It's not easy. The journey will take you three weeks at least. And what about the immigration authorities? They're watching all the time. I've heard you need to pay now. You can't just come and go like we used to.'

'No, Papà, don't worry. You don't have to pay. You need to show that you can look after yourself, that you have a job to go to. If you have five pounds they let you in.'

'Where will you get five pounds, Alfonso?' Cesidio had his doubts.

Alfonso almost jumped up with excitement. 'Here! *Ecco qua! Ecco qua! Guarda!* Here is the key to my future!'

With a flourish he pulled an envelope from his pocket and

carefully extracted a pale cream coloured, folded paper. He opened it out and smoothed it on the table. Here was a large, imposing scrolled note: The Clydesdale Bank Limited, Five Pounds Sterling. He passed it round, all the boys looking at it in wonder. Where in heaven's name had he got that?

Alfonso had the knack of making things happen that seemed impossible.

Emidio examined it carefully and handed it back.

'That's all very well, Alfons'. . . that will get *you* past immigration. It won't do *me* much good!'

'*Non ti preoccupare!* Giovanni says you show it to the immigration man, cause a bit of a rumpus and when he isn't looking you pass it to the man behind. Last year twenty-six Neapolitans got in with one five-pound note!'

They all laughed and cheered again. The combination of the wine, the feast day and the camaraderie filled them all with an infectious, ingenuous optimism.

Now they all wanted to emigrate.

Cesidio was still not swayed. A quiet boy, cautious and thoughtful, he had seen much hardship already in his family from this obsession with immigration. Half of his family – cousins, uncles and aunts – were all over the place.

'Look at you, Zio Giovanni' he went on, a little agitated, 'You tried all this. You've been to Paris and to London. What happened? Tell them the truth! Tell them the truth!' He almost shouted, 'You lived in a dirty room in a filthy tenement with twenty families all around you, with rats and disease and dirt. What fortune is that? Tell them. Tell them. It's not as easy as it sounds!'

Cesidio stopped almost as soon as he had started and went quiet. He felt bad, because in fact he admired all the men who had had the courage to take the chance. It was the strong ones who left, the ambitious ones. The cautious, apprehensive ones stayed here.

So many had gone, so many: from every family in every village, gone. To Paris, London, Cardiff, Glasgow, Manchester, Edinburgh, New York, Moscow, so many names, so many places. They had all gone, anywhere to get away from this vanishing way of life, anywhere to get a new start.

While he was thinking, Marietta came across and joined the

group. She nodded to the young men, modest in her behaviour, and kissed her uncle, Tadon Michele, and her father.

'Papà, it's getting late. I'm going down with my cousins to prepare the meal. Francesco will be wondering where I am.'

Her father smiled at her, '*Vai*. I'll be there in half an hour.'

She nodded and turned to walk away. As she turned she caught sight of Cesidio looking at her. It was as if something dawned on him as he looked at her, as if something had suddenly become clear. She didn't know why, but she blushed. Before her father noticed, she called her cousins, moving away quickly down the hill.

The Crolla boys stood up as well and said their goodbyes. It was past three o'clock now and it was time to get home before dark. It might even snow by the looks of things. The stall-holders were starting to tidy up. There was debris and discarded rubbish all over the now muddied piazza. The band members were hanging around the door of the church, packing away all their instruments. They were hoping for a share of Don Dioniso's collection, but they would be disappointed.

Alfonso went to look for Maria, excited to show her the letter.

Marietta was quiet as they walked down the hill. She sent her cousins on ahead to start the fire. She needed a moment to think. She went to the top field where the goats were waiting. The sky had turned into a glorious tapestry of watery blue and apricot cloud, the setting sun's rays rippling out all over the horizon.

Would she ever go back to Britain to live? Should she warn Maria how hard it had been? And Cesidio? Had she imagined it? Why had he looked at her so oddly? She had known Cesidio since she had returned to Italy. They were second cousins. He was twenty, four years older than her, but she hadn't seen him for about a year since he had been away in the army.

She gazed at La Meta, lost in her thoughts. It was beautiful here: so peaceful.

When she heard a twig snap she turned round with a start. It was Cesidio. Standing tall above her, he looked straight into her eyes and held her gaze. He screwed up his eyes a little, giving them a sleepy inquisitive look. Not a word passed between them.

She felt herself blush again.

He put out his hand and took hers. The rules in this peasant community were clear. Young people of the opposite sex did not talk to each other, far less meet alone. Girls were strictly chaperoned and their innocence was protected fiercely. Marriages were often arranged, and any hint of scandal meant the girl would never marry.

Marietta was shocked that he had touched her. She opened her mouth to object, fearful of his intentions. He immediately realised his mistake and dropped her hand, taking a step back.

'Forgive me. *Mi scusi, Marietta, carissima.* I know I shouldn't have followed you but I cannot help myself. Do you understand? I had to talk with you.'

Somehow, without even thinking, she nodded. She did understand. Her heart tumbled in her breast, the feeling making the back of her neck shiver and her legs buckle beneath her. She sank to the ground. Cesidio knelt down in front of her.

'Marietta, I need to tell you something. I need to tell you that I love you. *Marietta, ti voglio bene.* While I have been away I have thought of you all the time, only of you. I know now I can love only you.'

Marietta was overwhelmed. She knew only that she felt completely safe, secure with this young man beside her.

'Will you wait for me? I need to go away again, but will you wait for me?'

He took her face in his hands and gently traced her features with his fingers. She held her breath, transfixed. He traced her forehead where her dark brown hair was pulled back from her face. He traced each eyebrow, and gently smoothed her frown. He lightly drew his finger round each gentle, almond-shaped eye. He cupped his hand over her cheek, running his fingers tenderly under her chin. He traced the strong line of her nose with his forefinger. Then with the finger suspended inches from her lips so that he could just feel her warm breath, he looked into her eyes and whispered quietly, 'Marietta, I dedicate my life to you, my love. I will be your friend and your protector; I will be your father and your mother. I will be your brother and your lover. I will be your self.'

Then, without another word, he stood up, playfully squeezed her cheek with his thumb and finger, just like her older brother did, and turned and walked away.

The next time she saw him it was three years later when he came back to marry her.

5

Fontitune
1913

It did snow that evening, as Don Dioniso, Tadon Michele and Marietta had all predicted. By the time the Crolla entourage climbed back up to Fontitune the track was already thick with snow, slowing them, so much so that it was well after dark before they got home. The cold had settled down to a new, fierce intensity. In the dark valley between the mountains the silence was wonderful. They knew that once the snow came it stayed. They were all subdued, contemplating the weeks ahead.

Life settled into the daily grind of winter in the mountains, all the excitement of the *festa* now a distant memory. The cold was unforgiving, settling into the bones, gnawing at the spirit. But there was no time to complain; there was plenty of work to do preparing for the spring when the sheep would come back from the coast.

Like all other sheep-raising communities in the Abruzzo, the families in Fontitune followed the age-old practice of *transumanza*. In the autumn they moved their flocks of sheep down from the mountain pastures to the plains of the coast as far south as Apulia. They would walk, often with their womenfolk and children, along the age-old *tratturi*, tracks that had been followed by shepherds and their flocks since Roman times. In spring, as the weather warmed, they drove their flocks back up to the cool pastures in the mountains.

Tadon Michele's nephews and their families had moved with the sheep this winter, leaving Alfonso, Emidio and Pietro here in the Fontitune. This was the problem facing them. Larger extended families meant there was not enough work for all; an insidious unemployment was driving them out. They were a hard-working self-sufficient people. They had survived on their wits and ingenuity

42

for centuries. This was a new problem they were facing and it required a drastic new solution.

The men spent their days repairing tools, building walls, repairing roofs and mending the reed baskets they would need, ready to make the cheese. The women completed their daily chores: clothes to wash, by hand in cold water in the trough by the well, clothes to mend, garments to make. The children had their own chores: picking wild herbs and nuts, sweeping the area outside the house, chopping wood. All the women and children were illiterate. Some of the men had been taught to read and write in the army but they had no books to read, no paper to write on.

The daily preparation of food was the most pleasurable task. The diet was made up of warm heavy food, food to fill them up: *tordiglione,* golden polenta, flavoured with spicy bitter greens, or pasta, made by hand from wholemeal flour. From the start of the day, big pots hung over the fire, steaming with thick, nutritious soup cooked with vegetables and flavoured with slices of *sals-iccie.* Slabs of *lardo* were pounded with dried *peperoncino*, parsley and garlic and slowly melted into the broth as it simmered. The warmth and smells filled the stark room, transforming it into a haven.

Bread was baked once a week in the communal oven. Old dried bread was used in all manner of ways to subsidise the meagre food: steamed with winter greens and garlic or grilled by the fire and rubbed with garlic and thick cloudy olive oil. Sometimes it was simply splashed with water, drizzled with oil and dried herbs and left to go soft and soggy, juicy and comforting to eat. In this cold the peasants had hearty appetites and the pork fat and olive oil helped provide welcome calories.

The animals had to be cared for. Housed in the bottom room, they also were dulled by the cold. Each day their mess was swept out, piled behind the house, ready to be spread into the ground as soon as the snow melted. Pietro's pig was given pride of place and extra *polenta* was cooked for it. The goats were cared for by the women. As soon as the spring came their welcome supply of fresh goat's milk would return.

Time passed slowly; reserves of food became low. The cold was relentless. When the sun shone it was glorious but once it dipped behind the mountains the women sat huddled at the fire and crocheted by the light of an oil lamp, praying and longing for respite from the discomfort.

It was a dull and overcast day, not a shaft of light brightening the sky. It was Candlemas day, the second of February, forty days after the birth of Christ, the day of purification. Maria was now quite heavy in her pregnancy and was anxious about the impending labour. She had helped her cousins when their time came, and was apprehensive of the ordeal ahead.

The calendar was intrinsically bound up with their pattern of life. This day was the dawn of the year: the day half-way between the winter solstice and the spring equinox, the end of the winter and the beginning of spring. The men knew the jobs they needed to do. The dull day bore a good omen that winter would soon pass. Tadon Michele, Alfonso and Pietro began to spread the composted manure over their meagre fields. As they worked with the land, they anticipated the change and their spirits rose.

At the end of the day, after their work was done, the men settled down in the hut half-way up the hill, in the *forestelle*. They wouldn't go back to the village for a week or two, until everything was prepared for the returning sheep. They built a fire and shared some hard, dark bread, chewed on some slices of spicy *salsiccie* and broke off chunks of strong pecorino cheese. They warmed themselves with a goat-skin of wine and wrapped up in their dark, heavy over-cloaks worn on top of their sheepskin, *mastruce*. Their wide black hats were pulled down over their foreheads.

Twighlight was magical: as they looked across the valley they saw the lights flickering in houses dotted all around. Families lit their holy candles, kept from Christmas, to celebrate the coming of spring. In every home the women prayed to the Madonna and St Bridget, for their daughters and themselves.

Pietro used a long tube to blow the fire from below to keep the flames from dying down. He too lit a candle at the Madonna, a weather-beaten statue which had been in the alcove outside the hut for countless years. The men started to say their prayers, a rhythm of gentle chanting, natural between them. When they had finished they fell silent, filled with their thoughts.

'*Ragazzi, figlie mie, tutto sta cambiando,* everything is changing.'
Tadon Michele had tears in his eyes. He knew they would never
spend time like this again. For him it was all over. He spoke with
an air of resignation, soft words to give confidence to his sons.

'*C'è niente da fare.* There's nothing we can do. The world that
I have known is disappearing before my very eyes. My father and
his father before him travelled the same path but you boys can no
longer follow.' He shook his head in resignation. 'It's all changed.
Alfonso, my son, your path will be the most difficult, the most
dangerous. Have you made up your mind?'

'Yes, Papà.'

Tadon Michele looked out over the valley.

'Look at all these lights. Look at all these families that pray to
God and follow the rituals of centuries. These are the traditions
that bind us together.' He put his hand on his son's shoulder.
'Alfonso, when you go, don't forget your God. Don't forget your
traditions. Don't forget us. Remember what Don Dioniso said? He
had a point. If you put money and riches beyond your family you'll
lose everything. That is so true. *Ricordi,* Alfonso?'

'I know, Papà. You know we have no choice. We cannot survive
here. My child will be born soon, *se Dio vuole.* What future is there
for him? There's a chance for us in Scotland. It's not like London
and New York, not like Manchester, full of Italians that have already
set up business, all competing with one another. In Scotland there
are still so many small towns, so many opportunities. We need to
go now, before it's too late. Before others go. We'll lose our chance
if we don't go now.'

Pietro, the quiet one, was listening to everything.

'Alfonso, if you agree, I have decided to stay here. I'll look after
the sheep and the family; you are free to go. Emidio can go with
you. We'll manage more easily with fewer mouths to feed. If you
can, send some money.'

The men fell silent, contemplating the changes ahead.

'When will you go, Alfonso'?

'As soon as the baby is born. I'll wait until Maria is well again,
please God, then Emidio and I will go. We'll get on well, Papà, I'll
look out for him.'

'Alfonso, never forget you are a shepherd. You are a shepherd of shepherds, a man who thinks, a man who cares for his family and his flock. Don't change. Be a shepherd there, Alfonso. Be true to yourself. Be strong for the families that follow you. Be honest. Look out for the weak. Some of the young lads have been in trouble. Some have been fighting over money or gambling. Be careful. Try to set a good example. Work hard, protect your family. Don't be driven by success. Be driven by loyalty to your family and your country. Be honourable to God and Italia and you won't go wrong.'

The two men looked at each other. Both had tears in their eyes.

The next morning, spring arrived. The clouds had lifted, revealing a glorious blue sky, clear all the way across the valley. The view was magnificent: rolling hills, houses perched precariously on the steepest of slopes, the River Melfa sparkling in the distance. Birds twittered in the trees, chattering excitedly together.

'*Buon giorno, Papà. Come stai?* How are you this morning?' Pietro hadn't slept. He had worried through the night about his father. They were going to have to say goodbye to Alfonso and Emidio and then to Maria and her new baby. They might never see each other again. Now that the decision had been made, Pietro realised the enormity of it all. '*Come stai?*'

Tadon Michele was courageous. These boys had to find their own way in life, even if it hurt him. That was nature's way. That was God's way. He wouldn't let Alfonso know that his heart was broken. Alfonso was full of hope, full of ideas. He need not understand the agony of his father. His own time would come.

When Pietro asked him again how he was feeling, Tadon Michele slapped his son on the back.

'*Benissimo!* Couldn't be better!'

The snow gradually melted, first on the rough track and then at the edges of the streams. About two weeks later, their work all completed, the men walked back down to the village. Alfonso noticed the crocus and the blue hyacinths pushing through the snow, creating a tinselling effect of pastel colours.

The air was delicious and as the sun rose it warmed their backs. They removed their cloaks and jackets and strode towards the village with their sleeves rolled up, their hats in their hands. When the children heard Alfonso's familiar call they came running to greet them, jumping around and screeching with delight. The goat had given birth. The first kid of spring had been born through the night. The winter was definitely over!

As if motivated by the goat, Maria went into labour. Pietro set off to I Ciacca to fetch her mother, Arcangela. Meanwhile Filomena took control. The poor girl was kept moving around, up and down, up and down until she felt faint with exhaustion. When the pain became too intense she was given small sips of wine and infusions of wild herbs to relax her. Arcangela arrived just in time to support her daughter as she squatted in preparation for the birth.

Alfonso was chased from the house out of the way. He needed a job to do. He could kill the chicken.

'*Vai! Amazza il pollo!*'

The chicken was similarly despatched, its protesting and screeching doing nothing to distract from the cacophony coming from the bedroom. Its throat was wrung, it was bled and plucked and, once washed, Filomena put it in a pot, covered it with cold water and put it on the fire to simmer. She hovered nervously over the hearth, skimming the broth frantically every time she heard Maria cry out.

Maria had a boy.

She was overwhelmed by the disproportionate surge of love she felt for this squalling creature they laid on her breast. She had never experienced emotion as overpowering, such unconditional love as this, not even when she was with Alfonso.

The child was born, according to Arcangela, with an open hand outstretched immediately to his *nonna*. This was a sure sign that Alfonso's first-born would be generous of nature. Born on a Sunday, he would be called Domenico. Satisfied, the women cleaned the baby, then the mother, then fed her some chicken broth.

News travelled fast. A stream of visitors and well-wishers made their way up to Fontitune. Don Dioniso himself made the journey up the hill, the ass that was carrying him sweating and snorting under the strain. Immediately the priest descended from the animal, the baby was baptised. They all heaved a sigh of relief. They knew that a baby that died without being baptised would be abandoned in limbo for eternity, a fate worse than death itself.

Maria's spirits lifted with the arrival of her baby. Spring on La

Meta was lovely. Alfonso was sweet and attentive, proud of his healthy wife and their beautiful son. While he was working in the fields she walked for hours on the hills, Domenico strapped to her breast with a linen strip of cloth. She looked for wild herbs and roots. She knew each by instinct, its season and its properties. Young leaves of *cicoria* to eat in salads, the same plant that in winter she would stew with olive oil, chilli and garlic. *Dentedilione* and *finocchio*, *chenopodio* and *crescione d'aqua* were all collected for salads. She knew where to find *la rugetta* and the thin, succulent leaves of *barba di prete*. In the winter she had collected the root of this to use when they roasted the *porchetta*.

As she walked on the meadow she crushed oregano and thyme underfoot and their aroma pervaded the air. *Asparago selvatico* was good, cooked with eggs, and later on, in May, when the elderflower showed its abundant bunches of star-shaped flowers she would fry the highly perfumed flower in a light batter of egg and flour as a special treat for her husband.

Sometimes she walked to Prato di Mezzo, the field half-way up the mountain, to see Alfonso, courted by pink and apricot almond blossom and the citrus scent of orange. Clumps of violet crocuses prompted her to sit dreamily and pick the stems, forgetting the time as her baby slept beside her. She saved the stems in a folded leaf, ready to dry and store, making precious saffron for flavouring special dishes.

Alfonso found her like this one morning, propped against the bark of an almond tree, suckling her baby, dozing in the warm April sun. He knelt and kissed her. How blessed they were to have this peace and joy between them. They gazed at the child sleeping at her breast, enraptured by his beauty and presence. They wept gently, praying that one day his life would also be blessed with a loving wife and son of his own.

They sat quietly, treasuring the mountains, the river sparkling in the sunlight and the clear view away down the valley. Birds flitted among the trees. They soaked up the warmth of the sun. Alfonso kissed her gently on the lips.

'*Cara, ti voglio tanto bene.* I love you.'

'*Ti amo, Alfonso. Per sempre*,' she breathed, contented.

'Maria, as soon as the sheep arrive, I'll go.'

'I am prepared, Alfonso. Now that the baby is here I know it's for the best.' She lied to him. Deep down she didn't believe that, but she knew he had to go.

'Don't worry about anything. I'll send you money as soon as I can. You can come by train; it'll be much easier for you. I've already spoken to Giuseppina. She will come with you. She's going to join her husband in Manchester. She'll help you with the baby.'

'I'll miss La Meta so much. I can't believe we are going to leave all this beauty.' As she spoke she pushed her fingers into the earth as if she could put roots down just like a plant.

'*Coraggio, carissima.* Scotland is beautiful too. There are hills and mountains as well. You'll be surprised how beautiful they are. Lakes and rivers, wild flowers and blossom, just like here. You'll be enchanted, my darling, and you will learn to love it as well.'

Maria didn't answer. Her heart felt as if it had stopped beating and time had frozen. She felt that, at that moment, her life had stopped and from now she would have to learn to live again. She felt in a way as though part of her had died.

6

Italy
May 1913

In Fontitune news came that the sheep were on the way. They were at Ponte Melfa. They would arrive any day. It had taken over a fortnight to travel from Castel del Monte, south of Bari. It was a slow journey. Twice a day the lactating sheep had to be milked, and then the milk had to be made into cheese. The shepherds and their wives shared the work but it all took time.

Collective flocks of sheep belonging to different families and landowners were kept together, thousands of sheep moving as one flock. Few shepherds owned any sheep. Most of the flock belonged to wealthy landowners, *massari di pecori*, who had amassed great wealth over centuries. It was they who had kept the peasants impoverished.

As the flocks made their way along the dirt tracks, the shepherds paid taxes at tolls positioned on the ancient Roman tracts, *tratturi*. For villagers en route there was great excitement and anticipation. Not only was there the first fine fresh cheese of the season to sample, there was news to be exchanged and gossip to be savoured. The only method of communication was by word of mouth. These itinerant people traded tittle-tattle as well as cheese.

News from abroad, *all'estero*, of families who had emigrated, was top of the list, keenly devoured. The Crollas had made a fortune in Manchester, Valvona from Atina was selling tons of pasta in Edinburgh, Angelo Conetta from Perella owned a factory in New York.

The truth was less impressive. The Crollas were renting a shop, Valvona was almost bankrupt and Conetta had been laid off as factory foreman. But only success stories were welcomed. The dream of emigration and its seemingly unlimited rewards was precious to them all. As long as some of them were successfully on the ladder of success, those left behind could live in hope.

The women thrived on scandal and intrigue, bad news preferred to good: Donato was in prison, Filomena had died of pneumonia, a young Italian girl had burned to death in Edinburgh, Eduardo had two wives, one in Paris and one in Ponte Melfa. What fool of a man would want to keep two women? Surely one is bad enough! Word spread of babies born out of wedlock, adulterous wives, and priests with mistresses. The men discussed politics, business and war with shrewdness, cunning and bravado.

In the last few years, for the first time in Italian history, most of the young men like Alfonso and Cesidio had been called up for National Service. Some of them had also unsuccessfully fought in Libya, a war they didn't understand and certainly didn't want to fight.

Garibaldi was the great hero of the unification of Italy. The modern leaders were a mixture of incompetents and opportunists. Out-of-date newspaper reports told of pacts with Germany and Austria–Hungary or Britain, France and Russia. Europe was unsettled.

There were other rumours that the villagers found simply unbelievable. They say there's a school in London for Italian children, set up by our government. That's surely impossible since there are not schools for all the children here!

And most alluring was the myth of untold wealth, tales of roads paved with gold. It was true, more and more families were receiving letters with English notes and American dollars. Most people knew of someone who had seen the evidence, though fewer than expected had received such letters themselves.

This generated mixed feelings of envy and ambition. When no one had anything, the community spirit had been fierce. Everyone could depend on the family, on mutual support. Now that some had more than others, the balance was changing. It was bad enough to be poor among the rich, but very disconcerting to be rich among the poor.

As the flock weaved its way up towards Picinisco, it was not unlike a long white snake of gossip and intrigue it had picked up along the way. Higher and higher they came, causing great

51

excitement as they passed. Wives ran to embrace husbands they hadn't seen for months, sweethearts dragged along aunties as chaperones to get a sight of their betrothed, *fidanzati*. Asses, cockerels, hens and goats created a great hullabaloo running up and down, worrying the poor sheep.

The families that lived in I Ciacca joined the trail. Up, up the sheep came until they ran through the very heart of Picinisco, jammed from wall to wall of the narrow streets, not unlike the procession of Sant'Antonio, except this time the sheep were real.

Don Dioniso joined the tailback of stragglers at the end. Every year he blessed the shepherds and their flocks before they went up to the highest, cooler pastures for the summer. In truth he would have liked to go up to the Prato di Mezzo with them, but the climb would surely kill him. He was tempted. The villagers said that the ricotta the shepherds made there in the mornings was the sweetest, creamiest, most delicious cheese you would ever taste.

Nearly all the people of Fontitune ran down the hill to greet the sheep. The whole entourage made camp in and around the piazza, sheep spilling out at both ends of the village. They would spend a last night together before the final leg of the journey. There was a lot to do but the women in Fontitune had prepared, cooking big pots of *pasta e ceci*, *frittata* with potatoes and onions, and *guanciale con piselli*, pork cheek cooked with spring peas, served with a rough home-made pasta. Extra loaves of bread had been baked, and the children had collected *misticanza* of salad leaves and herbs full of nutrients.

Emidio and Pietro had gone down earlier to Picinisco to get two young lambs, *abbacchii*. They had carried them up on their shoulders ahead of the shepherds. After they had been born, the *abbacchii* had been strapped to the bellies of the sheep so that they had only been milk-fed, making their flesh tender and sweet. They had already been slaughtered and butchered. The men had dug a pit in the earth and covered the base of it with glowing embers.

Filomena pounded garlic, wild rosemary, thyme and preserved anchovies with green cloudy olive oil in a wooden mortar. She rubbed the mixture all over the lamb then laid it on a grate over the embers. Covered with twigs, the lamb roasted slowly. Occasional whiffs of rosemary and garlic and sparks of burning splinters of wood escaped with the smoke, creating an extraordinarily good aroma.

Once they had secured the sheep safely for the night, everyone sat round the fire to eat and gossip. Both the food and the *chiacchiera* that night were magnificently juicy!

With plenty of wine and the first coffee they had had for months, the night was long and merry. They played music on the pipes and sang ballads, happy to be together again. Most slept that night camped out under the stars. Even Don Dioniso slept in the open, though he did snore quite heavily and had to be prodded awake more than once. Oblivious, he dreamt that the last of the snow that capped the mountains was ricotta dripping down into his mouth. He would follow the sheep tomorrow. He must taste that ricotta.

Alone in the house Alfonso passionately made love to his wife, holding her as if for the last time. He was leaving at dawn. As soon as she slept, he kissed his child and went to sleep outside alone with his thoughts.

Maria woke as soon as the first light appeared through the narrow slit in the wall. She left the baby slumbering peacefully and climbed downstairs. The piazza was almost empty. A small fire had been lit and some women were making cheese. The milk from the sheep had been warmed with salt and some rennet from the *abbacchio*'s stomach. The women were scooping the solidified curds out with their bare hands, packing them like soft cotton wool into reed baskets to make pecorino.

The pale creamy whey that dripped through the baskets was collected in a pot and would be warmed again just to simmering. It would solidify again, producing soft grey-white curds that would be packed into smaller baskets to make the ricotta. The whey that dripped from these baskets would be collected and heated a third time. The spring milk was so rich that another curdling would produce even more ricotta.

The very last of the whey that wouldn't set was collected again, this time for the lucky pig which was already snorting around the women, nuzzling the ground, waiting for his treat.

Maria looked up to the hills. She could see nothing: the sheep and the shepherds, the dogs and the donkeys, Don Dioniso and his ass, had all disappeared. They had left well before dawn, driving the flock up to the pastures before the day was awake. She walked slowly to the small wall at the edge of the piazza, her heart thumping in her breast.

Away down in the distance, just past the third bend in the track, she could just make out the two men. Their heavy packs were strapped to their backs, their jackets were slung jauntily over their shoulders and their hats were pushed to the backs of their heads. Alfonso and Emidio had gone.

She put both hands to her mouth and called out as loud and long as she could. She waited. After a long minute, once the sound travelled down the valley, she saw one of the men stop. He turned round and looked back up to the Fontitune. Seeing the figure waving at the edge of the village he took his hat in his hand and waved wildly back. Maria was sure she heard Alfonso's call carried on the wind as he turned and walked away.

Alfonso felt no apprehension. He was convinced he had to go and he trusted that Maria would follow him as soon as he asked her. He was in fact very excited, optimistic, full of expectations. Life was going to be good.

Travelling on foot was natural to these two men who had trekked with the sheep all their lives. They followed the *tratturi* north as far as they could, then made their way to the coast. The roads were busy. They passed shepherds and farm workers going up the mountains towards the pastures. In the lower lands, peasants were working the fields, ploughing with oxen up and down, up and down, sowing seeds and pruning vines.

They met soldiers returning from duty, guns strapped to their backs, keen to talk of what they had seen. Other men were moving north, towards Roma and Genova, taking their chances on finding work in the cities. They came across whole families, grandparents, fathers with battered suitcases and women with cloth bundles piled on their heads, young children carrying babies, making their way south.

'Are we going the wrong way?' Emidio asked Alfonso, doubting his brother's lead.

'*A do vai?* Where are you going?' he asked one of the men as they passed by.

'*A Napoli!*'

The man's dialect was different from theirs and they found it difficult to understand.

'*Perche?*'

'*Per la nave per l'America.*'

These people were heading for America. What strange times they lived in, thought Alfonso. It was as if the world was upside down and back to front.

They too had thought about going to America; a lot of men they knew had. They had heard mixed reports, talk of people dying on the ships. It was a long journey. The thought of being on the sea, away from land for a whole month, was too much for them. They would not risk that. Also it was not as easy to get into America as it had been. They had heard horror stories of gangsters and shootings. They had heard that the Cosa Nostra had already taken a hold.

'A cousin of De Marco went all the way to New York only to come all the way back because they said his eyesight wasn't good and would not let him enter.'

'I've heard of children dying on the boats with typhoid and cholera.'

'Never mind typhoid. What about that ship that went down when it hit ice! Thousands of people drowned! That would put me off ever going to America.'

Only the year before, the news all over Europe had been of the *Titanic* sinking in the freezing water of the Atlantic. They had never really thought much about the sea but after that story they were both secretly afraid. Neither of them could swim. Living on a mountain why would you need to? America! They were not tempted. My God, Scotland was far enough!

It was lovely weather, sunny and warm, with a cooling breeze from the coast. At night they slept in fields or in the *pineta*, pine forests that stretched up the west coast of Tuscany at the edge of the beach. When they could, they washed themselves and their clothes in streams. They enjoyed the luxury of sleeping in the sun while their clothes dried. Now and then they worked on farms, helping with spring chores for a few days, in exchange for some provisions or a lift further north.

They made a handsome pair these two southern Italian boys, singing as they walked along. Emidio looked very like his brother, a softer, gentler, rounder-faced man with very dark brown eyes. He was slightly shorter and perhaps more reticent. He admired Alfonso and was happy to share this time with him.

They ate simply: bread and cheese, some salami or *salsiccie*, marvelling at the different types they were offered as they moved north. They ate cheese made from cow's milk, *Parmigiano Reggiano*, and mortadella, a huge pink salami studded with pistachios: good food but different from their own at home.

The countryside was also groaning with free food: glorious pink-red cherries, juicy and sweet, and the first golden apricots. There were plenty of wild greens and herbs, which they picked as they walked. If they were lucky they spotted spring *funghi*, spiky hedgehog or field mushrooms. Emidio carried a small frying pan in his pack. They lit a fire and cooked the *funghi* with some lard, *strutto,* wild garlic and eggs collected from a nearby farm. When they could, they bought some local wine, though it never tasted as fine as their own.

They heard talk of war. As they approached the main cities on the way north, they were aware of a political tension that was not as apparent in the south. Men in the street told them the news. They would be allowed to vote for the first time, a reward to all the men who had fought in the war in Libya. The next general election would not be until October. They would be far away by then.

They planned to get as far as Torino in the north, then stop and work for a few weeks to earn some money for the rest of the journey. As they approached the city, they hitched a lift from a farmer. His horse-drawn cart was piled high with boxes of his produce, which he was taking to market. He took them right in to the market, at the Porta Palazzo where the Via Milano meets the Piazza della Republica.

What an abundance of food! They had never seen anything like it. There were stalls upon stalls piled with all the produce of the surrounding countryside. Trestle tables and boxes piled on the streets, carts acting as impromptu shops; everything was for sale. Gnarled pepperoni, green, golden yellow and garnet red, were piled precariously in three stripes like an edible tricolour. Glorious golden trumpets of zucchini flowers, cranberry and white spiked radicchio and dozens of types of herbs in bunches and in pots.

There were leaning towers of wooden crates of *carciofi*, purple bulbous artichokes, and small delicate artichokes on long stalks, competing with creamy white bulbs of fennel with delicate green fronds. Cardoons and chicory, *puntarelle*, were being prepared for cooking by a gnarled old crone, sitting with a basin of water between her legs, trimming the vegetables to size, nothing better to do with the day.

Pock-marked Amalfi lemons and oranges were stacked beside gleaming ruby-red cherries, all brought up from Naples by a couple who looked like they needed a good wash. They aimed to sell their southern produce to these northern bandits and get out of there as fast as they could.

Other stall-holders looked more like zoo keepers, with cages of wild sparrows and starlings, live frogs and snails. A pig, just like Pietro's, had a price tag round its neck. Ducks and chickens, cockerels and geese were all wandering around pleading to be bought and cooked; surely anything would be better than the stench and chaos of this animal hell.

In the covered market, stalls were piled with pork and beef, horse and lamb, heads and tongues, tripe and trotters. Almost every part of every animal on God's Earth was there to be sold.

Alfonso and Emidio had been to the fish markets on the coast at Mondragone and Formia. They were familiar with dry cod, and with fresh-water trout caught in the lake high in the mountain. But here it looked as if all of the contents of the sea had been slapped onto the marble slabs. They heard the fishermen calling out the names and prices of the fish. Shiny purple-scaled *spigola* and bright-eyed *dentice*. Buckets of squirming cuttle-fish, *seppie*, squid and octopus, fighting for attention among luminescent, black slimy eels. Blushing, pink-red mullet, sensitive to the company of the ugly and surely inedible cat-fish, with its gnashing teeth.

The customers were as varied. Chefs and cooks fighting and arguing over quality and prices; sophisticated ladies with gentlemen on their arms, their feathers and plumes as exotic as any on the pheasants they wanted to buy. Their noses were affronted by the basic smells that assaulted them. They pushed past the workers, afraid of being contaminated. The wives of workers from the south laughed at them; dark and rough, full of a lust for life, they were the antipathy of the pampered rich *signoras*.

Emidio nudged Alfonso when a particularly buxom Sicilian woman passed.

'*Guarda, Alfonso. Vuoi due meloni?*'

Alfonso blushed at his brother and turned his head to look round his shoulder, sure that Maria was watching him. He slapped Emidio, good-naturedly.

'Emidio! *Fai bravo!*'

'*Ciao Bella!*' Emidio called after the girl. You never knew. He might get lucky.

The men took any jobs offered: unloading carts, lifting boxes and setting up stalls. Horses had to be fed and housed, straw and sawdust spread over their muck on the market floor. They worked from early morning to late at night sweeping away the debris that was left after the produce, live and dead, had been bartered and sold.

They felt at home here. There were plenty of Abruzzesi and Neapolitans working alongside them, peasants like themselves, desperate to find work. Many had come north after being in the army. It was in the army that Alfonso had heard the wonderful stories of the Fiat factory that was making more and more stylish automobiles, methods of transport that would one day take over the world. Many men came north to find work in Torino, dreaming of getting a job working in the factory. Most ended up just like them, sweeping up and carrying boxes.

The market was staggering. The abundance was incredible, the prices astronomical. Alfonso had no experience of city life. He was astonished to see so many lire changing hands for tomatoes and verdure, herbs and fruit, produce that they grew every year or harvested free. They talked in the dialect of Fontitune so that no one could understand them.

'Emidio, *guarda qui. La rucola costa soldi.* Imagine paying for rocket. It costs as much as cigarettes in Naples. And look at the price of the pecorino. It's five times what they give us in Picinisco, and it's not a patch on ours.'

'*Mannàggia!* We could bring our cheese here to the market and sell it. But, Alfons', even if we came by donkey the ricotta would be sour once it arrived.'

'Don't you see, Emidio? It is only a matter of time. Once we make money we can buy a horse, then we can bring Pietro's *formaggio* north and make a fortune.'

'If they built decent roads for us then we could buy a Fiat and drive the cheese to Torino! We could barter our cheese for cars!'

They loved this idea. It was a joke. The old bus that wound its way up to Picinisco twice a week usually broke down half-way up the winding dirt track because of the steepness of the climb. A Fiat car up to Fontitune! That would be the day!

They hadn't noticed a Neapolitan listening to them.

'*Ei, ragazzi,* you're dreaming. The North will never build roads to the South. They want to keep us down. They want to get rid of us, not help us get organised and work. And here in the market, what stall-holder would sell cheese from Abruzzo instead of from here in Lombardia or Piemonte. The people here wouldn't take your cheese even if you were giving it away.'

'But ours tastes better.' Emidio was indignant.

The Neapolitan shook his hand at them, three fingers joined together, an age-old gesture that accused them of not knowing what they were talking about. He walked off.

Alfonso felt ill at ease. It was better to keep quiet and act dumb. How could they survive in a city like this? These people had a different agenda. There was talk of Socialism and Liberalism; he had no idea what they were talking about. He could sense an aggression in the air, a mood of discontent.

In the inns at night the men heard talk of politicians, moderate well-off Socialists in whom the workers were losing confidence. They saw men reading free copies of a newspaper entitled *Avanti*, whose editor was a man called Mussolini. He called for the workers to take the initiative and stand up for themselves. Alfonso thought he might have a point. He frowned.

'Emidio, we'd better get away from here. There's trouble brewing by the sounds of it. Something in Torino disturbs me. The mood is unsettled. There's work, but even more workers. There's food aplenty, but it is so expensive you could hardly afford to live. There are trouble-makers around, Emidio. Somebody wants power, or even revolution.'

Alfonso was missing Maria and Domenico very badly but he could not allow himself to think about them. Instead, he planned how to send more money so that they could follow as soon as possible.

After two weeks they collected their wages. Almost as if the Devil himself was on their tails they pushed on over the border and set off towards Paris. They didn't stop. They didn't care. Something changed in their mood after they left Italy. Their bravado disappeared and they travelled as fast as they could towards Dover.

7

May 1913

They reached Calais within four days. Exhausted, they headed for the port. Two large ferries were moored at the quayside. They saw a huddle of families, and men milling around the ticket office on the pier. The official in the booth marked for '*emigranti Italiani*' was making a big deal about whom he was allowing a passage. The next ship to Dover was at seven the following morning. Alfonso did not want to spend a day longer on French soil.

He joined the crowd: 'Stay right behind me, Emidio.'

Every time a space opened out in front of him Alfonso pushed forward, his brother slipping in behind him. It was just like moving the sheep into the pen, he thought with a wry smile.

'*Documenti!*' the official was harassed.

Alfonso handed over the single sheets of parchment, passports issued to them when they had been called up to the army. In his letter from Edinburgh, Giovanni had prepared Alfonso. The ships would not carry passengers who could not prove that they had a place to go to at the other end, a secure job or a benefactor.

British immigration officers applied what they called the '£5 test'. Any immigrant entering the country had to possess five pounds sterling, 'a failsafe' to prove they would be self-sufficient and would not end up as dependants on the state. If the immigrant could not pass the test, the ship's owners were fined and had to bring the poor soul back again. The fool who issued the ticket would most likely get the sack.

Alfonso had the five-pound note, but only one. He was eager not to let any of these ruffians in the queue behind him see his money. Emidio and he might get ambushed during the night and be left with nothing. The crowd was pushing him from behind.

'*Aih!*'

He turned from the official and yelled at the crowd with his hand cupped at his mouth so that his voice carried over their heads. '*Aaaiiihh!*'

Even the ticket master looked taken aback. The crowd fell back. Instinctively Emidio turned his back to his brother and stood with his shoulders pushed back and his arms folded in front of his chest giving the impression he was a hard man or a bodyguard. The crowd took another step back.

These days the official never knew who was a big shot and who was a chancer, but he had learned to keep out of trouble. Alfonso put his hand on the counter and, looking the official straight in the eye, lifted the edge of his hand a little. There was the folded five-pound note. With pieces of crumpled paper between the folds, it looked more like a bundle of notes. The official saw it and, as he registered with a nod, Alfonso whisked it away, back down the front of his shirt.

'*Lavoriamo in proprio in Edimburgo.*' Alfonso flourished the picture of the shop with the words 'Crolla Newhaven' across the door and pointed out his name again on his papers. It looked as if he had his own business in Edinburgh. The official nodded. The deal was done.

The official looked Alfonso and Emidio up and down. He'd seen this type before. Dressed in filthy rags with the bravado of a magician in Turkey!

'Second or third class?'

Alfonso put his head to one side, lifted his eyebrows and gave the official a look that made him nervous. The man rubbed the back of his neck; it was warm in the office.

'First class, my friend, first class, if you don't mind.' Alfonso Crolla was not going to arrive in Britain on a third-class ticket. He pulled out the money that they had worked so hard for and gave half to the official. He watched as his brother's and his own name were added to the passenger list, took his tickets, touched his hat in salute and turned and walked away.

Emidio had been watching a rather pretty, well-dressed Italian girl in the queue, standing with an older woman, probably her aunt, so he didn't notice that Alfonso had gone. When the next man in the queue nudged him he looked around in a panic before he caught

62

sight of his older brother walking away through the crowd. He bent down to pick up their packs and, overloaded with the bags, tried to push his way through the crowd.

The people in the queue laughed, relieved that there had not been an incident. He's not as smart as his big-shot brother! They started pushing forward again behind him.

Emidio's pride was hurt. 'Alfonso, why did you have to buy first-class tickets? For God's sake, that's nearly half our money.'

'*Non ti preoccupare!* Don't worry, Emidio. You'll see at the other end. We want to make sure we arrive in Britain with our best foot forward. *La bella figura. Hai capito?* Trust me. We need to pass the immigration officer in Dover with no questions asked. You don't want to be sent back, do you?'

'No, of course not.'

'We need to start as we mean to go on. We'll travel first class because we, my dear brother, are heading for the top.'

'Will we have to walk to Scotland now? It'll take another week. My boots are worn through.'

'We'll see. I'll think of something.'

They slept rough that night. Waking at first light, they set off clutching their first-class tickets and boarded the ship before the rest of the rabble. They headed straight to the washrooms where both men had a good wash and shave, changed their clothes and, by the time the rest of the passengers came on board, they had made a pretty good attempt at looking like genuine first-class ticket holders.

As the ship's horn blew, Emidio gave a low whistle as he saw the pretty Italian girl come onto the fore deck. She was a first-class passenger as well! He slapped his brother on the back for creating such a good opportunity!

'*Bravo, Alfonso. Ci Vediamo!* See ya!' He removed his hat, smoothed his hair down, straightened his back and strolled across the wooden deck to pay his respects to the girl's aunt and offer his services.

Alfonso went to the front of the top deck and watched the rest of the passengers filing on board. He waited as the ship's anchor was pulled up: a loud, clanking clatter. His mood was sombre. He prayed to the Madonna.

'Santa Maria, Madre di Dio, prega per noi, peccatori, adesso e nell'ora della nostra morte, Amen.'

It was a fine, bright morning. The dazzling sunlight created intermittent flashes of light on the sea below. The ship moved steadily away from land. A rabble of people stood on the quay shouting and waving at their loved ones. Passengers were hanging over the edges of the barriers on the ship, almost as if they would jump overboard and swim back to land. Seagulls circled expectantly in the air above, shrieking to each other. The funnel puffed dark smoke and the horn hooted two long whoops, confirming the ship's departure.

An unexpected fear gripped Alfonso. He struck his chest. His stomach lurched with the ship as it dipped into the waves. A single seagull gave a shattering, piercing scream. It sounded as if Maria was calling, as if she was crying to him all the way from Fontitune. It was as if she didn't want him to go. For the first time, leaving the shores of France, the enormity of what they were doing dawned on him. He struck his chest again and, as the tears spilled, he prayed again to the Madonna to protect them all.

Once the ship was under way he walked around the deck looking for his brother. He spotted him talking to the girl. He smiled, his spirits lifting. That boy would get into trouble with a woman one day.

He looked around at the passengers sharing the journey. They were mostly families, couples with one or two children, well dressed with plenty of luggage. These were the lucky ones who could afford to travel all together; perhaps they had already made their fortunes or perhaps they were just going to Britain for a holiday.

Some men were alone and looked as if they were travelling on business. They were dressed in a particular manner with tidy, well-made suits, white shirts with small wing collars, covered by tailored waistcoats and a short black tie at their necks. On their heads they wore felt hats, the rim pulled jauntily over their foreheads. Many of them had a gold chain with a watch or fob dangling between two pockets. They ran their fingers over the watch as they walked around the deck, opening it now and then to check the time, as if to emphasise their wealth and importance.

Alfonso noted all the details. This was the uniform of a business-

man. He had left his shepherd's garb at home for Pietro. When
Maria saw him next he would be dressed as a businessman.

A tall, distinguished-looking man with greying hair caught his
attention. He had taken a small bottle of cologne from his inside
pocket, whisked out the handkerchief that decorated his top left-
hand pocket and dabbed it with cologne. He patted the sweet-
smelling handkerchief to his brow, signifying that he was slightly
distressed. He put the handkerchief back into his pocket with a
flourish, straightened the rose in his button-hole and took a turn
round the deck. As he passed Alfonso, there was a lingering perfume.

'I fancy that,' Alfonso laughed to himself, 'smelling of roses
instead of sheep!'

It was Alfonso's bravado and ingenuity that would be the making
of him.

When Alfonso and Emidio walked off the ship they almost looked
the part. They had given their de-mob army boots a good spit-
and-polish and, although neither of them looked as if they had a
penny to rub together, with their creased jackets and a kerchief
tied at the necks of their slightly grubby shirts, there was something about them that made them stand out among the other passengers. They were taller than most. Their hats were placed jauntily
on their heads, the rims turned down over one eye. Emidio had
the pretty Italian girl on his arm as he offered to help her down
the gangplank and Alfonso had given twenty cents to a porter to
carry their packs, giving the impression that they must have some
money.

With heads held high, the Crolla brothers from Fontitune stepped
onto British soil.

The immigration officer in the hall was impressed with Alfonso's
papers. Not only was Alfonso coming to work in his well-established
eponymous business, he had the means to support his brother as
well. These were the kind of immigrants that Britain needed. He
stamped their passports and wished them 'good luck, boys!' before
turning with a scowl to the rabble behind.

The men walked out of the customs hall, and as soon as they
were round the corner out of sight they hugged each other, slapped
each other on the back and laughed. They'd done it! They'd arrived

in Great Britain. What a relief! That was the first hurdle out of the way.

It was a dull day on this side of the Channel, a little chilly, with a breeze coming off the ocean. They walked away from the port and up what looked like the main street into the town centre. They wondered what they would do next. The signs were all in English. They understood only a smattering of words between them. They looked around. Nothing was familiar.

All of a sudden they felt foreign. They definitely looked foreign. Their skin was darker, they were rough looking and, to be frank, they probably stank. Their exuberance at landing on British soil was starting to wane. They were hungry and had no British money except for the precious five-pound note.

Just as they were starting to lose confidence, Emidio nudged his brother and started to laugh. On their left at the bend in the road was an ice cream shop, an Italian ice cream shop!

'*Dio mio, Alfonso! Siamo ancora in Italia!*'

They roared with laughter, so much so that the owner came out to see what the commotion was. A rotund, ruddy-faced man with an extraordinarily wide moustache and a spotless white apron that covered his ample belly from his armpits down to the ground, he didn't look surprised to see them.

Every day brought more Italian hopefuls off the boat. He had seen them all: Neapolitans, Sicilians, Toscani from Barga, Emiliani from Parma, Piemontesi from Borgotaro, Abruzzesi, Romans . . . It was as if half the population of Italy had passed this way over the last ten years. He and his brother had been here over twelve years, among the first immigrants to arrive. They had established a good business, converting a butcher's shop into a French and Italian café. What he didn't want was any more of his compatriots setting up stall on his patch. He had made it his business to watch who was coming in off the boats and make sure they weren't tempted to stay. Sometimes he gave the poor blighters a cup of tea and, if he felt sorry for them, some help towards their fare to London. It was an investment to get them out of the way.

When he heard their accent he knew these two were from south of Rome. He called them over. They looked like a personable pair and, anyway, he liked to know what was going on.

'*Ciao, ragazzi! Dove andate?*'

'*Edimburgo, amico.*'

As soon as he realised they had no intention of staying in Dover he asked them if they would like to take a table in his café. He gave them a plate of soup and some bread, the first food they had eaten in Britain. The cup of tea he gave them was very strange, quite bitter and not as powerful as the coffee they were used to, but fairly pleasing all the same. He accepted their francs in payment and once they had finished he talked to them. His family name was Mangilli.

His brother came out from the kitchen and shook their hands.

'We've seen lots of people from your part of Italy passing through Dover. They're mostly in London and Manchester now. And Glasgow as well, but usually those poeple come in at Liverpool on the west coast. Go to King's Cross rail station in London, take the train for Aberdeen and get off at Edinburgh Waverley Station. You'll be in Scotland by the morning if you're lucky. *Buona fortuna!*'

'I'm sending for my wife in a couple of months,' Alfonso said. 'I'll tell her to come to see you. Will you watch out for her? Maria Crolla. She'll be travelling with a friend and my baby son.'

'Sure. Sure. It will be my pleasure to look after her.' These lads thought they were pioneers. There had been thousands before them, the same story. How could he recognise this lad's wife from yesterday's or tomorrow's?

Anyway, they hugged each other and parted company as good friends. No doubt Alfonso and Emidio would see the Mangilli brothers again when they went back to Italy after they had made their fortunes.

'They've got it made,' said Emidio, full of admiration. 'They've found a great place to live. I'll bet they keep an eye out for all the Italians moving in and out of Britain. And they're closer to the boat home! Lucky so-and-sos!'

'Good luck to them!' Alfonso said. 'That's a good idea for us, Emidio. We should find a way of helping the Italians that come behind us. Once we understand English we can help them. Look at those chaps; they have the whole town sewn up!'

The men left in good spirits, with a full stomach and two new

67

friends. They waited at the side of the road and hitched a lift on the back of a horse and cart that was on its way to London.

King's Cross was a hive of activity, thronging with people and thoroughly confusing. The passengers, mainly men with bowler hats and severe pin-striped suits, had umbrellas swinging at their arms, much to the amusement of the two men; it had warmed up to be a dry sunny day.

Everyone was intent on getting to their train before everyone else. Well-dressed women, with maids looking after their well-dressed children, stood with boxes and parcels, more possessions than Emidio and Alfonso had ever owned in their whole lives. The noise was incredible. There were women sitting at stalls selling fruit, calling out with a comical accent, and newspaper boys screaming at the tops of their voices. Tall serious policemen with high navy hats and black rubber sticks walked around in pairs, eyeing everyone up and down and not missing a trick, chasing beggars away and politely greeting pretty girls who wanted to know where their train platform was.

Alfonso stood against the gate of what looked like the post office and waited. He had an idea that if they could find someone who could speak Italian they might be lucky. After an hour or so he saw an Italian-looking porter who was sorting out heavy sacks. Before long, Alfonso had managed to persuade the Neapolitan that he and Emidio would do all the work if he would help them stow away on the train. They worked for four hours loading mail sacks onto wagon after wagon and then, when they were beginning to think they had been conned, the porter came up to them and, thrusting some pieces of bread and jam into their hands, shoved the two men behind a pile of sacks inside a wagon, told them the train didn't stop until Edinburgh and slammed the wagon door shut.

After scoffing the bread, they fell asleep with exhaustion. The next thing they knew they woke to the sound of the brakes screeching as the train drew up at four in the morning in Waverley Station.

When the wagon door was opened they lay still until they could see that the way was clear, then they jumped out and ran hell for leather as far away from the train as they could. A platform guard spotted them and started to yell and blow his whistle, but to no avail. These two men were fit and within minutes had disappeared into the station.

It was early, and still dark outside, but they were in Edinburgh.

They took a turning to the left, went up some steps and, hearing a lot of bustle and noise, walked straight into the early-morning fruit market that was held in Waverley Market. That took the biscuit. They had left the market in Torino to end up in another market in Edinburgh!

Walking round, they looked in amazement at the produce: leeks, cabbages, cardoons and greens, plenty of herbs and salads and peas in their pods. Long pink sticks of something called rhubarb and wooden trays with small cardboard cartons of green sour-looking gooseberries.

They were walking round the potato stalls, which appeared to be the most abundant and busiest, when they heard a few Italian voices. They looked round and there in front of them were two older Italian men, up at dawn buying potatoes for their fish and chip shops.

'*Buon Giorno, amici! Da dove venite?* Where are you from?'

'*Madonna mia! Sant'Antonio!*' Alfonso was astonished. There were Italians everywhere!

It turned out that these were two men from Picinisco who had been working in Edinburgh for the last five years. They knew Giovanni Crolla and were aware that his brothers were on their way from Italy.

'*Bravi, ragazzi!* You've made it! Well done! Giovanni will be in his shop. Wait a minute till we finish our business and we'll take you down the road. Our shop is not far from his. We all work near each other.'

The men did their business, paying for the sacks of potatoes from a bundle of notes pulled from their back pockets. Emidio nudged Alfonso when he saw all the money this chap had. They spoke broken English with a strange accent. The man they were buying from was quite friendly. They obviously knew each other well. They piled six sacks of potatoes onto a barrow and Emidio helped pull it out of the market up to Waverley Bridge from where they made their way down towards Leith.

8

November 1913

Six months later Maria stepped down from the train, exhausted, into Waverley Station. She looked around and took a deep breath. The journey had been difficult, the train connections and boat journey daunting. Giuseppina had travelled with her from Italy but had left her at London, taking a train to Manchester to meet her family there.

Maria had sat in a carriage with strangers, foreigners in her eyes. She hadn't understood a word they had said but she had been aware that she was being talked about. Domenico had cried for most of the journey from London, and the other passengers in the compartment had not been pleased.

It seemed as if Domenico had been crying ever since Alfonso had left in the spring. Living in Fontitune with a new baby, being at the beck and call of her mother-in-law, had been intolerable for Maria. She too had been crying ever since Alfonso had left. For weeks she had had no news. She had been so worried about him.

She and Marietta had waited anxiously in Picinisco every Thursday for the post to arrive. Sitting together on the low wall at the edge of the piazza, they looked forlorn, scanning the valley to catch sight of the bus. Their hearts were thumping as they watched it snake its way up the hillside. Week after week they left disheartened, when the old driver said again, 'Sorry, girls. Nothing yet.'

Every week they kissed each other and returned to their homes, Maria up the hill, Marietta down, both disappointed and worried. The bus driver felt sorry for them. He saw girls like this in almost every village he went to all over the valley: young, beautiful Italian girls waiting for news from their lovers. At night he talked to his wife.

'Our country is making the biggest mistake of its history.'

'What do you mean?'

'We're losing our youth. Our young and healthy are leaving in droves. I see it everywhere. The young men go and take their wives and families with them. Mark my words, before we end our days we'll see these villages all over the mountains lying deserted.'

One Thursday the girls had been waiting as usual. Maria had brought Domenico and they played with him under the oak tree, splashing water at him from *la fontana*. They were so engrossed they forgot to look for the bus and didn't realise it had arrived, spluttering and chugging as usual round the last, steepest bend, until they heard its horn peep-peeping excitedly.

The driver jumped down and ran excitedly across to the girls.

'Girls, *bellezze!* Finally! A letter! *Ecco!*'

He waved the letter in the air and kissed both girls. The letter was addressed to Maria. He stood waiting for her to open it.

Alfonso couldn't write, so he had dictated his letter. Maria couldn't read, so she gave it to Marietta to read out. Maria stood with Domenico in her arms, with the bus driver, waiting to hear what it said. It was short and to the point:

'*Carissima Maria, siamo arrivati in Scozia.*

Edimburgo e bellissima e tutto è a posto.

Un bacio per te, Domenico e tutta la famiglia.

Tuo caro marito, Alfonso.'

'Darling Maria, we have arrived in Scotland.

Edinburgh is very beautiful and everything is fine.

A kiss for you, Domenico and all the family,

Your loving husband, Alfonso.'

All summer more letters had arrived, until eventually one had come with the money for her journey. Marietta had helped her get organised. Within a week she had been ready. Everyone from Fontitune and the whole of Picinisco had gathered to see her off and waved as Marietta climbed onto the bus with Domenico. With only a bundle of clothes and a *pacco di formaggio e salsiccie* she had sat in the front seat beside the driver, and left.

Now she stood on Platform 1 at Waverley Station with the baby strapped to her chest, the parcels at her feet, forlorn and almost in tears. Alfonso had said he would meet her but she couldn't see him.

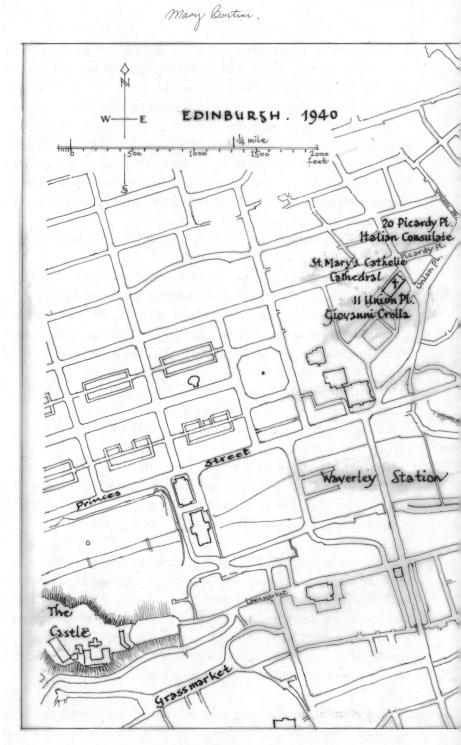

Map of central Edinburgh

Leith Walk

Montgomery Street

128 Easter Rd.
Alfonso Crolla
Confectioners

25 Easter Rd.
Alfonso Crolla Confectioners

19 Elm Row
Valvona & Crolla

Calton Hill

Holyrood
Palace

St. John's Hill

1 & 1a St. John's Hill
Valvona & Crolla

Holyrood Park

Ian Begg

She looked decidedly odd among the other people. Her clothes were grubby and crushed; her long peasant skirt, lacy long-sleeved blouse and coloured waistcoat incongruous in this busy city station.

Maria felt the other women looking her up and down. They were slim and well groomed, in graceful silk dresses with long velvet-and-wool coats that swept from their shoulders down to the ground. They wore wide-brimmed hats with feathers and flowers and carried beautiful little embroidered bags hanging on their leather-gloved arms.

The gentlemen were elegant, with smart top hats and neat jackets. Some of them smiled at her familiarly. Maria kept her eyes down, embarrassed. The noise of the steam from the trains, the whistles and shouts from the guards and the general hustle and bustle were strange and confusing. What would she do if Alfonso didn't appear?

Just as she began to lose hope, she saw him. Running along the platform, waving his hat high in the air to attract her attention was Alfonso, grinning from ear to ear.

'*Maria! Maria! Ecco mi! Ecco mi!*'

Her heart leapt. She reddened. Her cheeks glowed.

He scooped her up and twirled her round, kissing her mouth again and again as if he could hardly believe she was real. The people on the platform stood around and stared at this motley crew of foreigners. What a commotion they caused!

'*Domenico, carissimo*! *Un bacio per Papà*'! Kiss your daddy!'

Alfonso took the six-month-old child from Maria and held him at arm's length, studying his pretty face and broad forehead, his brown eyes and fairish hair. Was this his son? He had grown so big. He kissed Domenico again and again till the child started to cry and pulled away from this strange man, stretching his arms out towards his mother.

'Darling Maria!' he spoke the first word to her in English, 'Darling, wife!'

Maria laughed. She hardly recognised him. He looked older, slimmer, different. He wore a dark jacket over grey trousers and a waistcoat. His white shirt was open at the neck, with a blue cravat tied jauntily round his throat. A white handkerchief flopped from the top pocket of his jacket. He looked very happy, proud to be welcoming his family to their new home.

Emidio had come with him, so now it was his turn to kiss her and embrace.

Alfonso was desperate to show her everything.

'*Andiamo, carissima*. Let's go.'

Emidio lifted her parcels. Alfonso took the baby. He held Maria's arm and guided her out of the station up a steep road to Waverley Bridge.

In the fresh air, Maria immediately felt the cold, but was happy to see a clear blue sky.

'*Guarda! Carissima,* look at our new home. Look at this beautiful city.'

In front of her she saw an imposing tall monument with a statue of a man sitting underneath. On the left swept beautiful gardens landscaped with plants and trees. Ladies and gentlemen were strolling arm in arm, looking relaxed and sophisticated. Paths led down towards the railway line that was running along the lower side.

Rising from the gardens were austere tall buildings with small windows layered one on top of the other, seven or eight levels high. The stone was dark, grey-black, severe and imposing. Following the line of a craggy slope with her eyes, she came to beautiful white houses that looked like fairy castles. Then she saw Edinburgh Castle, perched high over the city on a steep rock face. She caught her breath. She had never seen anything so magnificent.

'See! It is wonderful isn't it? Isn't it? I told you.' Alfonso was thrilled that she was impressed.

'Now come and I will show you Princes Street, *La Strada dei Principi!*'

They walked up a small incline and crossed a busy road, with horses and carriages passing at great speed, and noisy, clanging open-topped trams pulled by sturdy horses along metal tramways. The ground was mucky with manure and mud and Maria had to lift her skirts to stop them getting even filthier than they already were.

They crossed a small road to a tall, dark corner building with wide glass windows decorated with gold gilt. Maria was entranced. In the windows were statues, each wearing splendid dresses and coats, wide-brimmed hats and leather shoes with delicate stitching

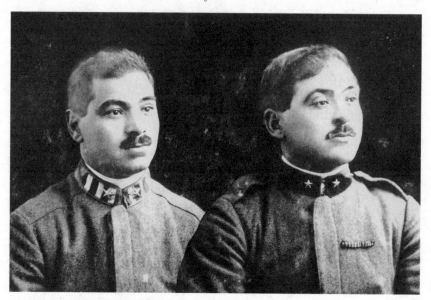

Emidio (left) and Alfonso, c. 1913

and slender heels. There were windows displaying babies' clothes, beautifully embroidered in the finest wools and silks. In another window was a large tree decorated with red velvet bows and golden baubles with piles of gaudily covered boxes and ribboned parcels underneath.

'What do you think? Isn't this incredible? One day we'll go in here and I'll buy you a coat like that one with the fur collar. You'll choose a hat to match, with the longest most outrageous feather it can hold!'

Emidio joined in. 'Look, you'll push Domenico in that pretty basket on wheels and he'll play with the toy as you walk.'

'Oh, Alfonso! It is exciting! I couldn't imagine such beautiful things and such fine quality. And look at this wonderful food. What kind of things are these? Pies and cheeses and cooked hams! Look how they decorate the cakes and the biscuits. It looks so tempting.'

'You'll see, Maria, we're going to be so lucky. You won't be lonely. There are about ten Italian families here, some of them you already know. Wait till you see. Come now, we have to walk about twenty minutes, then we will be home.'

He kissed her. He was very relieved that she had arrived safely.

Maria was happy too. She had been anxious and worried, but everything looked so wonderful. The shops and the castle and the ladies with their elegant men on their arms.

They started to walk east along Princes Street then turned down a long sweeping road towards Leith Walk. Alfonso pointed out buildings along the way: the North British Station Hotel towering above them at the east end of Princes Street with horse-drawn cabs outside and very important looking men sitting aloft. They passed the Vittoria Palais de Danse, which Emidio said people went to in the evenings to dance.

'I go there with my friend, Maria.' Emidio chirped up. 'We get paid to dance with the ladies! They call me a gigolo!'

Alfonso and Maria burst out laughing. Trust Emidio. *Che furbo!*

'Maria, *ecco la chiesa*: St Mary's Cathedral. This is where we'll go to Mass. It is different here. Only a few are Catholics. All the Italians are, of course. They all go to Mass, so you will meet them there. And that's the Playhouse Theatre. People dress up in their best finery and go there to hear people sing.'

Emidio gave the low-down on the night life. 'There's sometimes an Italian with a barrel organ outside or another lady called 'the Nightingale' who sings opera songs in the street for money. It's as bad as the piazza in Picinisco.'

They walked down further towards a wide street with tall trees lining it on both sides. As they walked, Alfonso and Emidio gave Maria a running commentary about which Italian families lived in which houses, and showed her some shops that had the names Coppola's, D'Agostino's, Marandola or Crolla displayed outside them.

'You're right, Emidio. It *is* like the piazza. They're all here!'

It was starting to get dark. A street lighter was going from lamp to lamp lighting the feeble gas lights, taking away some of the gloom that was settling over the city.

'*Sei stanca, cara*? Are you tired? Not long now.'

They crossed to the right-hand side of the wide street, lined with elm trees. The pale stone buildings were very tall and elegant. The ground floors of the buildings were all shop fronts with arched double windows of engraved glass. Flickering gas flames from the lights inside gave things a magical appearance.

They passed a shop with the name "Green's Furniture Stores". In the window was a wooden table with four chairs around it. There was a vase of flowers on the table and a photograph of a young girl in a frame.

Then they passed a lawyer's office, with a bright brass plate scrolled with letters and an imposing knocker at the door handle. After a few doors there was a shop called Lindsay & Gilmour with a gold pestle and mortar hanging outside. Alfonso said was where you could buy medicines and tonics if you were ill.

'This is Stocks, which sells stationery, and then we are nearly home.'

They stopped outside a wooden door.

'Down there is the post office and a drinking place called Pearce's. It sells beer and a drink called whisky. Never go in there, Maria, *hai capito*? Only *puttane* go in there.'

Maria blushed at her husband using such a word to describe women. She would never have gone into the bar in Picinisco. She would never even have spoken to Alfonso if he was sitting outside the bar with his friends. She could imagine what kind of women would go into a place that sells beer.

'Alfonso, there are so many shops! Where are the fields where you keep the goats for the milk?'

'We won't keep goats and sheep. We'll buy our milk and our food. Look down there, across the road, at the corner. That's the dairy where we'll get milk. There are shops further down selling meat and fish and everything you'll need.

'But where will we get money?'

'*Non ti preoccupare. Non ti preoccupare.* You'll see, it will be all right. I have work and I help Giovanni. Remember, if things get tough,' he winked at Emidio, 'I can always be a gigolo and dance with the girls in the ballroom.'

'No you won't, Alfonso Crolla!'

He roared with laughter. 'Now look, here we are. Your new home. *Diciannove*, Nineteen, Elm Row, *Edimburgo!*'

In front of Maria were two arched windows; faint glimmers of light could be seen inside. In the window was a display of jars of coloured boilings and sweets, and a pile of purple foiled boxes. There were tin boxes of red, silver and gold with pictures of cone-shaped biscuits with white ice cream painted on top.

'This is Giovanni's shop, Maria. What do you think? We'll have our own shop like this one day.'

In truth, Maria didn't know what to think. She had seen a castle and gardens, a cathedral and a dance hall. She had seen shops selling glamorous clothes and a man climbing a ladder to light a lamp with a flame. She had seen a shop that sells medicine and a bar that loose women go into.

She had seen trams and carriages pulled by horses, and children dressed like princes and princesses with beautiful mothers who had servants to hold their children's hands. She'd even seen a lady walking with a dog on a lead!

Most alarming of all to Maria was the number of houses she had seen, one piled high on top of the next, again and again, higher and higher. How many families lived on top of each other? How many people lived in this city?

Emidio opened the shop door and showed her into a high-ceilinged, long, narrow room. A wooden counter ran along the right-hand side. A cabinet behind the counter was filled with blue and white packets of cigarettes. Lining the walls were endless shelves, packed with bottles of sweets and chocolates, in different vibrant colours, stretching higher than you could reach. As she looked up into the gloom it seemed as if there was no ceiling at all.

Giovanni came hurrying out from a door at the back of the shop, wiping his hands on his white apron.

'You've arrived! *Siete arrivati! Bravi!'*

He came forward with his arms stretched out and welcomed Maria with a warm embrace and kisses on both cheeks.

'*Brava, Maria. Bellezza!'*

He was about twenty-eight, older than Alfonso. His face was narrower and longer than his brother's, his brown eyes edged with fine, smile wrinkles. He was a good-looking, strong man. His broad smile and warm welcome made Maria feel instantly comfortable with him. He looked very like his brothers with his dark curling moustache.

He hugged her and kissed her again, and in a torrent of questions and chatter asked her about the journey, about the baby and all about the family back in Fontitune.

'Are you OK? *Come ti senti?* Let me see the baby. Oh, he's lovely.

Congratulations. *Auguri, auguri.* Come through, come through.'

They went through to the back of the shop, a small dark space with a sink, a table and a small fire. Above the fire, a pot of soup was hanging from a chain. Giovanni's wife, Preziosa, a comely, well-built woman, came forward, her turn now to kiss and hug Maria. She took Maria's shawl from her and sat her down.

Preziosa had four children, aged seven, six, five and four. Two were asleep; the older ones hung near their mother, looking at the stranger suspiciously.

Preziosa took Domenico from Maria and offered to wash him and change his clothes. He had hardly been washed during the whole journey. She had some fresh clothes ready for him. He didn't object to being soothed in the warm water in the sink. There were a couple of gas lights creating a glimmer in the gloom of the room and the heat from the fire made it quite cosy, though very smoky and stuffy. The bare floor was covered in sawdust.

'Alfonso, fetch the *pacco*, please. I've brought a gift from Tadon Michele.'

It was important to Maria to offer a gift to this family who were welcoming her. Apart from a change of clothes for the baby and the three pairs of sheets that made up her dowry, she had nothing but the clothes she stood up in.

Alfonso put the small parcel on the table and opened the cloth that bound it together. The small room filled with the strong odour of sausages and cheese. They stood over the parcel expectantly as Alfonso pulled everything out. How wonderful to have some pecorino and *salsiccie* from Fontitune!

Giovanni put five small glasses and a flask of wine on the table. His wife brought out a large dark loaf of bread, sliced it and shared it among them all. Alfonso took a sharp knife and cut through the pale-skinned pecorino; it was creamy and moist inside. He sliced it into pieces and handed a piece on the edge of the knife, first to Giovanni, then to Preziosa, then to Emidio, the children and finally to Maria.

Giovanni smelled it, looked at its creamy, moist texture and tasted it. He savoured the flavour, full and rich in his mouth. A flavour he hadn't tasted for years.

'*Come è buono!* It is so good!'

80

He poured the wine into each tumbler and lifted his own, signalling to the others to do the same.

They were silent. The moment was as powerful as the consecration during the Holy Mass. Sharing the food from Fontitune, with Alfonso's wife and baby safely here, was a blessing. Nostalgia, longing and a deep sadness welled up within them all. It was good to be here, good to be together, to have arrived safely, but at the same time it was heartbreaking not to be with their family at home. *La lontananza*, the feeling of separation, overwhelmed Maria.

Giovanni lifted his glass. 'To our families in Italy. *Dio gli Benedica!*'

In the years to come Maria reflected on that moment many times. It was as if a bridge had been crossed, as if, when they had shared the bread and wine, they had turned their backs on their families and their country.

Maria shivered. She had nursed Domenico and changed his napkin and he had fallen asleep on her lap.

Alfonso was the first to make a move.

'*Andiamo!*'

Maria stood up. She wondered where they would sleep. She thought they might have rooms above the shop. She said goodnight to everyone and thanked them for their hospitality.

Alfonso took a candle and led her, with the baby in her arms, towards a door in the corner.

'Be careful, Maria, it's a bit steep.'

He took her hand and led her down a narrow wooden staircase, down down into a stone cellar. The candle flickered in the dark. Her senses were assaulted with a smell of stale, damp air and acrid smoke. In the dark she put her hand out and felt a cold stone wall. Dry sandstone crumbled onto the ground as she leaned against it. Alfonso took her along a narrow corridor and into a small dark room. He put the candle on a wooden table. There was one gas lamp, which gave off a dim light.

She could just make out a straw mattress on the floor, and a chipped chamber pot beside it. On a wooden chest against the wall were a wash bowl and a white tin jug. Above the chest hung a printed picture of Sant'Antonio Abate, the only familiar thing in the room. She noticed a small window at the top of the wall with a scrap of net curtain across it. There was a string hanging

81

between two nails with some pieces of Alfonso's clothes draped over it.

She sank down on the mattress, exhausted.

'*Maria. Mi dispiace, carissima.* This is not much, but it's the best I can do.' Alfonso crouched down on the mattress and put his arms around his wife and son. He kissed her. She felt tears on his cheeks.

'I'm sorry, my darling, I'm sorry.'

Maria could not bear to see him cry. What fault was it of his that they had nothing. Thank God they were together. Thank God the baby was well. She held his face in her hands. She started to kiss him, his lips and his cheeks. She kissed his eyes gently, each wet with tears. She held him to her and consoled him. At least they were together. She could cope with anything if they were together.

'I love you. Alfonso, *carissimo, ti amo.* Don't cry. Don't blame yourself. This is only the beginning. This is only the start. It will be better, you'll see. It will be far better. As long as we are together we can make it better.'

For the first time in her life she felt she had to be the stronger of the two. Alfonso was so full of enthusiasm and ideas, so eager to get ahead. She was shocked to see him despondent. She had never seen him like this.

They clung together and in the dark cold room in the cellar of a shop in Edinburgh they made love. She fell asleep with their baby at her breast and a rough blanket draped over them. Her first night in Edinburgh turned out to be beautiful after all.

9

The next day Maria woke to the sound of rain crashing against the window. She was chilled through from a draught whistling under the door. Alfonso had gone out at first light and now the baby needed seeing to. She nursed Domenico and then tried to tidy herself. She washed her face and hands in the cold water in the basin and pinned up her long dark hair. She tried to smooth her clothes but was ashamed of the state of them. She lifted her baby, left the room and went down a long dark passage leading to a dimly lit room at the back.

'*Permesso?*'

Preziosa was waiting for her and called her through. '*Vieni, vieni.*'

They were in the stone cellar underneath the front of the shop. There was no window; two gas fittings gave out a faint light. A large fire burned in a hearth set into the farthest away wall. Maria looked around. This was the living and sleeping room for Giovanni, his wife and four children.

There was a further cellar in the far corner that was half the height of the room. A trap door in its ceiling was used to deliver cases and boxes from the street at the front of the shop directly into the cellar. In the corner of this low space was a cupboard with a toilet and a low earthenware sink.

'Come in my dear.'

The two oldest children were upstairs in the shop doing chores for their father. The younger ones kissed their aunt and sat on the floor to play with Domenico.

Preziosa invited Maria to sit at the square wooden table in the centre of the room. She pulled a kettle from the fire and poured boiling water over some ground coffee in a pot. A glorious smell of warm coffee filled the room. She poured Maria a hot drink in a tin mug and offered her some dark bread and cheese.

'Give Domenico a crust of bread, he will be teething soon.' She

83

pointed to a tin bath under the table. 'I'm heating some water for you. After you've eaten I'll let you wash. The men are away to the market and won't be back for an hour or so. Do you have clean clothes, *cara?*'

'Only the clothes I'm wearing.'

Maria was uncomfortable. She had travelled in her best outfit, which now looked bedraggled and dirty. She had left her few other clothes for her sister in Italy. She wore wool stockings and two warm shawls, worn on top of each other because she had been so cold. She had nothing else.

'*Non ti preoccupare.* Don't worry. We're all poor here; *è la vita*. I have some things you can wear and we'll wash all your clothes. When Alfonso comes back he won't recognise you.'

Preziosa took some clothes from a chest and pulled out the tin bath, filling it with hot water. She helped Maria to wash. The clothes were plain but more like those Maria had seen the women wearing in the street: a long dark skirt and a high-necked blouse with a little pattern of roses on it.

As Maria dressed herself, Preziosa pottered around preparing some vegetables to make soup which she added to the pot hanging over the fire. She chatted away, in the dialect of the village, glad of another woman to speak to.

'This shop used to be a bakery. We're lucky, there's an oven in the wall here. When I have wood I light a fire in it and make bread and *pastone*. Look,' she pointed to a mound covered by a clean cloth on the table. 'I have some dough rising, I'll bake it later. Alfonso works for two Italian families and in the afternoons he takes his turn in the shop. He has been working really hard and has saved up some money already. You mustn't worry too much; if you work hard you can make a good living here and get on.'

When the men returned, Maria was happy to greet Alfonso now that she was tidied and clean.

'*Belezza!* You look lovely, *cara*, just like a Scottish girl!'

'Hardly!' Emidio snorted. Maria looked stunningly Italian, exotic and beautiful. She had colour on her face from the sun. The others had a pallid look; her complexion was bronzed and healthy.

'I doubt if any Scottish man would say that.'

The shop had closed for lunch. They all sat together round the table: Giovanni, his wife and four children, Emidio, Alfonso and his wife and son; ten mouths to feed. They ate hot cabbage soup and the warm bread from the oven, its appetising aroma masking the damp, dull smell of the cellar.

Domenico sat contentedly on his father's knee, fascinated by his black moustache.

Alfonso worked behind the counter in the afternoon. Preziosa took Maria out to buy some milk and provisions. Milk was cheaper in the afternoon, before the second delivery arrived. Preziosa always bought hers then. It was overcast outside and, although the rain had stopped, there was a biting wind that cut through Maria's shawl. She tightened her shoulders to protect the baby.

Preziosa couldn't speak much English. Maria was impressed by the way she managed to point her finger to show the shopkeepers the vegetables she needed or the cut of beef that she liked. Maria was fascinated by the strange coins. She noticed that Preziosa checked her money carefully, counting out the pennies and checking her change.

It started to rain again. They ran quickly back to the shop but were soaking wet by the time they reached it, and chilled to the bone. Maria's hands were freezing and her feet were soaked through. Her skirts were all muddied and her hair was wet. She felt overwhelmed. As soon as they were back indoors she excused herself and went down to the room that she had slept in the night before.

She didn't know how to light the gas lamp so she just sat on the mattress shivering. 'What has Alfonso done, bringing us here? God help us.' She lost all courage as she thought of the warmth of the sun and the beauty of the valley around Fontitune and was overwhelmed with a wave of homesickness. Completely distraught, she sat weeping.

Later on Alfonso found her asleep with the baby. She didn't tell him how frightened she was feeling. She tried to be brave. She couldn't let him down. She had told him last night it would get better.

And, bit by bit, it did.

In time, life settled into a bearable pattern. Mornings were spent preparing food, shopping for provisions and washing clothes. The women always seemed to be washing clothes.

Alfonso and Maria wanted to save every penny, so their meals consisted mostly of thick soups and pastas, vegetables and bread. Preparing food for them all gave Maria her greatest pleasure. This was one way she could help and make this feel like home. She learned to visit the shops at the right times of the week to get the best bargains. She couldn't find everything she was used to, especially the herbs and spices she had dried from the hills, but she made the food she knew with the ingredients she could find.

At the back of the cellar was a door with a few steps up to a small garden. Maria persuaded Alfonso to get a few hens. At least this way they could have fresh eggs and a pot of chicken soup from time to time. She noticed some of the Scottish women also kept hens. In the spring they might get a small pig and keep it, as they had in Fontitune.

'Now Maria, you'll have to buy some clothes.' Alfonso gave her one pound, and Preziosa took her down to the foot of Leith Walk. Joseph Hepworth and Sons was a large corner shop that sold most items of clothing. They bought two blouses, a pair of sturdy boots and some dark woollen material that Maria could use to make two skirts.

On the way home they passed Mrs Gibson's Haberdashery. Preziosa stopped and showed Maria.

'Maria, here the women wear garments under their dresses.'

'What do you mean?'

'Look, they wear tight-fitting corsets round their stomachs and garments under their skirts.'

In the window were elaborate lace corsets, nightwear and wool stockings, laid out in tidy piles.

'Why do they do that? It looks very uncomfortable.'

'They like to look thin at their waist so they tie themselves up.'

They laughed. At home in Fontitune, the women had never worn any underwear at all, never mind corsets.

On Wednesday afternoons the shop in Elm Row was closed; Alfonso liked to take his wife out. She particularly loved to walk down to the harbour at Newhaven; she liked the open space, away from the confines of Elm Row. The smell of the sea was invigorating. Domenico loved to watch the ferry boats, fishing boats and larger passenger ships sailing up and down the estuary and to wave to the trains crossing the Forth Railway Bridge further up the coast.

As they passed Valvona's grocery shop at 84 Newhaven Road, Signor Valvona was standing at the door with his arms folded. His dark suit, waistcoat and fancy neck-tie gave him an air of prosperity.

'*Buon pomeriggio*, Signor Valvona. *Come stai?*'

Alfonso had obviously met him before. Maria had noticed that Alfonso seemed to know everyone. Signor Valvona was a lot older than Alfonso. He looked established; less like an immigrant, more like a businessman.

He invited them in. His shop was full of Italian produce: wine, tins of tomatoes, garlic and pasta. Maria was impressed that he had chairs for his lady customers who sat and relaxed while the Scottish assistants made up their orders.

'Is this your lovely wife, Alfonso? *Complimenti.*'

Signor Valvona took Maria's hand, bowed gracefully over it and kissed it.

'*Complimenti.* How are you settling in, my dear?' He spoke in a dialect from south of Picinisco. 'It's difficult, I know. Once you learn to say a few words you'll see that the people are very friendly. They like it if you can talk to them; otherwise they are a bit suspicious.'

He looked sideways at the two girls working behind the counter and lowered his voice. '*Guarda*, Alfonso. *È meglio lavorare con gli Scozzesi*. It's better to employ Scottish staff. Then the customers are not shy to come in.'

They bought a few provisions, including a bottle of wine to take to Alfonso's uncle, Benedetto, then said their farewells. Alfonso carried the shopping. Maria put her hand on his arm.

She felt slightly less conspicuous in her new skirt and blouse. But she noticed the more elegant women always wore gloves and a hat. Maria wore a scarf over her hair with the ends tied around at the back. She looked more like the working women who stood chatting at their doors or were on their hands and knees whitening their front steps with chalk. These women looked up and stared as the strange couple passed.

'More "Tallies" by the looks of them.'

'More trouble!'

Benedetto Crolla's shop was in the main street of the fishing village of Newhaven. The houses here were very pretty: two-storey low cottages, whitewashed, with sea-blue window ledges. Outside stairs led to flats above. Women sat at the bottom of the stairs baiting the lines for their menfolk. Old, bushy-bearded fishermen sat with cowled sweaters and pipes in their mouths, repairing their nets. Children ran up and down the street, barefoot and poorly dressed, playing with skipping ropes or kicking tin cans around.

Benedetto Crolla had come over from Italy more than a decade before. His shop was a stone's throw away from the port at Newhaven where he had come off the ship from Antwerp. He was settled in Newhaven and was a driving force in helping others from Fontitune come across to Scotland and get started. He had helped Giovanni start; now he would be happy to help Alfonso.

Benedetto saw them through the open door and came out of his shop to greet them. He was a gentle-faced man with swarthy skin, sultry eyes and a thick head of dark hair. Zio Benny's moustache was fabulous, curling at the edges giving his face a look of authority. He was an incongruous Italian in the middle of this Scottish fishing village but looked very much at home.

'*Vieni, vieni.*' He ushered them into his shop and after kissing Maria and the baby he enthusiastically gave her a seat at a table behind the counter. He thanked them for the wine and immediately opened it, calling his wife to bring out some fennel biscuits.

'These taste exactly like your mother's *biscotti di finocchio,* Alfonso.'

'They should, my dear,' Zio Benny laughed. 'They are made exactly the same way.'

Benny's wife took Maria through to the back shop to show her how to make the biscuits and to let her feed Domenico. The men sat and talked.

'Well, Alfonso. How are things settling down?'

'Not bad at all, Zio. Maria is over the shock of the journey and I think she is settling. She's very shy. She's unhappy living with Giovanni and his family. It's very cramped in the cellar. Once we get started on our own I'm sure she'll be fine. She's expecting again so we need to find somewhere quickly.'

'*Senti,* Alfonso. Here the bars can't open on a Sunday because they're not allowed to sell alcohol. If you have a café and sell tea and coffee, you can open on Sunday when all the other shops are closed. There's a shop in Easter Road, about ten minutes from Elm Row. Signora Rossi, who owns it, is a widow. I've been to visit her. She tells me she's not managing. She has no family so she may be happy to talk to you, to sell her shop. Have you any money?'

'I've saved a little, not much. Giovanni has some money he can lend me to get started. Emidio is going to take the Elm Row shop. Giovanni has found another place in Union Street for himself and his family. Fish and chips, *Pesce e patate*.'

'*Bravo. Bravo*. Tell him to come down to the market in the square here to buy his fish. He can buy them straight from the boats.'

'What about moving out of the city, Zio Benny? I sometimes think Maria would be happier away from so many people.'

Benny knew all about it. 'There are shops just outside Edinburgh, further down the coast in Portobello. They do good business in the summer. Valvona's family have a café there and the De Marcos. Further east again is a fishing village called Musselburgh. The Di Rollos and Scapaticci families are there. They do very well, very well.'

'What about the next village?'

'Prestonpans? Antonelli is there. He is the cousin of your Di Ciacca relations. Talking of which, look at this.'

He brought an envelope out of his back pocket. His address, 'Crolla, Newhaven', was written in a beautiful sweeping scroll, three lire Italian stamps were on the top right-hand corner, stamped with Frosinone. Benny showed Alfonso the letter inside.

'It's from Cesidio. You know, the Di Ciacca boy? He's coming over to help me. I've sent him the five-pound note so he says he'll be here within a month.'

They both laughed. The 'five-pound note' was now a standing joke.

'He's twenty-two now and he's done his National Service. He wants to marry young Marietta and bring her to Scotland. Your Maria will be pleased about that. They get on, I understand.'

'Oh, yes, that's good news, very good news. Maria!' Alfonso shouted through to his wife, who came with Domenico in her arms, his mouth covered with his first taste of Cadbury's chocolate.

'*Guarda*, Alfonso. Look, he likes *la cioccolata!*'

Maria was really happy to hear that Marietta was coming. What a difference it would make to have one of her friends here. They all talked together for another half hour, about her relatives at home and how Don Dioniso was. Somehow the conversation always returned to Italy.

As they made their way back up towards the city centre, Maria felt really contented and happy, for the first time since she had arrived. Perhaps Alfonso was right. There was a chance they could survive here.

She moved towards him and reached up to kiss his cheek. He didn't kiss her back, just patted her hand on his arm and straightened his back proudly. He felt pleased with himself. If he could do a deal with this Signora Rossi, things might take a turn for the better.

By the spring of the next year, Alfonso and Maria were settled in a new shop and a new home. Signora Rossi had been relieved when Alfonso and Giovanni had called on her. She had no idea how to run a business and had been more than happy to accept the hundred pounds Giovanni counted out in front of her.

Alfonso had not taken on the shop lightly. He had walked the length of Easter Road from top to bottom to see what other shops were trading. There was a good selection: two post offices, the Buttercup Dairy, Rankin's fruit shop and a grocer's shop. Simpson, the newsagent and tobacconist, sold some chocolates and cigarettes.

Alfonso made sure there were no other Italian shops that sold confectionery. There was Demarco's, but it was a good distance away, right at the bottom of Easter Road. Italians didn't open shops in opposition to each other. He called on D'Agostino in Leith Street and Valente in Great Junction Street, his nearest Italian neighbours. They were happy to hear that he was taking the café.

The front windows of the shop were decorated with Fry's and Cadbury's brands. The travelling representatives from these manufacturers dressed the windows with their products free of charge for a commitment of steady orders. Inside, the shop was long and narrow, with a high ceiling, and walls lined with wooden shelves. The backs of the shelves were mirrored, making them look deeper and full of stock, even if there was just one row of goods. A wooden counter stretched down the right-hand side with a till and scales at the door.

Behind a glass partition was a small seating area with six or seven round marble tables and chairs. A fire at the back wall and glass lamps made the whole area cosy and warm.

Alfonso felt very proud to stand behind his own counter. The customers were suspicious at first, but were gradually enticed by his charming manner. As soon as he knew their names he greeted them personally, making them feel important. He was especially careful to treat the women with the utmost respect, but was gracious and flattering to them as well.

He took Valvona's advice and employed Scottish women to help behind the counter and serve the teas. Mrs Glen, a tall, thin, pernickety woman, lived next door. When she saw the new Italians putting a sign in the window advertising for help, she went in. Alfonso liked the look of her and offered her the job. Alfonso needed two other assistants. Mary Praties and Lilly Rough fitted the description perfectly: young, fit, hard-working girls.

Alfonso and Maria rented a first-floor flat across the road in Rossie Place. It had a living room with a fireplace, a gas ring and a sink with cold running water. The small bedroom held a double bed, with enough room for Domenico to sleep between them. Some of the flats in the stair shared a toilet but this one had a toilet of its own, a huge luxury for the couple.

For the first time in her life, Maria had a room she could share alone with her husband. Even though he spent most of his time in the shop, she felt happy looking after their new home, cooking, washing and caring for their boy. The new baby was due soon. She felt very hopeful.

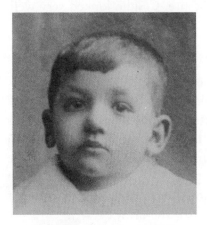

Domenico Crolla, aged 3

At the end of the night, after a busy day, Alfonso counted out the pennies that he had collected in his till with satisfaction. They owed Giovanni the money for the shop but Alfonso was convinced he could pay it off in a few years.

At last, everything started to make sense. They were on their way.

10

On a Sunday evening when their own shops were closed, Emidio and Giovanni would go down to Easter Road. They liked to sit in the back room of Alfonso's café with a bottle of wine and a pack of cards. They talked and shared problems but, best of all, they relaxed, playing *scopa* for farthings, often well into the small hours.

One evening, a little later than normal, Giovanni and Zio Benny arrived with a young man.

'*Ragazzi, guarda!* Look who's here? You'll never guess.'

Alfonso stood up to see who it was. 'Cesidio! *Hey, guaglione!* Welcome! Welcome!' Alfonso embraced his friend and kissed him on each cheek. He hadn't seen him for over a year, since that day in the piazza on the feast of Sant'Antonio.

'How are you? You look great.' Alfonso poured his friends glasses of wine. Maria had made some pizza. Alfonso told the men to help themselves.

'Sit down, sit down. Tell me all the news.'

The men sat down in front of the fire. Cesidio looked very well, more confident.

'When did you arrive?'

'Just yesterday. I left Picinisco five days ago.'

Emidio wanted more pressing news.

'How is your romance progressing, *amico*?'

'Oh, pretty well, I think. Marietta and I are engaged. As soon as I have saved enough, I'll go back to marry her. She is really keen to come over. Zio Benny is going to help us.' He slapped his uncle on the back in appreciation.

'Have you finished your National Service?' Emidio thought Cesidio looked as if he was just out of the army.

'Yes. It was not exactly strenuous. Good fun. But don't tell Marietta.'

'What's the mood in Italy?' Giovanni asked.

'No better than when you left, maybe even worse. They say Italy is unified but the North doesn't want to know. The politicians are not really interested in the South.'

'Are there still a lot of men going north for work?' Alfonso was concerned. He had heard rumours of trouble in Europe. He hadn't mentioned anything to Maria, afraid to worry her.

'Yes, but there's still a lot of unrest; the factory workers are striking for more rights. They work something like seventy hours a week. It's as bad as on the land!

Alfonso nodded to Emidio.

'We saw that when we were in Torino, didn't we? A lot of strong men ready to stand up to the politicians.'

'Yes, but it's more sinister than that, Alfonso.' Cesidio lowered his voice. The shop was closed but he was afraid in case anyone should hear. 'I've heard that the Fiat factory is increasing production.'

'That's good, isn't it?' Emidio couldn't understand what Cesidio was going on about.

'Production of rifles! Not cars. Rifles! What does that tell you?'

The men were all shocked.

'What do you mean? Come on, Cesidio, tell us.'

Cesidio didn't like to arrive among them and bring bad news:

'Fiat is planning to supply the warring parties, whoever they are. Whatever side they are on.'

Alfonso took this in.

'What warring parties? They must know something. They wouldn't switch production if they didn't know war was coming?'

Cesidio had more bad news. '*Mi dispiace, ragazzi*. When I was in London I called in to see Marietta's family. They're really worried.'

'How do you mean?'

'Well, the word is Austria–Hungary is going to war with Serbia, and all the signs are that Germany will join them. Italy could be stuck in the middle. Who do you think we'll side with?

Emidio stood up. He was agitated. 'What are they saying in London? Will Britain go to war?'

'I hate to say it, but it looks as if it's on the cards. In London they think Britain will be at war in months.'

Emidio was anxious. He had married by now, and his wife,

Carolina, was expecting. He had responsibilities, and a lot of debt. He couldn't see how they could survive here if there was a war. He looked to Zio Benny.

'What should we do? Zio, should we pack up and go home? What will happen if the Italians join in and we're called up? The women will be left here alone.'

'To be honest, Emidio,' Benedetto said, 'they're much safer here. Scotland is far away from Europe, you know. They would be in more danger in Italy than here.'

Cesidio agreed: 'Emidio, I don't think we'll be called up. It really looks as if Italy will stay neutral if there is a war. Our government is in such a mess. I doubt they could even work out how to call us up! They'll do better to sell Fiat's rifles than try to fire them!'

Alfonso was quiet. They all had wives and children here now. My God, if they had to go to war!

Giovanni had been listening intently. He spoke up. 'Boys, we need to keep our heads. We need to make sure our families are not in danger, and the best way is to make sure people here see us as friends.'

Benedetto spoke next; these two had lived longer in Edinburgh. 'Listen, lads. I've got an idea. There's the National Relief Fund, to help needy causes, war widows, that sort of thing. The business people always give money, help the community, you know.'

'We give every year, don't we?' Giovanni remembered giving money to this fund before.

Benny had given ever since he had arrived, as had nearly all the Italians.

'Yes, every year. Alfonso, you and I, we'll go round all the Italians and encourage them to give as much as they can. The amounts are printed in the *Scotsman* newspaper, usually with the names and addresses of the donors. That's good. It lets the local people know that we're still contributing, that we're doing our bit.'

'Good advice, Giovanni.' They all agreed that at least it was something to do.

Alfonso lifted the flask and poured some more wine. 'Have another drink, Cesidio. What a conversation to have on your first night. Here, deal the cards. Let's see if your luck is any better than your news.'

*

94

They had been right to be worried.

Events moved quickly and, like all the people of Europe, one way or another, the next four years of their lives were going to be caught up in a war.

On 28 June 1914 Archduke Franz Ferdinand and his wife were assassinated in Sarajevo, triggering the bloodiest slaughter the world had ever seen. If they had known what was coming, would the men have decided to take their wives back to Italy? Who knows? As it was, by the following year, when Italy eventually decided to join in the war, the British and the French had been fighting for the best part of a year. Hundreds of thousands of men had already died.

The effects of the war were all around them. There was no peace of mind. News filtered through from their customers, dreadful news. A neighbour's husband had returned with no legs. Another had lost an eye and was in a hospital, having gone mad with the horrors he had seen. One lived with the news that her son was 'missing presumed dead'. What kind of agony was that to live through?

The Italian wives, feeling vulnerable in a foreign country, were particularly frightened. Powerless to do anything, they turned to their faith. They prayed incessantly: for the men fighting in the war, for Italy to remain neutral, for their children. The Cathedral at the top of Leith Walk became a refuge. They went to Mass daily, praying fervently for peace. They prayed alongside the Scottish Catholic women whose men were already fighting, wounded or dead.

By Easter 1915 there was talk that Italy would soon take sides. On 23 May, news came that Italy was joining forces with Britain, France and Russia. Italy had failed to side with its traditional ally, Austria. Instead, Prime Minister Salandra had signed the secret Treaty of London on 26 April 1915. In return for their invasion of Austria, the allies promised significant parts of Habsburg territory as a reward. Italy, the youngest and weakest of the European nations, wanted to support the British and hoped to become a stronger member of the Alliance.

When Alfonso told Maria, she slumped against him, shocked. She had been living with the terror of this thought for a year and, now that the inevitable had happened, she collapsed. They had

Margherita Crolla, aged 2

a new baby girl, Margherita. Domenico was nearly walking. Maria was expecting again. When you married, babies came, one after the other.

'*Oh Dio! Madonna mia! Oh Dio, aiutaci!* God help us!'

Alfonso stroked her hair and gently reassured her.

'*Cara, senti.* It had to happen. We couldn't escape this. I don't want to leave you. But I have no choice. I must join with our new country and fight for peace. How could we men stay here, safe, when our neighbours are at war?

'Now listen, I've been preparing. You and the children will be all right. I have saved up some money and I have already spoken to Mrs Glen and the women in the shop. They're going to stay with you and help you. It's best if you keep the shop going for as long as you can.'

'What about the children? What about the new baby?'

'The other wives will be here, Preziosa and Carolina. They'll help you. We haven't had our call-up papers yet, but I doubt if Zio Benny will be called up. He's older. He'll be here and will help you if you are in trouble. We've spoken about it.'

'Can I not go home? Can I please go home? Alfonso, I could just pack everything up and go with the children.'

'It's too late, Maria. The borders are all closed. *C'è niente da fare.* There's nothing we can do. There's no way back.'

What if Alfonso never came back? She convinced herself this was impossible. It was too terrible a thought to contemplate. He had always been lucky. He was right. There was nothing they could do. Once she accepted the inevitability of the situation Maria's stoicism took over and she made up her mind to be calm for Alfonso and do her best. Like so many millions of women around Europe, the last thing she wanted was to allow her husband to go to war worrying or distressed about his wife. She held him close and promised him she would be strong.

That night Alfonso went to the shop at Elm Row to meet the men. They were all there, about twenty of them, sitting round the table or standing by the fire: fine, young Italian men, cousins, brothers, in-laws, strong, handsome and full of life. There was an air of expectation about them. The anticipation of returning to Italian soil, even at this price, was exhilarating.

The older men were subdued. Emidio and a cousin had their call-up papers already. Giovanni read the instructions for them.

Emidio listened carefully.

'I'm relieved in a way. Waiting all year, not knowing what would happen, has been hell. Selling cigarettes to women whose men are fighting for peace is demeaning.'

Alfonso was trying to be up-beat. 'Look, lads, we need to make the best of this. I've heard that there have been big marches in London and Manchester supporting the Italians joining the war. We would have had to fight anyway. Thank God we're with the British.'

Giovanni agreed: 'We'll be fighting in the mountains, on the Austrian–Italian border. I've been there. When I came over to Scotland I took the route through the west edge of those mountains, through Bolzano. The terrain is not unlike the peaks of La Meta, but much higher. They'll most likely be frozen, even in summer. But we're used to living outside, hardened to the elements. You'll see, it'll be just like watching at night for the wolves on La Meta.'

Alfonso spoke. 'Only this time the wolves will be the Austrians. Poor souls.'

Cesidio's English was good. He had picked up more news than the others.

'There's a report that the Germans have captured thirty thousand Italian civilians, women and children who were trying to get over the Austrian border. They're holding them as hostages. That's reason enough to fight. This is a bad business, boys, a bad business.'

He turned to Alfonso, worried about his *fidanzata*, 'I wish Marietta was here already. I am afraid if the war moves south she may be caught up in it.'

'As soon as you get leave,' Zio Benny patted his back to

reassure him, 'go straight home. Marry her, and when things get better bring her here. Have you spoken to her father?'

'Yes. He knows. *Oh Madonna!* It's agony not to have her safe here beside me.'

'She'll be safe. Picinisco is remote. It should escape the fighting, surely.'

The men started to make plans and talked late into the night. They gave each other details about their wives and children, their businesses and private things that they would not have shared before. Each took their turn. They trusted each other implicitly. They agreed who would look after their shops and keep their suppliers at bay. If they all worked together they might have businesses to come back to once this was over. Each promised faithfully to look after those who were left behind. The older men promised to keep an eye on the women, especially the younger ones.

'Thank God we are on the side of Britain. I would not leave them here alone if we were on the other side. God knows what would happen.'

Alfonso felt confused.

'Governments! They play with our lives and our families just like footballs.'

As the night wore on, the older men started to reminisce.

'We had great leaders. Leaders who loved their men; they inspired us to fight for Italia. Garibaldi, Mazzini, Mameli – the sword, the brain, and the heart!'

The camaraderie between the men was strong. They were in this thing together. They were used to spending long periods away from their wives. The bond between them was in-bred.

As the wine bottle was emptied, their spirits rose and they toasted Garibaldi and the king, Vittorio Emanuele. Then they toasted King George V. They sang the National Anthem and then substituted the words to include their new allies. Things became increasingly hilarious.

'*Dall'gli Alpi a Sicilia!*'

'*Dall' Fontitune a Dover!*'

'*Dall' John o' Groats a Picinisco!*'

Their allegiance to the Church and the family had expanded to take in an allegiance to their Motherland and their new adoptive country. They felt a purpose and a goal and were inspired with the idea of fighting. This was a chance to show their worth, a chance to prove themselves.

Their call-up papers arrived over the next two weeks. The postman knocked on the door and, handing them the official envelope with the unusual Italian stamp, shook their hands.

'Good luck, Mr Crolla.'

'Good luck, Mr Coppola.'

In the shops and cafés the regular customers who had always been a bit formal with the newcomers over the counter started to tip their hats and nod approvingly at these new allies.

'Good lads, these Italians. Hard-working.'

The women resigned themselves and prepared for the parting. They were used to the men leaving for months at a time; they convinced themselves this was not very different. Alfonso had said they were going to the Alps. It would be beautiful. He was going to Italian soil. Maria felt quite excited for him. He seemed strangely happy. He was optimistic. She noticed, however, that in church the Scottish women looked over at her with a look of pity. They knew what anxious nights she would have to spend alone, what agonising worry was ahead of her.

Within weeks the men were gone.

On Thursday 3 June they went with their wives and families on the train to Glasgow. The men joined a highly charged demonstration in George Square to celebrate Italy's entry into the war. What a great day. Spirits were high, the Italian tricolour and the British Union Jack were flying together outside shops and government buildings. Their women and children joined the crowds on the street, waving flags and handkerchiefs, cheering and singing, wishing them well.

The men looked handsome and romantic in their olive-grey uniforms, their swarthy skin and dark moustaches adding an air of recklessness that excited the crowd.

An Italian band was playing enthusiastic war anthems alternating with popular British tunes, which the Italians didn't hesitate to join in. They carried a banner high above the crowd showing a cartoon of the Austrian Emperor being kicked by the boot of

Alfonso, Maria and young Domenico c. 1915

Italy, with the slogan 'This boot is a bit *cheugh* for me!' They had no real idea why they had to put the boot in. They didn't think for one minute that 'the boot' would kick right back at them with double the force.

They were naïve. Their Mother Country had called them to defend it and, as millions of other young men of other nationalities did, they marched to do their duty.

> The trumpets sounded the beat.
> Parapum, Parapum, Parapum!
> They would die in their hundreds of thousands.

> They marched straight-backed and proud.
> *Uno, due! Uno, due! Uno, due!*
> They would be massacred by bullets and bombs.

> The drums thumped out the march.
> Boom, Boom, Boom!
> They would fall silently to their deaths.

> The crowds cheered in support.
> Hurrah! Hurrah! Hurrah!
> They would be blown to smithereens.

The new front stretched 375 miles along the Austrian–Italian border. A war front fought on stunning mountain peaks at altitudes of 3,500 metres: frozen peaks that were rugged and dangerous, peaks that fell uncompromisingly to precipitous valleys along the Isonzo River, which flooded constantly in frequent torrential rain. Mountain peaks that were impossible to attack and foolish to defend.

Alfonso and his compatriots joined other Italian emigrants from Manchester and London, New York and San Francisco. They joined mixed battalions of men from all over Italy. Sicilians fought alongside Milanesi, Abruzzesi alongside Venetians. For the first time in Italian history they fought as one nation, one country.

It was a brutal, vertical war. The few kilometres of mountain tops that became the battleground were pulled and pushed between the two armies like a macabre tug-of-war. The loss of life was relentless, obscene.

The rough, hardy Italian peasants of the South fared best. Luck was perhaps on their side. They had experience of the extreme temperatures and high altitudes, hunger and lack of good food were not unfamiliar, the sheer drops and deadly terrain were exactly like those of the mountains they came from.

Nevertheless, some of these men were among the half-million Italians who lost their lives. They died from cholera and shrapnel, from grenades and bullets, from sinister splinters of brittle limestone that flew from blasted rocks and killed instantly, tearing through flesh like lethal arrows. Climbing up to the peaks in nighttime marches they slipped from icy passes and fell pitifully, silently, to their deaths, without a cry so as not to alert the enemy.

Corporal Alfonso Crolla was assigned to the artillery. There were chronic shortages of ammunition. To maintain stocks, the generals reduced the number of attacks on the enemy to separate intense battles, fifteen in all over the four years of the war. The temporary advantage gained in these battles cost unspeakable numbers of lives. The army resisted attack after attack and succeeded in maintaining the security of the plains of Italy behind them. It was a heroic endeavour.

In between battles, when they left the front line and descended the mountain to the relief camps, life was more bearable. They could attend Mass and Confession, eat better food, wash and mend clothes, de-louse and generally build up their strength.

They were taught to read and write – something that excited Alfonso. They met with other emigrant Italians and in the later part of the war fought alongside British regiments; therefore many learned English with London or American or Scottish accents, depending on who was in their battalion.

Alfonso started to write letters to Maria. She still couldn't read but he poured his heart out to her nevertheless. He told her how he missed her, how he longed to see her, how he was desperate for news of their baby and of his young family.

How he longed for her. Moments of longing came when he least expected them. The sheer force of the feeling and raw emotion always caught him by surprise. It shocked him, delighted him and caused him physical pain, more severe than the freezing cold or the cuts on his body. He marvelled that he loved this woman so completely. It made him feel alive. He was so desperate to touch her again. His love for her left him overwhelmed and exhausted with unfulfilled desire. He willed himself to survive so that he could hold her again.

One of the captains had a gramophone which he played most evenings: Italian opera, Verdi and Puccini, music that Alfonso learned to love. He recognised inspiring marching songs that he and his men had heard in Libya, 'A Tripoli', a rousing call to arms. They joined in, the words imprinted on their minds. The fast-moving tripping 'March of the Bersaglieri' had them up in droves mimicking the double-time march of the fearsome elite corps, and the 'Garibaldi Hymn', which Alfonso and his cousins had sung in the cellar of Elm Row with Zio Benny and Giovanni, brought tears to his eyes.

So shocking was the raw destruction he witnessed that he hadn't shed a tear in the battleground. But two bars of a familiar song had tears rolling down his cheeks.

Alfonso was a courageous soldier. He used all his cunning and ingenuity to survive. Like the shepherd he was, he shone as a natural leader and was promoted to Senior Corporal. To him it was a true labour of love to lead his men, to inspire their courage. He felt their distress, fear and hopelessness in his own heart. As one by one they were maimed or killed, he grieved. Often they were simply shot through the head and tumbled from frozen ledges to their death. His anguish tore him apart, his spirit was crushed with pain.

What excuse was there for war like this? What reward for those who were not lucky enough to die? Who could imagine hell like this?

Through this journey of terror, hardship and longing, Alfonso found his Faith. His belief in God became the Truth. There had to be a higher reason beyond this futile waste. To watch death as random as this, to see one man die in the same second that another's life was saved had to have a justification.

Surely there had to be a greater reward for those whose lives were taken. It was the one who died who was blessed by God, taken from this living hell. He who was already in the arms of God, whose desires and longings were satisfied by a greater being: he was the one who understood and was at rest.

Alfonso had found his God in the Now. His life became a prayer.

11

Maria's faith was of a more practical nature. She thanked God for Mrs Glen.

Maria was relieved when she realised the baby was on its way. She was anxious to get the birth over with. Mrs Glen sent a lad along to Elm Row to fetch Carolina, Emidio's young wife.

Carolina arrived just in time. Mrs Glen was trying to keep Domenico and Margherita away from their mother. They sensed something was happening and wanted to be near her. A farthing bar of Cadbury's chocolate did the trick.

The Scottish women living in the stair also sensed something was happening. They congregated at the front door so that they wouldn't miss anything. They were suspicious of the Italian woman living alone with her two children. Her man was away at the war. Some of them fancied him; he was a 'looker' and always quick to hold the door open or say good morning in his husky voice with the lilting accent. They liked him. But she seemed odd to them.

These women were even poorer than Maria. Since the war had started, there was precious little money in the till at the end of the day, but Maria had access to the produce she used in the shop. They watched enviously as she had a pint of gold-top milk delivered every morning. That was more than they had in a week.

But their hostility towards her was temporarily put aside. She was having the bairn now. No good her dying and the poor wee bairns left on the parish. They nodded to the midwife when she arrived and moved aside to let her in. If things took a turn for the worse they would be happy to help: take the bairns for a while or get the doctor. It was unlikely they would be asked to help though.

As it was, it took no more than three hours before they heard the baby cry, a loud healthy cry. It was a relief. It hit you in the stomach, that sound. A new-born Italian baby sounded much the same as one of their own. They had to admit, we're all cut from the same cloth when you get down to basics like having a child.

All week there was plenty of coming and going in Rossie Place. Everyone was thrilled that the baby was a boy! Alfonso would be so pleased. They must write a letter to let him know. Zio Benny's wife arrived with a huge pot of chicken soup. The DeMarco and Valente women came bringing some hand-me-down baby clothes. The priest came and baptised the baby. Alfonso had left instructions: if it was a boy he was to be called Vittorio after the king of Italy.

Maria asked the priest to add 'Fortunato', a lucky name that would bring this baby's father home safely from the war.

The women in the stair were kept going with gossip for a whole month, watching all these peculiar women and swarthy Italians coming and going. When they eventually bumped into Maria some of them had the courage to say hello and congratulate her and steal a look at the wee boy strapped to her chest. He had a shocking head of straight jet-black hair and sallow olive skin.

One woman felt encouraged by his smile and slipped a farthing into the baby's shawl as a lucky token. Maria didn't understand this gesture of good luck and stepped back alarmed. The woman was affronted and thought Maria was rude. She walked off, insulted. 'Bloody Eyeties!'

An Italian Flag Day was being held the following weekend. The Italian women were all working feverishly, embroidering the Star of Italy on the corner of squares of white linen. The handkerchiefs were so delicately sewn and beautifully embroidered they would be able to sell them for sixpence each, along with little badges of the Italian national flag. The funds would go to the Italian Red Cross and the dependants of the men who had gone to war.

It was a glorious day, the kind of unexpected Indian summer that delighted the Scots and Italians alike. The streets of Edinburgh were cheered up with young Italian girls dressed in national costume walking alongside young Scottish girls from Newhaven dressed in traditional costume.

Members of the Boys' Brigade joined in, selling the badges and handkerchiefs in aid of the Italian war effort.

Maria dressed the older children with ribbons on their clothes in the colours of the Italian flag. She walked with them, the new baby strapped to her chest, down to Newhaven to see Zio Benny. She felt very happy. All along the way she was smiled at, people clapping her pretty children and wishing her luck. There was a general feeling of goodwill towards the Italians since they had joined the war. Maria felt it and it gave her new courage, made her feel less alien in the community.

Before long, she started to work again. The children played behind the counter in the shop and she laid the baby in an open drawer and gave him a rag to suck so that he didn't cry. Little Vittorio Fortunato spent the best part of the first six months of his life in a drawer in his father's confectionery shop.

Maria still couldn't speak much English. When the local kids came in with their farthings to choose their weekly bag of sweeties, Maria could do no more than point to the jars with a long stick and weigh out the sweeties in the brass scale. She learned the value of the coins by their size: the small farthing and the large flat brown pennies. When she was given a half-crown to pay for cigarettes she knew by memory which coins to give in return. In the evening she sorted the coins into bundles ready for Mrs Glen to count them and write them in the accounts book.

Maria worked through the day and in the evening crossed the road to her small flat with her three children to feed them, wash them and put them to sleep. When they were asleep, she washed their clothes, did any mending and scrubbed the flat clean. At night she lay in bed with her children, exhausted but often unable to sleep.

She worried about Alfonso, missing him more and more as the days and weeks passed. Night after night she lay awake in the cold dark room and prayed incessantly, imploring La Madonna to protect him for another day.

Was he alive now, now, still alive now? She was tormented that if she stopped praying for him, even for a moment, he might be killed. If she kept praying for him he would surely survive.

Autumn faded into winter, and the long dark nights left Maria depressed. She lived only for her children and did everything to keep them healthy and clean. On Wednesday afternoons when the shop was closed, she would visit Preziosa or Carolina to see if they had any news of the war. The *Scotsman* newspaper had fairly frequent war reports from the Italian Front. Zio Benny gave the women abridged versions to keep their spirits up.

She spent Christmas alone with her three children. She knitted socks and scarves and made up parcels of chocolate and cigarettes to send to her husband. She and Alfonso had been married less than four years. The feast days of the New Year came and went: La Befana, Sant'Antonio, La Festa della Luce. She clung to the rituals of the Church to put order in her life. She showed the children the only photo she had of their father, looking handsome in his Corporal's uniform. At night, before going to bed, they all prayed for him and kissed his picture.

To try to forget her worries Maria took the children outside as often as she could. If she crossed London Road and walked down the hill she reached Arthur's Seat, a large hill to the south of the city. The children loved to chase the ducks at the pond, or pick the daisies to bring to their mother. Maria recognised some plants from the hills at home in Fontitune: crocuses, dandelions and wild garlic. She picked them with the children. She would cook with them that evening.

She made pasta and, while it was boiling, she warmed some oil in a frying pan and added the chopped wild garlic. The aroma filled the house. She felt she was at home. She drained the pasta, tossed it in the olive oil and added some young dandelion leaves that wilted in the heat.

She sat at the table with Domenico and Margherita.

'*Mangia! Mangia! Come e buono. Pasta con aglio e olio*, pasta with garlic and oil. Isn't it tasty?'

'*Si, Mamma, Si, Mamma.*' They were hungry after the walk.

Vittorio was six months old by now and, sitting him on her knee, she offered him a tiny taste of the pasta with her fingers. He smacked his lips and opened his mouth for more.

'*Ecco, Vittorio.*' Domenico stretched out to put some of his pasta into his brother's open mouth.

'*Bravo, Domenico, bravo.*'

Just as Maria was about to start eating, there was a knock at the door. She was not expecting anyone. With Vittorio in her arms she opened the door.

She was shocked to see a policeman. Her neighbour across the landing was standing at her door, a scowl on her face, her arms crossed.

Maria's heart stopped. Alfonso? Had something happened? She knew the policeman from the shop. He came in to buy his cigarettes and to make sure everything was in order. He removed his hat and tucked it under his arm.

'Good evening, Mrs Crolla.' He smiled oddly at her.

'*Buonasera.*'

She moved out into the stair and noticed Mrs Glen was behind him as well. He had brought her to help him by the looks of things.

'Mrs Crolla, I'm sorry about this but your neighbour here has complained to the police that there is a terrible smell coming from your house. She thinks it's gas.'

Domenico came to his mother's leg and tugged at her skirt. He had his empty plate in his hand and wanted more pasta.

'Oh, Mrs Crolla,' Mrs Glen realised it was the smell of the cooking. She had smelled this before in Mrs Crolla's flat. 'What a lovely smell.' She burst out laughing and turned to the policeman and neighbour. 'It's not gas leaking. Mrs Crolla is cooking with garlic. She uses it a lot in her cooking. It's really delicious. There's nothing at all to worry about.'

Understanding the word 'garlic', Maria went into the house to fetch some of the bulbs to show the policeman. He laughed with Mrs Glen and looked at the neighbour with his eyebrows raised.

She turned away, embarrassed at her stupidity, and went back into her flat mumbling something about stinking Italians.

'I'll never understand women,' thought the policeman. 'The sooner this war is over the better. The men can sort out their wives' problems themselves. I've got far more important things to do.'

Secretly he would have liked to have tasted the food. It smelled pretty appetising.

Maria with her children, Domenico, Margherita and Vittorio c. 1916

More letters came from Alfonso. Maria asked Zio Benny to read them to her. She kept them in a tin in the kitchen, happy knowing that Alfonso was alive and well. He had still not seen their new baby. Maria had gone with her sister-in-law to Ledbury's, the photographer on Montgomery Street, and sat with the three children to have a picture taken to send to their father. She wore her pretty blouse with the roses that he liked and borrowed clothes from the photographer for the children so that they all looked really smart.

By June it was very warm. The children were happily running barefoot in and out of the shop. Vittorio was starting to sit up now and they enjoyed playing with him. Lilly Rough and Mrs Glen worked in the front shop. They kept an eye on Domenico and Margherita as they ran in and out. Vittorio slept in his pram at the

110

door, oblivious to the stream of customers coming in and out of the shop. There was plenty of business for a 'penny slider' on a sunny day.

Maria had got into the habit of sitting in the shop with the women, knitting, or sewing in the back room. The shop was as much her home as the dark room in the flat.

One day she was sitting in the back room finishing sewing a button on a dress she had made for Margherita. The children were growing so quickly she was constantly sewing and mending clothes for them. She put the needle into her blouse to keep it away from the children and bent over to pick up the dress that had slipped to the floor.

As she straightened, the sun from the front shop dazzled her eyes. She blinked; they watered a little. As she rubbed them she thought there was someone in front of her, looking at her. She blinked again but still couldn't see. She stood up and, clearing the trimmings of the material from the table, turned to call Margherita to try on the dress.

As she turned round she stopped dead in her tracks. She dropped everything. Her hand flew to her mouth as she drew her breath in shock.

There in front of her in an olive-grey uniform with the badge of a Senior Corporal of the Third Artillery of the Italian Army was a tall, slim, suntanned soldier. He was standing quietly at the door, the light shining behind him.

He stepped towards her and held out his arms. She ran to him, tears filling her eyes. Alfonso was home.

They kissed and clung to each other, whispering *Grazie a Dio* over and over again. The children had followed the man and were now standing at the door, looking on as their mother kissed the soldier.

Domenico moved into the room, closer to his parents. He stood near to his father and tugged insistently on his trousers. He looked up.

'*Papà, Papà. Un bacio per me!*'

Alfonso looked down at his darling three-year-old son speaking such beautiful Italian words. He knelt down and held Domenico close to him, tears brimming in his eyes. He kissed him again and

Maria with Vittorio, Easter Road, c. 1916

again and then his pretty daughter, laughing and crying at the same time.

When he stood up, Maria handed him his third-born child for the first time, Vittorio Fortunato.

12

Easter Road, Edinburgh
October 1919

Alfonso survived another two years of intense fighting before the war ended, and it was a further year before he was finally released from active duty. When he returned home, he had been decorated with the Ordine della Corona d'Italia, awarded to long-serving soldiers who had served Italy with honour. He had seen Italy defend its borders, achieve great successes and suffer disastrous defeats.

He was fighting in November 1917 when over 30,000 Italians died in a dreadful, bloody massacre at Caporetto, resulting in a humiliating retreat. Nevertheless, fighting alongside British and French battalions, they regained lost ground and finally, a year later, they fought the great victory of the battle of Veneto Vittorio, which ended on 3 November 1918 and won their war.

Alfonso had changed. He had gone away illiterate and returned educated and bilingual. He had gone to war unconditionally to do his duty and returned with a burning patriotism and loyalty to his country. He had fought in a war that had forged friendships between nations and had, they all believed, made the world safe for justice and for truth. He had fought in the 'war to end all wars'. There must be no more secret plotting and scheming by powerful men, robbing the lives of the young.

Gradually many of the Italians returned to Edinburgh, going back to their wives, their families and their shops, ready to take up their lives where they left off. And many of the Scottish soldiers also returned to their families.

Many never came back at all.

The flow of emigration from Italy was now stemmed both by the experience of the war and new opportunities opening up in Italy. Both governments gradually changed legislation to curtail the movement of people. Italy needed to keep its men, with so many having perished and emigrated already. Britain needed to protect its workforce; post-war unemployment was increasing.

Cesidio had taken Zio Benny's advice and, during his war leave, had returned to Picinisco to marry Marietta. Sadly, they lost their first child, Michele, at birth, but they now had a beautiful little girl called Lena, and another baby on the way. By the autumn of 1919, Cesidio was happy to leave for Edinburgh ahead of his young wife, just as Alfonso had done seven years earlier.

After the war there were still a lot of food shortages; business was slow to pick up. Laws had been introduced to restrict hours of business, so the shops had to close at eight o'clock. But if a customer happened to pass and knock on the door they were more than happy to open and sell a packet of cigarettes or a bar of chocolate. Every penny counted, with takings no more than a couple of pounds a day.

The men felt unsettled. They missed the company of their fighting units, the camaraderie that had bound them together with strangers, strangers who daily saved each other's lives. Selling ice cream and fish and chips could not live up to the life-and-death drama of the past few years.

They started to congregate again in one or other's shops, talking together, sharing a glass of wine, relaxing, playing cards. They couldn't talk to their wives about the horrors of the war. They felt a need to discuss their experiences over and over again among themselves. Few of them had fought together. They were hungry for each other's experiences.

On an evening like this, the friends were all in the back shop at Easter Road: Benedetto, Giovanni, Alfonso, Emidio and Cesidio.

Alfonso was concerned. Maria had told him she wanted to return to Italy. If Marietta arrived it might help her to settle and not feel so interminably homesick.

'Cesidio, are you sure Marietta still wants to come across here? Maybe, now that the war is over, things will change for the better in Italy?'

'She's made up her mind. As soon as the baby's born at the end of the year she's going to come. We've saved every penny, though my army pay won't get us very far!'

The Italian army stipend was meagre and deductions were made for food and uniform, leaving very little over.

'We have some good gifts of sterling cash at our wedding; they will help.'

Zio Benny was Cesidio's *padrone*, helping him find work. 'Cesidio, there's a shop in Cockenzie, about ten miles east of here, along the coast; it sells ice cream and fish and chips. One of my boys opened it a few years ago. It's a good site. There are no other families down there. You work with him, get started and build it up. It's a lovely village, built on fishing and mining. I think Marietta will settle well there; she speaks English already, after all.'

'Don't you think we should look for a place in the city?'

'I'm not sure.' Zio Bennie liked to encourage newcomers to open shops in other towns and villages, partly to spread the competition and also to protect his own patch. It suited him if Cesidio took the Cockenzie shop. 'Try this first. See how you get on, then we'll see. I'll keep looking for you.'

Emidio was having doubts as well. The shop at Elm Row was making hardly any money; there was so little to sell. This business was not as easy as they had all made out.

'Zio Benny, do you really think we should stay? Why don't we all go back to Italy and try again. We could sell our cheese in the market in Torino. Remember, Alfonso?'

'It's no use, Emidio, believe me. Things are still unsettled in Italy. There's huge unemployment now that the army has been disbanded, and there are strikes across the whole country. Who knows what will happen now that the war is over?

'I think we'll have a better chance if we work hard here. If we save everything then in ten years or so we can afford to go back in a position of strength.'

Cesidio agreed. 'Inflation is running riot. You get seven lire for a day's work in a factory but it costs seventy lire to feed your family. You think things are tight here. This is *paradiso*, believe me. There's no way we can go back to working in the old ways. Those days are really gone.'

Giovanni spoke up, trying to calm them down. '*Senti, ragazzi,* don't you see the opportunity you have here? If you go back you'll end up a slave of a big company, making cars for Fiat or clothes for a sweat factory in Naples. Going back on the land waiting for the wolves to attack the sheep will never satisfy you now.

'Remember we've learned to look after ourselves now, we're used to making our own decisions. Here at least we can do that, *è vero*, Alfonso?'

Alfonso agreed. 'Think it through. The sums are obvious. If we work here and save, we can change sterling for lire in ten years, then we can go home well-off. I'm for staying.

'We've not fought for nothing. We have proved our allegiance to both countries. We're all valued *ex-combattenti*. We're respected by our own Government as well as the Government here. You'll see, we'll reap the benefits.'

Alfonso had spent the last six months working in the artillery stores. He had had dealings with the big companies in Turin and Milan that had made fortunes supplying the war machine, companies like Fiat who were now one of the major employers in the North. He had seen the food shortages, seventy-five-hour weeks and strikes. He had heard of anti-communist riots and street warfare. There was no way he was going back to Italy until things had settled and there was a strong government.

It was agreed. Cesidio would go down the coast. They would keep helping each other with loans so that they were not dependent on banks and interest. The opportunities ahead of them were there for the taking.

Maria came in from the flat across the road with some of the *pastone* she knew Alfonso liked. The children were with her, now aged six, five and four. They loved to sit with their uncles and watch them play cards.

The conversation changed to more relaxed homely matters as Alfonso poured some wine for his friends. Emidio put a few more logs on the fire and took the cards down from the mantelpiece. He needed to take the eights, nines and tens from the British pack so that they could play *scopa,* so he called the children over to play a game where they pointed to a card every time he dealt one of the offending numbers.

'Eight! *Otto!*'

'Ten! *Dieci!*' They squealed with delight every time they recognised a number.

117

'*Sette Bello*! *Sette Bello*! *Scopa!*' shouted Vittorio, picking up the seven of diamonds, using the winning word that he had seen the men shout out when they lifted all the cards from the table and scored two points.

The men all cheered. '*Bravo, Vittorio!*' He was going to be smart this little Vittorio Fortunato.

Alfonso lifted up his son and sat him on the table so that he could clap his hands and shout out '*Scopa! Scopa!*' to his heart's content.

He smoothed his son's hair. 'This is what we are working for, boys: a safer future for our children. For us the die is already cast. We have their future to build, the future of Italia and Scotland.'

Maria sat on her husband's lap. 'You should have been here when the Carabinieri came during the war. They were playing in the big concert hall; what is it called, Zio Benny?'

'The Usher Hall.'

'They were in full uniform, magnificent with their cloaks and their wide hats with wild feathers and dazzling medals. We watched them march up the Mound and the crowds cheered and clapped as they played our wonderful music.

'Alfonso, you should have seen your children! They're Italian through and through! They were shouting "*Viva l'Italia!*" and all the Scottish people were laughing.'

'I had no idea that the Carabinieri came here. They inspired us so much at the front, kept our spirits up.' Alfonso was thoughtful.

Emidio spoke up. 'Alfonso did you fight with the storm troopers, the Arditi? We came across them in the second winter. They saved our skin many a time.'

'Yes, Emidio. What brave men! Mad as well, I think. They were fearless. Without them, and help from the British and French battalions, we would have had it. Things could have turned out very differently.'

Benedetto had not been called up. He had felt left out but had followed the war eagerly, desperate for every bit of news, keeping newspaper cuttings of anything written about the Italian front.

'Alfonso, I spoke to some of the Carabinieri. They told me a story about the whole army singing in the face of the enemy. Is that true?' Benny lifted Vittorio from the table as he spoke. He had heard about a magnificent night when the war had stood still for a moment, for Italy.

'Yes. I was there; it was after the battle at Monte Santo. I'll never forget it.'

'Me too,' Cesidio remembered.

'And me,' Emidio said.

'What happened?' Maria had not heard any of the men talk about the war before.

'I remember exactly. The eleventh battle of Isonzo. Over fifty divisions fought, Cadorna was our General. Do you remember, boys?'

'How can we forget?' Cesidio would never forget.

Alfonso continued. 'It was the night of 26 August, two years ago. We were fighting between Gorizia and Trieste, in the north-east. It was terrible terrain, terrible. We fought man to man, face to face with the enemy.'

He paused. 'It was impossible. Freezing cold. Ice. Ice everywhere. Imagine, so high, ice even in August; they were the worst ice and rock faces we had to climb in the whole campaign. You've no idea. We just battled on and on, every step agony.

'The Arditi fought alongside us. They took the hardest ridges. When we could do no more, were finished, they carried on, led us forward.

'Most of them were boys from the South, young mountain men like us. And a lot of Siciliani; a lot of Siciliani. They fight like madmen.' He laughed. 'No thought for their own skins, blindly loyal to their leaders.'

Benedetto was engrossed.

'What happened?'

'Eventually, I don't know how they did it, our second army took the Bainsizza Plateau, which is north-west of Gorizia, and pushed the Austrians back. It was a great success, a great boost to our morale. We had been pulling and pushing like a bloody tug-of-war up and down the mountains.

'You know, you have to understand. From day to day we never knew what was happening along the front; if the enemy was above us or below us; if we were getting ammunition; if we were getting any supplies. This time, I don't know why, the news that our *Tricolore* was flying on the summit of Monte Santo swept all along the mountain ridges like a dancing flame.

Alfonso in soldier's uniform c. 1917

Cesidio (2nd left, standing) in soldier's uniform c. 1917

'We had lost so many, hundreds of thousands, *Madonna mia*, so many. In one hour five of my men died before my eyes; knocked down like flies. But, even so, this time it felt as if we had made a huge advance. This time it seemed as if it was worthwhile. We had saved Italy from being overrun by the Austrians. My men had not died in vain. Not this time.

'I can't explain it. The victory was intoxicating. We were drunk with relief. It was as if for two years we had fought and resisted the Austrians sweeping down into our land, down the staircase of the Alps into Italy. Two years of living with death, of walking with the devil, and finally a victory. *Finalmente!*'

Alfonso stopped. He was lost in his own thoughts, oblivious of his wife, still on his lap, oblivious of his friends, who were listening captivated, oblivious of his children sitting at his feet.

He lowered his voice as if whispering to an angel, reminding himself that he had not forgotten his fallen comrades.

'The sky was clear. The moon was high, a strange violet glow bounced off the mountain tops. Now and then a flair or shot would ring out, a defeated Austrian's final barefaced act of defiance against us.

'We were silent. We were terrified that these fiends would start back at us again, starting it all over again, robbing us of our moment of victory. We leant against the mountainside, looking towards Heaven, rejoicing that our country was protected for another day, thanking our God.'

He looked up, remembering that the other men were listening.

'*Ragazzi*, you remember when in Fontitune we used to call across the mountains using the echo to carry our message for miles? That night the mountains carried news of our victory and a requiem for our fallen heroes. Out of the blue, and startling us all in the quiet, we heard the opening clash of symbols of the Marcia Reale.

'It was coming from the white walls of the convent on the summit of the Monte Santo, ruined by gunfire but still standing like a monument to the dead. It was the Divisional Band of the four Italian regiments that had taken the mountain. After a moment of stunned silence, soldiers answered the call to salute our country.

'One after another, hundreds upon tens of hundreds of men sang out the words of our National Anthem.

'A colonel from somewhere called out an echo: "*Soldati, attenzione!*"

'Others repeated it, as did I when it reached my ears, cupping my hand to make my call travel as far as it could around the mountains; calling so that no Italian soldier dying in agony or lying deserted on a ridge would not hear and be consoled.

'It's true, Zio Benny, it was beautiful. We each stood to attention, one after the next. We echoed our response to the booming of the music from the mountain above us.

'*Viva l'Italia! Viva il Re! Viva i Soldati!*

'Like the swelling of a great ocean, again and again rebounding from the mountain-sides, and in the face of the cowed Austrian army, we called out a salute to our country and to our king. We prayed to the Gods with our cry of victory.

'I've never experienced anything like it. A wave of pride, of love and sorrow, of elated joy, swept over us all.'

He shook his head and swallowed, his emotion choking him. He gently pushed Maria to the floor beside her children. He looked at her.

'To fight through the horror, to go forward through hell itself, you have to strip your heart of love or you would surely die of

Cesidio (1st left, standing) with a group of soldiers c. 1917

sorrow alone. But the music made us alive again, resurrected us from the living death. Then we wept. We cried. To a man, we shouted and cheered.

'The band played on: the Hymn of Garibaldi, the Hymn of Mameli, the fighting songs of triumph.

'Gradually the music faded away. We stood enchanted, spellbound. Then in a breathless magnificent communal cry of ecstasy, a final huge cheer rang out across the hills. Every last one of us called out to God to save Italia and save our souls.'

Emidio and Cesidio had also been there; they understood. Quietly they hummed the tune, a hymn to those who had fought with them, those who had died with them.

'*Le ragazze di Trieste,*
Cantan' tutte con adore,
O Italia, O Italia del mio cuore,
Tu ci vieni a liberar!'

123

They wept together, remembering the sufferings and losses of the last four years.

'Do you know, we heard that Toscanini himself had climbed up to the Convento to conduct the band and it was he who had inspired the intensity and beauty of the music?'

Giovanni began the opening bars of the Marcia Reale and there, in the back shop of the confectioner in Easter Road, they sang the Italian National Anthem:

'Red from the hearts that were pierced for thee,
White as thy mountains are white,
Green as the spring of thy soul everlasting,
whose life-blood is light.'

Alien's Order, 1920

With Maria and her children sitting among them, they laid to rest some of the horrors of the war, pushing to the depths of their souls the disastrous defeat of Caporetto that followed this moment of salvation barely three months later. They felt proud that they had fought with the Italians, the British and the French to preserve peace in Europe.

Therefore Alfonso found it hard to understand when, a year later, they all received notice from the Edinburgh City Police that they and their families had to register under the 1920 Aliens Order and that they would now be under police surveillance and be deported if they broke the law.

13

Cockenzie lay ten miles to the east of Edinburgh, an old fishing village on the Firth of Forth. The café was in a great location, right in the middle of the village, between the Auld Kirk and the Thorntree Inn.

Every morning the warm smell of freshly baked bread came wafting across the street from the bakery at the Co-op. Twice a day the milk cart came round with warm milk. Children ran out, barefoot in the summer, with a jug to be filled and a few pennies to buy butter or eggs. Beef and lamb sold at Harkes the butcher was raised in the fields behind the village. There was even a local slaughter-house at the harbour at Port Seton, the adjoining village five minutes' walk away.

Behind his grocery shop in Elcho Place, Dan Buchanan made oil-skins for the fishermen. The 'bomb' skins were put through a process of dipping in yellow oil until they were stiff and waterproof. The fishermen wore them over their heads like a strange yellow cloak over their all-in-one knitted undergarments and their heavy cotton trews and crew-neck sweaters.

Stewart's, the boot-maker's store, was opposite the café. It was a small cupboard-like shop, lined with boots, sheets of leather and all manner of tools and nails. Mr Stewart sat in his den with the door open, tapping away with his hammer, high on the smell of leather, polish and glue.

The harbour and boatbuilding yard were at the west end of the village, alongside the Salt Pans. Here sea water was boiled in twelve-metre metal pans, the steam leaving the surrounding walls pearly white. The salt that was scraped off was used for curing and preserving the fish. Lying between the harbour and the café was the Boat Shore, a natural harbour in the rocks widening to a sandy cove.

The big trawlers, with coal-fired engines, went to sea for days on end, returning to harbour with huge catches of haddock and cod. In the summer, when they were following the herring, the boats were away for weeks, fishing as far south as Lowestoft and Yarmouth. The smaller sail-boats went out nightly in the Firth of Forth, often landing their catch at the Boat Shore to avoid harbour taxes.

If the weather was bad and the boats couldn't go out, there was no catch; the whole community suffered.

The fishing families lived in low whitewashed cottages along the shore, their front doors opening directly on to the beach. The fish-wives sat on their doorsteps baiting the lines with clams, coiling them into baskets layered with grass so that their men could cast the lines without catching the hooks.

Poorer families lived in a decaying block of flats rented from the Fishermen's Society. Each room-and-kitchen housed a family of six or more, the dozen families sharing an outside privy. They took turns weekly to boil water and scrub their clothes by hand in the communal washhouse.

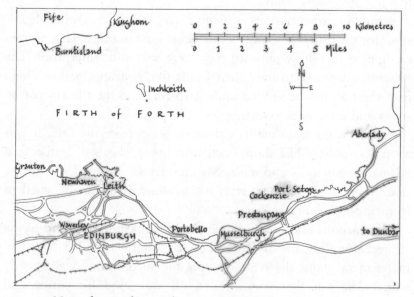

Map of coastal route between Edinburgh and Cockenzie

Fisherwomen at the Boat Shore, Cockenzie c. 1920

The flats were right on the shore. On a wild night, when the tide was high and the sea was rough, the waves would wash up, crashing terrifyingly against the back of the building. The wind would whirl around, shaking the foundations to the core.

On the ground floor of the flats was the Cockenzie Café. The shop was split into two, selling ice cream and confectionery on the left side of a wooden partition, fried fish and chips on the other.

The Italian man who had taken over the shop had been the subject of much local interest. Now that news of his wife and two children had arrived, the local women were disconcerted. They didn't know what to expect; they'd never had a foreign woman living among them.

They didn't have long to find out. The day after she arrived, early in the morning, Cesidio took Marietta and his two children to the Boat Shore. It was a bright, clear morning. Four boats were waiting in the shallows. The water was calm, the waves lapping against the sand.

A dozen or so fishwives were already there. They made a colourful sight in ankle-length, striped woollen skirts, covered with long

127

'peenies', aprons, full-sleeved blouses buttoned modestly at their throats. Hand-knitted shawls thrown over their shoulders, and brightly patterned head scarves tied over their heads and round their necks, protected them from the wind.

They looked across at Cesidio. 'Morning, Sis.'

'Good morning. Good morning, Mrs Brown.'

Mrs Brown nodded, unsmiling, at the young woman standing beside Cesidio.

The other women nodded as well.

The first of the small boats sailed between the rocks and made its way into the cove.

Mrs Brown shouted at her man and her son. She hitched up her skirts and waded into the shallow water. Her son jumped out of the boat and between them they hauled the boat up onto the sandy shore.

'How many huddies dae ye need, Sis?'

'About two stone.'

The men handed the fish they had caught out of the boat and Mrs Brown laid it on the foreshore, sorting out haddocks for Cesidio, packing the rest into lidded wooden fish boxes to be taken off to market at Newhaven.

One by one, the other boats came ashore; the women hauled them in and sorted the catch. Some packed creels with the fish, tied them to their backs and carried them away for salting or curing.

Marietta stood and watched the proceedings, full of admiration for these hard-working women.

When they got back, there was a wiry, fresh-faced man in the shop. Cesidio introduced him to his wife. 'Marietta, this is Tommy Dougal. He's deaf and dumb. He helps me with the fish.'

Marietta nodded to the man, who smiled and clapped, pleased to see this lovely girl.

Tommy took the fish from Cesidio. He immediately went to the sink and set about cleaning and gutting them with a long, narrow, sharp blade and a dexterous flick of his wrist. Marietta watched, fascinated.

She fed and washed the children then, smelling a wonderful aroma, took them through to see what their father was doing.

Twice a week a gallon can of warm fresh milk was delivered to the back door.

In the back room, Cesidio was standing over a deep pot of simmering milk, balanced on a square gas ring. He had added sugar, double cream and butter and two or three pungent oily vanilla pods that he kept in a jar. He was stirring the creamy mixture rhythmically with a long wooden spoon with a metal paddle attached at the end.

'What a wonderful smell.' Marietta breathed in deeply. 'It reminds me of when I was in London when I was young. Oh, Cesidio, it seems like a lifetime away.'

'Here, taste it.'

He took a small cup and scooped out some of the custard. He caught the drips on the side with his finger and, after licking it, handed her the cup.

She tasted the creamy, sensuous vanilla custard and closed her eyes, breathing in deeply and savouring the flavour.

When she opened her eyes she smiled with pleasure. Cesidio was looking intently at her. He didn't say a word, just moved towards her and kissed her lips, which were sweet with the sugar of the custard.

'Do you like it, sweetheart?'

Marietta burst out laughing and kissed him back.

'Watch, Cesidio. You'll burn the custard if you're not careful.'

She took the wooden spoon from him and handed him the cup.

'I'll do this. Here, let the children taste the custard.'

Marietta knew what to do. She had seen her father make ice cream. She knew that the paddle at the end of the spoon had to keep contact with the bottom of the pot to stop the custard sticking. She worked rhythmically, taking her time.

As soon as the custard coated the back of the spoon, she turned off the gas. She opened the tap in the pot, siphoning the shiny mixture into sparkling clean metal pails. Then she covered them with some clean muslin and left the cream to cool.

The Newhaven ice-man delivered blocks of ice to the harbour for packing round the fish. Cesidio had some dropped off at the shop. He stored it outside in a cool cellar, covered with a cloth and straw, so that it didn't melt.

Once the custard had cooled, Marietta called to her husband: 'It's ready!'

Cesidio prepared the hand-cranked freezer. He lowered a cylindrical metal pail into a round wooden barrel. He crushed some of the ice with a hammer and filled the space between the pail and the inner rim, adding coarse salt to make a brine solution. Then he poured the custard into the metal pail.

Tommy Dougal stood and churned the handle round and round. After a time the mixture started to chill, solidify and change as if by magic into a mouth-watering ice cream.

Cesidio scooped some ice cream onto a cornet, smoothing it round the edges so that it wouldn't fall off. He bent down to Lena, who was sitting on a step behind the counter watching him, her baby brother snug on her knee. He handed her the cone.

'Now, Lena, taste Papà's ice cream. Is that not the best ice cream in the whole wide world?'

Lena licked the cone then pushed the delicious ice cream onto her baby brother's lips.

'Taste Papà's ice cream, Giovanni. It's lovely.'

Cesidio smiled at his wife and pulled her close to him. They looked lovingly at their children, thinking that they would each do everything they could to give them the best chance in life.

Cesidio and Marietta didn't realise it at the time, but they would enrich the lives of their neighbours and customers as well.

The fishing families in the village had few home comforts, minimal cooking equipment, no running hot water; few houses had gas. They survived on potatoes, thick soups, mutton and smoked fish. Porridge, tea, bread and jam were the staples.

A scoop of frozen, sweet, vanilla-flavoured ice cream between two thin wafer biscuits was an exotic treat, adding colour and luxury to their lives. For a halfpenny they could experience the taste of a different world. Pennies were keenly saved so that visits to the Di Ciacca's shop could be more frequent.

When the fishwives had a spare ha'penny they would buy a bottle of Dunbar's ginger beer or a bar of Cadbury's chocolate to take home to last the week, a square of chocolate enjoyed every evening when the bairns were in bed.

Marietta was in the shop in the afternoon. Two fisherwomen

Marietta, Cesidio, Johnny and Lena, c. 1920

came in. They were taken aback when they saw Marietta behind the counter. So this must be Sis's wife.

The first woman looked Marietta up and down, feeling slightly intimidated by her dark good looks, her beautiful thick black hair, her pretty brown eyes. She nudged her friend. 'Yae tak,' you speak, she whispered in broad Cockenzie dialect.

'Na, yae dae it.' Her friend nudged her back.

Taking a deep breath the first woman spoke in a slow clear voice, trying to make herself understood. 'Can . . . I,' she pointed to herself then to the penny bar of Cadbury's chocolate on the counter, 'Can . . . I . . . have . . . cho . . . co . . . late?'

She put her penny down on the counter and took a step back, frightened that the strange woman would do something. She whispered to her friend.

'She disnae understand. What will I dae? I canny speak Eyetalian.'

Maria picked up the chocolate bar and put it into a paper bag. 'That's a penny, thank you very much. I'm . . .'

But before she could say another word the woman grabbed the chocolate and the two scuttled out of the shop, embarrassed. Nobody had said the Italian woman could speak English.

The children in the village all did errands after school. On Saturdays they did chores, cleaning, helping in the fields to 'houk tatties' or pick peas or strawberries. The pennies they earned were mostly given to their mothers to augment the family budget, but spare farthings were excitedly spent in the shop. 'Soor plooms', Duncan's toffee, a thirty-minute teeth-rotting chew, or a lucky tattie, a flat crunchy toffee sweet dipped in delicious-smelling powdered cinnamon. These were sucked and salivated over for hours of pleasure.

The young girls liked to spend their farthing on two strips of liquorice. They would pass it round their pals for a 'sook' before taking it home to make 'sugar'ally' water. They soaked the 'liquorish' in a jam-jar full of water and left it under the bed until it melted and left a sweet, murky sugary drink.

By that evening Marietta had met most of the children in the village. They were not worried that she was foreign. They had tripped in and out and hung around the shop all afternoon. They told her all about their favourite sweeties, giving her lots of the information she needed about her new customers, their fathers, mothers, aunts and uncles. They played with Lena and, when Marietta wasn't looking, let the baby have a 'sook' of their sweeties.

After an eventful day, Marietta was glad when her own children had settled for the night. Cesidio was sitting at the table, his jacket off, shirt sleeves rolled up, relaxing with the remains of their supper in front of him. He looked at his wife, who had stood up, ready to clear the table.

'Well, *cara*, how do you like your new home?'

Her new home was a room at the back of the shop with a bed in a recess and a mattress underneath, which was pulled out at night. A sturdy wooden table and four wooden chairs were the only furniture. A crucifix and a picture of the Sacred Heart hung on the wall. Beside the store room, where they prepared the fish and potatoes and made the ice cream, was a small kitchen, dark and windowless, with a two-ringed gas stove and a water boiler. In an ante-room was a toilet with a small sink.

'Do you know what? I think it's going to be just perfect.'

'Are you happy?'

Marietta came across and sat on her husband's knee. He put his arm round her. She stroked his hair.

'Happy, my darling. Very, very happy.'

Cesidio smiled. 'Jimmy will be in shortly. We'll be busy tonight. The local women will have told everyone you've arrived. The men will be wanting to see what you look like.'

Marietta stood up and, taking a step back, put her arms on her hips and looked at him.

'And what do I look like, Signor Di Ciacca?'

'Beautiful, my darling. Very, very beautiful.'

Jimmy Caulder, a tough ex-army cook, had arrived and was lighting the coal fire under the fryer. Cesidio introduced him to his wife.

Then he took Marietta through to the ice cream shop. They stood behind the wooden counter, both in spotlessly clean white cotton coats, waiting for customers.

There was a wooden bench along the length of the shop for their customers to sit on. Usually, from first thing in the morning

Cesidio in the shop at Cockenzie c. 1920

till last thing at night it was full. There was no extra room in any of the houses, so the local men, rather than stay at home with their wives, found the bench in Di Ciacca's just the place for sitting, talking and placing the odd bet between each other.

In the evenings they came after work. There were different groups: the miners, mucky and sooty off the trams from Prestongrange, in for a packet of Woodbine or a bag of chips. Or, if the boats were in, the fishermen came down before or after they visited the Thorntree, sometimes wild with drink, boisterous and rowdy. The unemployed and retired just sat around day and night.

Few of them had been in during the day. Cesidio had been busy showing Marietta all the jobs, so hadn't paid attention; tonight though, it was unusually quiet.

He went through to the fish and chip shop. Everything was spotless. Jimmy Caulder was standing with his arms folded, with nothing to do. There were no customers.

'I don't know what's wrong, Marietta. We're usually busy by now.'

They waited another half hour. Nothing.

Cesidio went through again to the chip shop.

'Jimmy, what's wrong tonight? Where are all the lads?'

'Have you not noticed, Sis? They're all out in the street.'

'What do you mean?'

'Have a look.'

Cesidio went to the front window and peered through. Outside in the street, spilling off the pavement into the road, were his usual thirty or so regular customers. They were all spruced up with their best jackets on, clean shirts, ties and hats. They stood silently, not saying a word.

'What's going on, Jimmy? Why are they all dressed up? They look like they're going to the kirk.'

'They've heard your wife's arrived. The word's got round that she's a braw lassie.'

Cesidio burst out laughing. He felt a surge of pride. The men were shy of his wife.

'Right Jimmy. Get the fish frying. We'll just have to persuade them to come in. Marietta!'

Cesidio called his wife from the ice cream shop. He stood her behind the counter and showed her how to lay out a piece of old newspaper. Then he showed her how to scoop a generous serving of hot, crispy chips on to a smaller sheet of greasproof paper in her hand, put it onto the newspaper, then lay a piping hot, crispy battered haddock on top. He showed her how to use a clean wet cloth to wipe her fingers, then sprinkle the fish and chips with salt and vinegar.

'Now, fold the newspaper like this, then close the parcel at the bottom end and pass it to me with the top end opened.'

She did this perfectly.

'Right, Jimmy, are you ready to go? I'll get them in. You do the money, Marietta'll wrap the suppers.'

Cesidio winked at his wife, and with a thumbs-up to Jimmy Caulder he went outside.

He stood among the men in the street. He nodded to them but said nothing. Putting his hand into the 'poke', he took out a piece of crunchy, white-fleshed, fried haddock. The warm smell of fat and salt was even more intense in the open air. His mouth watered. Their mouths watered.

He took a mouthful, licking his lips, savouring it. 'Mmm.'

That did the trick. First one, then a second, and within minutes all the men were in the chip shop, their sixpence slapped on the counter, queuing for their turn to order their fish supper and gawp at the 'braw Tally lassie'.

That night most of them secretly fell in love with her. She was an alluring creature, full of fun, not shy, always with a ready answer. She had the disconcerting knack of encouraging them to be familiar while keeping them at arm's length. She was so unlike their own women who in comparison were always worn down and exhausted. Life had suddenly become far more interesting.

Months later, by the end of January, Marietta was expecting her third child; she was working in the shop as usual. As she served the queue of customers, she felt a sharp pain in her back. She looked at Cesidio.

'The baby?' Cesidio knew by her look that it was time. Without saying a word, she went into the back of the shop.

'I'll go and fetch Nurse Swan.' One of the customers ran along to the midwife's house to get help.

The men eating their fish suppers stood anxiously outside the shop.

Marietta, Lena, Johnny and Cesidio outside the shop at Cockenzie c. 1921

Nurse Swan arrived. It was just past midnight. The men waited. They were like twenty waiting fathers, pacing up and down in the cold and dark.

After one o'clock, some of the wives came out looking for their men. They stood around, like sisters and mothers, rubbing their hands in the cold, determined to wait for news.

Sis came out at five minutes to two. 'Marietta's had a baby girl!'

The waiting crowd cheered and patted Cesidio on the back. He looked around with tears in his eyes. This crowd of locals around him, wishing him and his family well, had become his friends. At that moment, he felt that he had arrived and that their future was secure.

Cesidio owed Zio Benny some money. He would have to go to Edinburgh.

'Marietta, would you like to go up to Edinburgh with me? We can take the children in the tram. You can see Alfonso and Maria.'

Alfonso and Maria had also had a fourth child, who was now nearly two years old.

'That would be lovely. Lena and Giovanni can play with their cousins. I haven't seen their young Olivia since Anna was born. I'll bring Maria some really nice *baccalà* I saw in the fishmonger's. I don't think she has been able to find it in town.'

In Edinburgh they got down from the tram at the top of Easter Road and walked to the shop.

When he saw them approaching, Alfonso came out to greet them, handsome and charming as always. He kissed Marietta and made the children giggle, nipping them affectionately on the cheek. He shook Cesidio's hand, kissed him and patted him warmly on the back.

'*Auguri!* Congratulations, my friends. You're looking great. Come in. Maria's inside. What a lovely surprise!'

Maria was sitting in the back shop with two-year-old Olivia on her lap. The little girl was beautiful, full-faced and dark skinned. She smiled at her aunt and held out her hand. She wanted to play with the new baby and kept reaching over to pat Anna's head. The children all endured kisses from their relatives, then settled to play with the new baby.

Johnny, Anna and Lena, August 1922

Marietta gave Maria the dried cod she had been carrying in her bag. It was wrapped in brown paper and in newspaper. As soon as Maria unwrapped it, Alfonso burst out laughing.

'Is that what the smell was? I thought you were all smelling like fishermen because you're living so near the sea!'

The *baccalà* had a strong smell of old fish, salt and smelly socks. Domenico and Margherita came in from school. They looked at the dried fish and held their noses and moaned.

'Take it away, Mamma. Ugh!'

'You are all very rude.' Alfonso apologised to Marietta. 'Forgive them, Marietta. They're town children! Come, we'll go across to the house for some lunch. We're just about to eat.'

Maria had made some *'sagne e fagioli*, home-made pasta and bean soup. It was thick and creamy, and the pasta was cut roughly into strips, making it easy to slip down. The children loved it. They ate it with some heavy bread. Maria had also baked some *shadoon*, half-moon pastries stuffed with home-made ricotta and baked in the oven with a brush of egg yolk so that they were crispy and lightly golden in colour. The pastry was as light as a feather and crumbled as you bit into it to reveal the creamy sweet ricotta inside.

'*Grazie*, Maria. These are just like my mother used to make.'

'Your mother taught me, Alfonso, but I still can't make mine as good as hers!'

They all laughed. The women went into the kitchen to tidy up. The children played happily together. The older ones jumped from dialect to English with ease, their accents a mixture of Scottish and Italian. Olivia and Lena sat under the table and played with some coloured wooden bricks.

Alfonso and Cesidio sat at the table.

'Is everything settling down, *compare*? How's business?'

'I can't complain. We're working all hours. We've rented a flat across from the shop so we can make the back shop into a café. I have some money for Zio Benny. Can you pass it to him for me?'

'Of course. I'll see him this evening. How's Marietta? She looks very happy.'

'She's very happy. She's really good with the locals. It helps that she speaks English so well. How's Maria?'

'Oh, I don't really know. She is quiet sometimes. She works in the shop half the day then looks after the children: you know, constant cooking, washing, ironing. She never complains but she is alone quite a lot. The older children are at school so I'm really glad we have Olivia. She keeps her mother company.'

Cesidio wanted to know what was going on in Italy. He got no news down in Cockenzie. Alfonso usually knew what was going on.

'There are even more strikes, one political group fighting against the next. If there's not a strong government in Italy soon, who knows what the workers will do. I don't blame them really. If you can't feed your family what would you do?'

'It's just as bad here, what with the miners striking. You wonder, what was the point of the war?'

'Some of the soldiers I fought with have told me they are thinking of voting for Benito Mussolini. He is against the Communists and the strikes. Even the Catholic politicians are joining him in some parts.'

'Well, let's wait and see.' Cesidio felt he was far better off having emigrated, so he was not too anxious about the future.

Alfonso lowered his voice and moved towards his friend, 'Don't tell Maria, for the love of God. I've had a summons from the police.'

'Alfonso! What have you been up to?'

'Nothing bad: well, I don't think so. You know we're supposed to close at eight at night? The bakery down the road finishes up at nine. I sometimes let the boys sneak in. I can sell another few packets of Woodbines or a bar of chocolate. If they don't buy them from me they'll get them from Simpson's in the morning with their paper.'

'What's the fine?'

'£4. Sssh . . . don't tell Maria.'

Cesidio laughed. 'Never mind the police. If she catches you out you'll get more than a fine!'

'Eh! You two. What are you up to scheming over there?'

Marietta always wanted to know what the men were up to.

'Nothing, nothing.' Alfonso blushed.

On the way home in the tram, Cesidio told Marietta all about Alfonso's antics.

'He's harmless, Cesidio. I am glad we are not living in town though. I think it's a lot harder there, by the looks of things. Maria told me he was already fined for selling sweets for a penny over the fixed price, 9d instead of 8d,' Marietta laughed, 'I've done it myself but I didn't get caught!'

'Don't be clever. We're doing quite well. If we just keep saving, in about a year we'll be able to pay off our debt to Zio Benny.'

'Cesidio, I've been thinking about that. If we pay off the debt too quickly they'll know we are doing well. Zio Benny might send another family down here and open another shop. Port Seton is just five minutes away. There's no ice cream shop there. Let's just keep a bit of money aside and, instead of paying Zio Benny, we'll buy the corner shop at the Links at Port Seton. It's a great site. We'll protect our future first. Then we'll pay Zio Benny back.'

Cesidio didn't answer. She had a point. She was *furba*! At the beginning the Italians worked together but one would eventually come out stronger than the other. Marietta was clever. He had

140

chosen well. Not only that, she was beautiful too. He felt they could tackle anything together. Lena and Giovanni were happy looking out of the window. Cesidio looked down at Anna and soothed her brow as she slept on Marietta's lap. He felt very lucky.

He bent over and kissed his wife on the cheek and whispered, '*Ti amo.*'

14

Maria banged on the shop door screaming for Alfonso. Her hair was in disarray, a shawl pulled hastily over her shoulders. It was teaming with rain. She was almost soaked through.

She banged again.

She saw the light in the back shop and just as she was going to shout again the door swung open.

'*Maria, chè successo?* What's happened?'

'*Alfonso. Oh Dio! Alfonso. Olivia è malata! Aiuto. Aiuto.* Get the doctor. *Forza! Forza!*'

She turned and ran back home, barely avoiding getting knocked over by a horse and carriage that was charging down the street in the dark.

Olivia was breathing very shallowly. Every time she tried to fill her lungs she made a sinister wheezing squeak. Maria had seen children ill before. She knew Olivia was really sick; something was very wrong.

The children were standing round their sister's cot whimpering with fright. Olivia coughed again, almost desperately trying to catch some air, a coarse barking cough that she had had for almost four weeks, almost since Ash Wednesday.

Dr Sinclair had already been called out twice. He had told Maria to keep Olivia warm and put lavender oil in warm water by her bed. It didn't do any good. The lady in Lindsay & Gilmour's pharmacy had told Alfonso to make a poultice of bread and grated soap and warm it to put on the child's chest. Nothing helped. Preziosa said they should take her out for fresh air but it was so cold and damp Maria had been afraid and had kept her in.

'Mamma, what's wrong with Olivia?' Domenico was nine now

and old enough to realise that his mother was really frightened. He took Olivia's hand and bent over to give her a kiss. He patted her head.

Olivia coughed again.

They heard a commotion in the stair. Margherita opened the door for the doctor and her father.

As the doctor examined the baby Maria took a step back from the cot, too afraid to look. She started to cry. Alfonso put his hand on her shoulder to try to calm her, but she pushed him away.

'Take the children next door, *cara*. Take the children away.' Alfonso insisted. Maria's heart sank. '*Oh Dio! Oh Dio!*'

She took Margherita and Vittorio through to the bedroom. Domenico slipped her hand and stayed back in the room, moving into the shadows, refusing to leave his father alone.

He heard his mother start to say her rosary and a chill gripped his heart. She only said the rosary when they were all in bed or if something was wrong. His mother still didn't understand English. He did. Over the last few days he'd heard the children in the stair whispering 'The Tally bairn's goin' to cop it, she's got the croup.'

Olivia coughed again, but by now her breathing was even shallower, making a whistling noise like Zio Benny when he played the mouth organ.

Domenico thought she looked just like a blue angel; her face was round and pretty, her lips cherub-like, delicate and gentle. Her big brown eyes were wide open, staring at him in the corner of the room. He covered his ears with his hands, not wanting to hear her cough again.

The doctor listened to the little girl's chest. He kept listening and listening as if he was looking for something, something that he couldn't find. Something that had disappeared.

The doctor stood up and put his hand on Alfonso's shoulder and moved closer to him, saying something very quietly in his ear. Domenico's father leant over the cot and kissed Olivia, then put his fingers over her eyes and closed them, as if he was putting her to sleep.

Domenico went into the bedroom and stood close to his mother. He understood. 'She's gone, Mamma, *Olivia non è più.*'

Maria let out a strange noise, a noise like an animal makes when you hurt it badly: a long, loud agonising wail. A terrifying noise to Domenico; it was as if his mother's heart had broken there and then, right in front of him. He put his arms round her and held her. Instinctively he pulled his sister and youngest brother beside him. When his father had been away he had sensed his mother's every mood, he had known when she was anxious. He had never seen her as desperately upset as this.

The news travelled quickly around the Italian community, one family telling the next, just as they would have done in Picinisco. The next day, when Cesidio and Marietta arrived, they were shocked when they saw Maria. She looked devastated.

The house was full of women, dressed in black from head to toe, sitting around talking with quiet voices, crying and consoling each other in turn. The men, dark suited, stood silently near the door, hats in their hands, black mourning bands already stitched onto the left sleeve of their jackets. Father Michael had come from the Cathedral, the first time he had been in their home.

Alfonso greeted his friends. He looked stunned, haggard in fact, worse than he had ever looked while at war. He took them through to the bedroom where Olivia had been laid out. Marietta had to cover her mouth to stop a cry escaping. The beautiful child they had seen only four weeks before was lying lifeless.

She was dressed in a white long-sleeved silk dress that stretched the length of her slight body. Peeping out from under the hem were her pretty bare feet. Her tiny hands were crossed over her chest, white rosary beads entwined in her fingers. Her olive-coloured skin was as smooth as porcelain and her tiny cherub lips had gained some colour and stood out like a pink smear on her face. Her dark lashes framed her closed eyes, her black hair fanned out over the white pillow. On her head was a garland of fresh yellow primroses that framed her head like a halo.

Cesidio and Marietta knelt down and whispered their rosary for the little girl, praying for an hour or more until the next family came in to take over the vigil. On the mantelpiece was a picture of Sant'Antonio Abate illuminated by two flickering candles at either side. The room was filled with the aroma of candles burning and the scent of the flowers.

Marietta stayed through the night, preparing food for the mourners and consoling Maria when she collapsed again and again into unendurable despair. Maria could not bear Alfonso to touch her, recoiling in shock if he came near. Instead she clung to Margherita and her two sons. She found solace only in her rosary. She prayed decade after decade to her Holy Mother, desperate to avoid every thought that struggled into her consciousness.

She blamed herself. Had she neglected her little daughter? Had someone pointed the evil eye? Would her child be alive if they had never left Italy? She wanted to scream at Alfonso for putting her through this. She wished they had never met, never married. How could their love cause so much pain?

When she looked at her other beautiful children she was tortured with guilt and beseeched God for forgiveness for her wickedness and her ungrateful thoughts.

The women in the stair were wary. They had listened to the sound of the coughing of the Italian bairn and knew it was the croup. They kept their doors closed and told their own children not to go near the Tallies lest they catch it. They had all seen bairns die of this curse and they were afraid for their own. They felt sorry for the Tallies of course, but they were wary in case their bad luck would rub off on them. They wished among themselves that the Italian family would go and live somewhere else.

The next day the white-plumed horse-drawn hearse stopped at the door. Spending the last moment with his little girl alone, Alfonso blessed his daughter and kissed her forehead. '*Addio, mia cara.* I'll pray for you every day, every day that I live without you. *Cara Olivia.*'

Before they closed the small white coffin, he sprinkled cologne over the flowers on her head. The scent of his "Ashes of Roses" perfume lingered in the air as she was carried out of the house.

Neighbours and shopkeepers in Easter Road were all standing in respectful silence at their doors. Outside the ice cream shop, Mrs Glenn, Mary Praties and Lilly Rough were crying. The Italian families were all waiting silent behind the hearse.

It was a strange sight, all these foreigners walking together. The men led the way, hats in their hands, their dark good looks adding an air of excitement. The women were dressed in severe long black

145

lace dresses with high collars buttoned right up to their necks, fine black lace mantillas covering their faces. They held their children beside them, all beautifully dressed and respectful: healthy, strong-looking children with dark skins and thick black hair.

The procession turned up Montgomery Street and made its way along to Elm Row then up to St Mary's Cathedral. Maria walked beside her husband. She was retracing the steps that she had taken that first afternoon when she arrived at Waverley Station and Alfonso had come to meet her. Only this time she was burying her youngest child.

If she had known the hardship she would have to face and the sorrow that would fall on her, she would have turned back then and given up this mad adventure. What kind of improvement had there been? Working day and night, a stranger in a city, and now a child dying before she was two? Anger swept through her like an irrepressible dark wave. She wanted to lash out, smash everything in her sight.

Laid out in front of the majestic altar, the small white coffin looked incongruous among the sinister splendour of Scottish Catholicism. The gloomy gothic ceilings and powerful images of the risen Christ made the children shiver in fear.

Alfonso knelt at the front right-hand pew and sat symbolically alone, his wife and children behind him. During the Mass, when the congregation filed passed the coffin, they each bent over and kissed it, then crossed themselves, put their fingers to their mouths and slowly bowed down in front of the cross. Each man moved across to place his hand on Alfonso's shoulder in an act of respect. Some bent over and whispered something. Some just nodded and murmured in dialect '*condoglianze*'.

This was the first time Alfonso had seen his compatriots all together. They all came: his brothers Emidio and Giovanni, Zio Benny, Carlo Crolla from Antigua Street, and Cesidio, of course. Then Achille Crolla, Church Street; Valvona, Newhaven; Demarco, High Street; Tartaglia, High Street; Pompa, Crichton Place; Di Marco, Leith Street; Sabatino Cervi, Dundee Street and his cousin Pia, Raeburn Place; Valente and Rossi from Leith; Crolla, High Street; and Marandola from Pitt Street. Then, from down the coast, Mancini, Scapaticci, Di Rollo, Antonelli and Coppola from Tranent,

Togneri from Dunbar; in all, about twenty families, most with young wives and three or four children, nearly all from Picinisco and the surrounding villages. He felt blessed by their presence.

Next the women processed up to Holy Communion, many weeping, some supported by each other. They too had tragedies in their lives. Some had lost a baby in childbirth, or an older child like Olivia; some had lost a husband or son in war.

All felt a yearning for their families in Italy. At times like this they felt strangers in this country, fearing their families were vulnerable and at risk. *La lontananza* came over them, that feeling of separation that haunted them. Even the Church, though familiar in many ways, did not offer the support and guidance they craved. Though the Mass was in Latin, the women mostly did not speak English and could not gain support or guidance from the priest.

There were few Scottish Catholics at the service; it was a private affair, this Italian funeral.

No one noticed two strangers at the back of the church standing aloof, watching. The younger of the two was distinctive in that he had only one arm. They were dressed slightly differently from the mourners, with expensive suits, and black shirts rather than black armbands. The pass-keeper asked them if they would like to move further up to join the funeral party. They politely refused in perfect Queen's English. By the looks of them, they were Italians, but different; he couldn't put his finger on it. By the time Alfonso carried his daughter's small coffin out of the cathedral balanced high on his shoulders, they had gone.

After the funeral, Maria slipped into a quiet depression and became more and more distant from Alfonso. He tried everything to help her, worried that she would fall ill. He felt bereft, alone. He wrote letters to Tadon Michele and Pietro, talking through his worries. He felt he had lost part of his wife as well as his daughter.

To calm himself he started smoking, chewing on a dark Toscani cigar. He started to sprinkle his handkerchief with Ashes of Roses, a private ritual that kept the presence of his little Olivia alive.

Maria kept her own vigil with a lighted candle beside her holy picture and prayed constantly to the Holy Mother. She had taken to bringing the children into her bed at night, as she had done when Alfonso was away at war. Alfonso slept on the mattress in the front room. He was patient and loving with her but spent more time alone, walking on Arthur's Seat, chewing on his cigar, thinking, trying to make sense of this tragedy.

The children were subdued, so he made a point of bringing them little treats. He kept some liquorice allsorts or boilings in his pocket, which he slipped to them when their mother wasn't looking, much to their delight. Sometimes, if the weather was good on a Wednesday afternoon, he would pick them up from school and take them on the tram to Portobello. They would walk along the promenade and visit the Demarco café for an ice cream. Their favourite treat was a visit to Signor Valvona's car showroom. He would let one of them sit at the wheel of one of the biggest cars and pump the horn, pretending they were driving, to the delight of the other two who pretended to be passengers in the back.

When they came back from these excursions with some flowers or sweets for their mother, she smiled at them and hugged them, grateful to Alfonso for distracting them from her distress. In the evening when the children were finally asleep he would try to talk to her:

'*Maria, cara, come ti senti?*'

'Oh, Alfonso, I am too afraid to feel. I pray and pray so that I can't hear myself think. But I wonder if there is any point. How can any God take a child away like that?'

'God took her to save her any suffering in this life, *cara*. He took her because she was so good and pure she did not need to travel this path of doubt and disappointment. We should be glad for her. She is already in his arms.'

'Do you think so, Alfonso? Is she already happy in Heaven?'

'Of course, my darling. God would not take her and leave her unhappy. She doesn't want us to be unhappy. She is in Heaven praying for us.'

This seemed to console Maria a little.

'Maria, you must remember the children. They need you to be strong for them. They need you to hide your pain so that they can show you theirs.'

Maria moved towards him and sat at his feet, laying her head on his lap. He stroked her hair. She was vulnerable, this precious jewel of his. She had been so brave when he had to leave her to fight in the war. She didn't deserve this to happen.

'Alfonso,' she looked up at him, doubtful if she should speak.

'What, darling, *dimmi*.'

'I dreamt last night that La Madonna came to me.'

Alfonso said nothing.

'She said I was to stop weeping. She consoled me, Alfonso. She said I would have another child. That she was looking after Olivia and I was to look after my children, and another child would come.'

'That's good, Maria. That is a blessing. How strong your faith is.'

He pulled her towards him and held her close, kissing her head gently. '*Brava, Maria.* You have been so brave.'

She looked up into his eyes and blushed a little. She kissed him gently on the lips, for the first time since the child had died, the kiss of a lover rather than a sister.

He stayed with her until she fell asleep, then carried her through to their bed where Margherita was sleeping. He kissed her and left her to rest. Her healing had begun.

The loss of his child affected Alfonso much more than the death and carnage he had seen while fighting. He had suffered then, terribly, but this was much worse. He sat up all night trying to lift himself from his despair. In Maria's final unburdening after almost fourteen months of mourning, his own anger and frustration rose to the surface as if a dam had burst. He wept until his tears no longer rolled down his cheeks. Then he wept more.

He felt destroyed by doubt. His life was a failure. He didn't know what to do next. He had encouraged Maria to come here against her will. He had left her to cope alone, through no fault of his own. Now he was working every waking hour to try to improve their lives. Domenico would be ten years old next year. What had he achieved? An ice cream shop in a Scottish town, a rented house, debts to pay and five mouths to feed.

Maybe Maria was right. Maybe they should have stayed in Fontitune. He felt unsettled. Here they were branded as aliens but there was no way back home. He felt unsure of the future.

Alfonso was lonely.

In Fontitune he spent many weeks with Pietro or Tadon Michele in the Prato de Mezzo, weeks when they talked, cared for the animals, protected their flock. He was a shepherd. He missed his father. He missed his flock.

It was four in the morning and he would have to start work at six. He shook himself from his self-pity and went through to the bedroom. The Devil was tempting him to lose courage; he was angry with himself. He should thank God for all his blessings and have some faith.

15

Alfonso was wearing the new suit he had bought in Wight's stock-taking sale. He felt just the thing, dressed in smart, pin-striped trousers, with a dark grey waistcoat and black jacket. His new fob watch hung between the two buttons on his waistcoat, and his starched wing collar finished a very pretty picture. He straightened the black armband on his jacket and sprinkled his handkerchief with some Ashes of Roses before tucking it into his top pocket.

'How do I look?'

Maria undid his tie and sorted it for him. 'There, now you look the part.'

She kissed him on the cheek.

'Where are you going, Papà? Can I come with you?' Domenico was working in the shop after school. He loved being with his father as often as possible. He loved being with the customers.

'No, son. Not this time. There's a man coming to talk about Italy. He's from Torino. Remember, I told you, Zio Emidio and I worked in the market there when we were on the way to Scotland.'

'Will he know you, Papà?'

'I don't think so', Alfonso self-mockingly puffed up his chest, 'but I look so good he'll want to know me!'

'Alfonso, your pride will be the death of you,' Maria loved Alfonso's bravado but didn't think it was good to encourage him.

She helped him put his overcoat on.

'I'll be late; *un bacio a Papà.*'

He kissed them all, lit up his cigar and took his hat from the table. The aroma of smoky tobacco and cologne lingered after he'd gone, leaving a warm sense of security with his little family.

The meeting of the Scoto-Italian Society was being held in the New Café Hall. Alfonso, Emidio and Giovanni often attended these monthly meetings. They enjoyed the contact with other people: lawyers, officials, doctors, Scottish people who all loved Italy.

The Italian professional community also attended: the Consul, his officials and pen-pushers, a few teachers and translators. The immigrant women folk rarely came with them. They preferred sermons in the church, and felt intimidated by the so-called educated community.

When he arrived, Alfonso was warmly greeted by the Edinburgh Italian *ex-combattenti*, about twenty war veterans who had fought in the war. They usually met informally in the back of one of their shops, but this time they'd all had a letter from their regiments encouraging them to attend this evening's meeting. Mr Nicol Bruce, a Scottish lawyer and the Italian Consul for Edinburgh, had invited Signor Carlo Lupo, from Torino, to talk about Italy.

'Oh, look at you! *Che bello!* You must be doing well!' Giovanni patted Alfonso on the back and whistled at his new get-up. He was glad to see him looking better; he had watched his brother suffer after losing Olivia. It had knocked him back a lot.

Twenty-five minutes after the lecture was scheduled to start, Mr Nicol finally stood up to introduce the speaker. Everyone clapped.

'*Buonasera*. May I extend a warm welcome to our Scottish friends.'

A round of applause.

'And to our Italian *ex-combattenti* who fought so bravely in the war and defended our freedom. Stand up, stand up!' Consul Bruce signalled to all the ex-soldiers to take an applause.

Alfonso and the others stood up, a group of immigrant shop-keepers, recognised by many in the audience.

'*Grazie, Grazie amici.*'

The audience clapped enthusiastically. A ripple of acknowledgment whispered round the group, 'I didn't know Mr D'Agostino fought in the war. Mr Crolla too. How marvellous.'

Carlo Lupo stood up. He was a tall, slim man with a handsome narrow face and a very impressive moustache. He was well dressed, sporting a serious selection of medals and badges on his lapel.

The lecture was in Italian. For the non-Italian speakers in the audience, Miss Cornwall, a pretty spinster who had blushed when Alfonso had bowed to her at the door, translated each point with a gentle, Morningside accent. Some of the immigrants found both the northern dialect and the Morningside accent difficult to understand, but Alfonso sat entranced, concentrating on every word.

'Thank you, *gentile* Signor Bruce, for inviting me to talk this evening.

'After the war, so bravely won side by side with our Allies, Italy has had a period of turmoil. The red Socialists thought they sensed disunity and strife among our people. They used cunning and propaganda to encourage strikes and street fighting. They thought to break up our new country again and take control.

'But they misjudged our new, awakened patriotism. They misjudged our strength and brotherhood. They underestimated our new leader, Prime Minister Benito Mussolini.'

Alfonso was surprised at the warm response this brought from the audience. He sat quietly, studying the lecturer, assessing his tone.

'With audacity and braveness, firm action and genius, Prime Minister Benito Mussolini has destroyed the threat of civil war in our beloved country. He has offered salvation and vision to our people. He has guaranteed for us all the peace that our men have died for in war.'

Another, more enthusiastic, round of applause.

'He is a labourer, a workman's son. He fought alongside our men in the war. When he was shot down in action, his iron will helped him survive his wounds. He fought on with his heart and his pen to raise morale and maintain our spirit.'

More clapping.

'At last we are in safe hands. He knows what he wants. His aim is to make the Italian people a true nation. He will instil a collective responsibility and a desire for the common good. He will create a valued, protected workforce. He will inspire increased production. He will create unity. He will maintain peace. Peace at home and peace abroad.'

This made sense to Alfonso. He joined in the even louder applause.

Signor Lupo, fired up by his oration, stopped, waiting deliberately to allow Miss Cornwall to translate. She stood entranced by his passion – and not unattracted to his dark good looks and fiery brown eyes.

'Our saviour, the great Generale Garibaldi inspired the *Risorgimento* to unite our beautiful country, *Italia Nostra*. We have suffered war. We have suffered social injustice. We have suffered poverty and hunger. Our children have died and our mothers have wept. No more. Never again! *Mai più!*

'Benito Mussolini, *Il Duce*, puts the love of mankind first; the love of the family first; the love of our country first. He has shown us a new patriotism, a purified patriotism, a selfless patriotism.

'In a vision of genius, Prime Minister Mussolini has created *Fascismo, Il Partito Fascista. Fascio*, a bundle of reeds, a bundle of reeds, . . . signorina . . .

'Signorina!'

He translated the last word himself almost in a screech to startle Miss Cornwall back into translating.

'Binding the nation, holding us together with strength and vision. This is the true revolution in Italy.

'A revolution which has the blessing of the King Vittorio Emanuele!'

Applause.

'A revolution which has the backing of the great General Armando Diaz, who led us to victory with the brave British and French armies in the battle of Vittorio Veneto.'

Applause.

'A revolution which has the blessing of our Holy Father, Pope Pius the 11th.'

A cheer reverberated round the hall, the audience carried away with the drama enacted before them. The orator, cunning in his approach, now lowered his voice so that Miss Cornwall and her audience had to strain to hear every word, had to force their very beings to hear the conspirator's secret.

'More importantly, Italians are joining the Fascio, joining all over the country, from Sicilia to Napoli, from Roma to Trieste, and in London and Manchester, Glasgow and Edinburgh; in every city where even a single Italian citizen exists.

'Our Messiah, Benito Mussolini, will collect his flock and lead us to peace and prosperity. He tells me to inform you of the truth. *La verità!*

'*Onore, Famiglia e Patria! Onore, Famiglia e Patria! Questo è il cuore del Fascismo. Onore! Famiglia! Patria! Viva Il Duce!*'

He pounded out his message. He held his hand in a fist, stopped and thumped the air, his whole being vibrating with passion. He looked into the souls of every man in the room so that each personally felt that Mussolini was calling only to them.

He waited, then looked down into the eyes of Miss Cornwall.

'*Signorina, Il Partito Fascista, puoi fare la traduzione, per cortesia, signorina gentilissima?*'

Miss Cornwall was an educated young lady, exemplary in her training, equipped to cope under every situation, a woman of independent means. Trained to act efficiently, she unwittingly affirmed the message from Mussolini with as much enthusiasm as Signor Lupo.

'Honour, family and motherland! This is the heart of Fascism. Honour, family and motherland!'

'*Viva Il Duce!*' Lupo encouraged her to continue.

'Long live the leader!'

She looked up at Signor Lupo for approval. Was he happy with her translation? He looked down into her eyes and nodded gravely. He lowered his face towards her and pulled his eyebrows together.

Then, without moving a muscle on his face, he winked.

Taken aback, she blushed till her neck broke out in a sweat, her heart lurched and she promptly fell in love!

The Consul stood up, flushed and pink, drops of perspiration on his forehead. '*Grazie, Signor Lupo.* Thank you, my honourable friend, for taking the time in your busy schedule to give us this important message from Signor Mussolini.

'My dear compatriots,' he turned enthusiastically to his audience, overlooking the fact that they were mostly Italians and not his compatriots at all, 'I remind you that on 17 September of this year we will be holding the Centenary Celebrations of the great Manzoni, who is, according to Mussolini, "The Italian Walter Scott". May I respectfully suggest that, if you have not already done so, this would be an ideal opportunity to read his greatest work, *I Promessi Sposi.*'

He then signalled to the audience to rise as he led the singing of the Italian National Anthem, loud and resounding in the hall, followed by an equally enthusiastic 'God Save the King'.

By the end of this rousing finale there was much thanking and bowing, much kissing and back-slapping, enlivened discussion and talk. There was also a huge sense of relief that at last Italy had a strong leader, at last Italy and Italians could hold their heads up high and be counted. The mood in the hall was electric.

In a small side-hall the *ex-combattenti* gathered together, sharing a bottle of wine. Some had heard about Mussolini; some of their Arditi comrades had fought alongside him. They needed a vision in their lives. They needed hope. They were Italians, after all. They were proud and loyal. They felt as if they were in combat again; they had a sense of mission and objective to finish the job and make Italy great – this time by peaceful means.

Nicol Bruce came over to them accompanied by two Italian officers who had been standing at the back of the hall during the talk. 'May I introduce Signor Carlo Tronchetti, the Fascisti delegate for Scotland, and Father Salza?' Father Salza was a much decorated ex-officer and priest who had lost an arm in the war. Both men were in army uniform but, unusually, with distinctive black shirts instead of the olive green ones the *ex-combattenti* had worn.

After much hand-shaking and introductions, each man waiting in order of rank for the right opportunity to be acknowledged, Signor Tronchetti spoke to them. '*Soldati! Compagni!* I have an invitation for you all from Prime Minister Mussolini himself.'

Alfonso noted that Giovanni was standing slightly apart, listening, but not as animated as the rest of them. He caught Alfonso's eye and raised an eyebrow but said nothing.

'Prime Minister Mussolini, Il Duce, wants me to report to you all that he respects every soldier who put his life at risk for his country.

'He especially respects those of you who have been driven from your homes, driven from your families and heritage, driven from your country by the corruption and bad government of the past. He respects those of you who have had the courage to make your own way in the world, abandoned by your government.

'He has instructed me to say to you, to all of you in the country:

no more. No more! He recognises that *you* are the strength of Italy, the courage of Italy, the heart of Italy. No longer will you be despised as an *emigrante*; you will be honoured as *lavoratori Italiani all' estero*, Italian workers abroad. At last you will be given the respect and dignity you deserve.

'No more will you feel afraid, called aliens, distrusted.

'Join us, *amici!* Il Duce wants you to join us; join the Fascio here, to support each other and protect each other. *Onore, Famiglia e Patria!*

'*Ma senti,* his instruction is clear. You must accept the discipline and responsibility of being an Italian. You must respect the laws of the country that has given you a home. You must set an example to every citizen. You must not take part in the politics of the country. You must take responsibility to keep good relations with other Italians living abroad. That is your Fascist duty.

'Men, Il Duce says you must set an example of public probity and uphold Italian traditions, you must perform charitable works and discipline yourselves in the same way he demands that citizens of Italy must.

'Men, join us. Join us for the good of peace and the good of your families.'

That night, Alfonso arrived home late and very excited. It all made sense. If this were true, if Italy really had a great leader at last, maybe things could change. He felt empowered. No longer would he have to be regarded as an alien in a foreign country and an exile from his own. Mussolini understood that they were still Italian citizens, even although they worked abroad. Mussolini knew that their hearts longed for home.

He felt that this was the path he had been looking for. This was the way he should go.

Onore, Famiglia e Patria. This was the truth that was in his heart. Benito Mussolini might be right.

The next day, out of the blue, a parcel arrived from Fontitune. It was wrapped up securely in white muslin and string and sealed with big stamps of red wax. Alfonso brought it across to the house, excited like a child, wondering what was in it. This was the first time they had had a *pacco* since the war had ended.

'*Il Pacco! Il Pacco!* Children, look at what has arrived from Nonno Michele.'

The children had never seen their Nonno Michele but were told stories constantly about his wisdom and courage, about the sheep he cared for and the wolves he frightened away. They knew about the cheese that he made and they had wished many times that they could taste Nonno Michele's *salsiccie.*

'Open it, here, Domenico. Help me open it.'

Maria came out of the bedroom. She was expecting another child at last, due next month, God willing. She looked very beautiful, pale and with a gentle smile that warmed her sad eyes. She sensed the excitement and came over to Alfonso and kissed his cheek.

'How wonderful, I wonder what's in it. It smells pretty strong!'

She laughed and, unexpectedly, hooked her arm round Alfonso's as she stood and watched the children pull the packet open.

Alfonso pulled her towards him and held her close, his heart full of love. She was so much happier now that the new baby was nearly due.

'*Papà, aiuto.* Help us, *per favore.*' Vittorio interrupted them. He had sensed that there was food in the *pacco,* something that smelt unusual. Mamma didn't kiss Papà very often, but now wasn't the most convenient time, not when something more exciting was about to happen.

Alfonso took a knife and cut the remaining string, pulling the cotton away. Vittorio knelt on the chair and prised the lid open. Margherita climbed up and settled herself on the table so that she could see everything that was going on.

'Vittorio, you are in charge of the *pacco.* You have to unpack everything and tell Domenico what is inside.' Alfonso gave Domenico a pencil and a small black notebook. Alfonso was teaching him to write Italian at home as he was doing very well with his lessons.

First Vittorio pulled away some newspapers that were packed on top and discarded them. A pungent smell of mature cheese mixed with a spicy chilli smell hit them all.

'*Oh Dio. Papà! Che puzza!*' Margherita got a clip across the ear from her mother for taking the Lord's name in vain.

Vittorio pulled out the first bundle, again wrapped in old

newspapers. He opened it and revealed the booty inside. '*Cinque salsiccie. Scrivi, Domenico*. Five sausages. Are these Nonno Michele's *salsiccie,* Papà?

Alfonso was as excited as the children. He hadn't tasted *salsiccie* from Fontitune since Maria had brought them with her when she arrived. He lifted one up and smelled it, taking in the aroma of pork, pepper, spices and chilli. He took the knife and sliced a bit of the dry, hard sausage. He put it in his mouth and chewed it. The children were silent. Were these the famous *salsiccie* of Nonno Michele? Alfonso smacked his lips and smiled at the children.

'Well,' he said, slowly and deliberately, enjoying the moment of suspense, 'well, do you know what? I think I'll just have to try another slice.'

'What?'

'Alfonso! Stop teasing them!' Maria laughed and pushed him aside; taking the knife from him, she started to cut slices of the sausage. She gave a piece to each of the children and cut some more for herself and Alfonso. They all waited in suspense for a declaration from their father.

'*Questa è la salsiccia migliore nel mondo. Fonteluna*! This is the best sausage you will ever taste, this is the sausage of Fontitune, the sausage of your past and your future.'

They all cheered and clapped, then they tasted the sausage. It was chewy but moist, not too dry, quite sweet, tasting of juicy pork. There was a mixture of spices and flavours with whole spices that released an unexpected punch of flavour when they were bitten into. It was delicious.

Vittorio stood up on the chair. At seven years of age he felt entitled to be the centre of attention.

'I would like to say that *questa è la salsiccia migliore in tutto il mondo!*'

They all laughed. So this was the famous sausage – the *Fonteluna*. Now they understood why all their uncles kept talking about it, missing it and scheming how they could make it here or, better still, get it sent across from Fontitune.

'What else is there?' Maria wanted to taste some pecorino. She knew by the smell that there was some inside.

Vittorio pulled the three parcels out of the *pacco,* each wrapped in more newspaper. '*Tre formaggi*. Write it down, Domenico.' He was quite bossy to his big brother, sharper and sometimes impatient of Domenico's laid-back nature.

'Give me the newspapers, Vittorio. Margherita, collect those from the floor and lay them on the sideboard. I'll read them later.' Alfonso wanted to read the precious Italian newspapers, even if they were months out of date.

Maria took the first cheese and lifted it to breathe in the aroma. 'I hope Mrs Wilson doesn't pass the door or she'll be phoning the police again.'

It was now a family joke that Mrs Wilson, who had never warmed to her Italian neighbours, had called the police when she smelled garlic cooking. To be fair, sometimes the smell of Mrs Wilson's cooking was so awful to Maria that she felt she had to hold her own nose when she passed the door. She put the cheese on the table and looked at Alfonso for instruction.

'Just cut it in half, Maria, we'll eat it tonight. I noticed you made some fresh bread this morning.'

Maria cut the cheese in half, straight down the middle. It opened out revealing a creamy, pale soft cheese, slightly sharp on flavour with a soft buttery centre.

'What is that in the middle?! *Oh Dio!*' Margherita earned another clip across the ear and a second one for screwing up her nose at a mass of translucent maggots squirming in the middle of the cheese.

Maria and Alfonso laughed. They found nothing unusual in this. At home this was regarded as the best part of the cheese and was savoured as a bit of a luxury.

Alfonso winked at Maria. These city kids needed a rude awakening. Maria took a spoon from the drawer and handed it to Alfonso, who immediately dipped into the middle of the cheese and scooped out a spoonful, offered it to his wife who ate it with real pleasure. He then took another spoonful and offered it to Vittorio.

The boys screamed in disgust and Margherita, devastated that her mother had just eaten maggots, went off into the bedroom in shame. What a disappointing *pacco*. What other horrors were buried deep inside?

The boys stayed and tasted the cheese from the edges; and were glad they had. It was really good, and strangely familiar to these two young boys, whose parents had chosen to turn their backs on their inherited livelihoods.

Later, in the evening, when the children had gone to bed and the house was quiet, Maria sat contentedly beside Alfonso as he set about reading the precious newspapers that he had rescued. The cheese and sausage had been covered with a cloth and put on a plate on the window-sill, to keep them cool. The rest of the contents of the *pacco*, a bottle of olive oil, six ruby-red beer bottles filled with tomatoes, three heads of hard, dry garlic and bunches of dried herbs, were displayed proudly beside the sink. Maria couldn't read but she sat with the letter from Pietro, thinking about all the news from Fontitune. *Grazie a Dio*, everyone was well.

She was tired and thought that she would go to bed. Alfonso might come with her. She stood up. '*Alfonso, caro*. I'm going to bed now. The children are in their own beds and are all asleep.'

She bent over him and kissed him on the cheek. He put his hand up and pulled her down towards him. 'Look at this, Maria. Look at this man.'

In the newspaper, a sheet from *Il Popolo d'Italia*, 31 October 1922, smeared slightly by oil from the sausages, there was a photograph of an attractive-looking man. He was about forty, five years or so older than Alfonso. He was sturdy and strong-looking, muscular and healthy, with short cropped dark hair and a slightly receding hairline. He had a distinctive Roman nose and a firm-looking, sensuous mouth. He was clean shaven and wore a beautifully tailored black suit with a black shirt underneath. In his hand he carried an incongruous British bowler hat.

Maria was struck by his piercing eyes; even in this crumpled newspaper picture you could see a fierce determination and power in his eyes.

'Who is he?'

'Il Duce. Benito Mussolini. The new Prime Minister of Italy.'

'Since when?'

'Since three months ago. In October he marched on Rome with his supporters and offered his services to the king. He says Italy needs a strong leader who will put backbone into the government and avert civil war. They told us all about him last night. He will be a great man, Maria, he will be Italy's Saviour. What do you think of him?'

161

Maria thought for a moment. He was unlikely to affect her life, but somehow she didn't like the look of him. Her instinct recoiled against something in his arrogant look and aggressive stance. '*A me non mi piace.* He'll be trouble, Alfonso, he'll be trouble.' Maria kissed Alfonso again and went to get ready for bed.

She had the knack of taking the wind out of his sails. Here he was, enthralled by the idea of a strong leader in Italy, and she thought he'd be trouble. Could she be right? But surely Italy needed a strong leader, one who would unify her and prevent any more disruption? The trouble was, Maria didn't understand war. She'd had a hard time during the war, on her own in a strange country with a young family. She'd had to suffer the loss of her child, which was tragic for them all. But women didn't understand war. How could they imagine the destruction and useless carnage, the slaughter and bloodshed, the agony and futile waste? Thank God, she didn't know; but if she did, she would see things differently.

He knew that peace could only come with strength. A weak leader leaves the way open for more strife, for another war, God forbid. No, she was wrong. Mussolini was the right man at the right time.

He smoothed the paper and put it into a drawer. He would show it to the men on Wednesday when he met them after work. He was keen to know what they thought. How many of them would have the courage to stand up and be counted?

Alfonso couldn't resist. He took the sausage from the window-sill and cut another few slices. He poured half a glass of wine and drank slowly, looking out over Rossie Place. This trial package had worked well. He would write to Pietro and send him money for three packages. He would sell this sausage and cheese easily to the Italians in Edinburgh. Valvona already sold some in his new shop in George IV Bridge, but it wasn't a patch on this.

One day he'd take his family back to Italy. He understood Maria: that was what she longed for; one day, but not yet. First he had to make money. He would work every hour he could and save up every penny he could. He closed the window and locked the front door. He drank back the last of the wine and smiled to himself. If he was lucky, she wouldn't be asleep yet.

16

Edinburgh
1924

Looking back, Alfonso always considered the day he heard Carlo Lupo as the moment he found his vocation. Until then he had been lost. He had turned his back on his past but had not yet found his future. That day was a turning point in his life. He felt that it was his lucky chance, his *sette bello*, the moment when he chose his destiny.

Maria was not convinced.

'Alfonso, be careful. Why are you getting involved with politics? What do you know about things like that? It's a waste of time.'

'*Cara, tu non capisci*. The strength of the Fascio is that it will keep us all together. We need to be bound together, a *fascio*. Think about it, our new countrymen don't know where we stand. To some, we are heroes who fought alongside them. To others, we are foreigners who look and behave differently, foreigners not to be trusted. To the Scottish churches and Jews we are Catholics. To the officials and the police, we are "aliens" to be watched and penalised for every misdemeanour.'

Maria immediately smelled a rat. She understood Alfonso better than he understood himself.

'What misdemeanour?'

'What do you mean?' Alfonso scratched his leg nervously.

'What misdemeanour?'

'Well,' Alfonso put his head down and looked up at her. Then he tipped his head and shrugged his shoulders. 'Nothing. It was nothing. I have been fined for selling cigarettes after hours. It's not a big deal. All the boys do it.'

Maria knew he had been fined. The other wives had already told her.

'Oh, Alfonso. Be careful. Please don't get into trouble. I know Emidio and the D'Agostino boy were fined as well.'

'Don't you see? That's precisely my point. The other shopkeepers sell a packet of cigarettes out of hours as well, but it's the Italians who are watched, so it's the Italians who are caught.

'Mussolini understands what we're up against. Suspicion arises from fear of the unknown. Mussolini says we have to stand up and be counted.'

'What has Mussolini got to do with it? You shouldn't sell cigarettes out of hours and that's that!'

'I know, I know. I won't do it again. But, Maria, we need a strong leader. All the leaders of the Alliance agree. Read the *Scotsman*.'

'I can't read.'

'Well, you know what I mean. Read the newspapers. Many politicians approve. People like Churchill.'

'I don't know who you mean.'

'A lot of world leaders are impressed with Il Duce. The Holy Father, the Archbishop. The King, for God's sake!'

'Alfonso, there's no need to raise your voice.'

'Mussolini says that, as immigrants, we have to honour the country we are living in, obey their laws and set an example. Tadon Michele said to me that discipline is the only way to survive: discipline the dog; discipline the sheep; discipline yourself.'

'And I suppose the wife comes into that as well?'

Alfonso sensed his victory. He put his arms round her and kissed her on the cheek with a flourish. 'My darling,' he patted her slightly swollen belly, 'how could I ever discipline you. You can have anything you want. Now, . . .'

He knew he had won when she kissed him back. Maria was afraid she had pushed him too far; she didn't want to quarrel.

But Maria wasn't as easily convinced by Alfonso's ideas as he thought. She saw his point and she knew from talking to the other wives that they wanted some structure in their lives, something of the old way of life, some help to discipline their husbands. Some of the younger men were being lazy or staying out later than they needed to. One of the wives thought her husband was having an affair with a Scots girl who worked in their shop.

Alfonso had a point. They needed discipline but she didn't want her husband to be the one to take the responsibility. Let Mussolini find someone else.

Alfonso subtly changed the subject, 'I need to buy a black shirt. Do you want to come shopping with me and we'll buy you a new hat.'

She agreed to go. A day out would be nice.

Alfonso wanted to take her to the sale at Jenners department store on Princes Street but, since that first day when she had looked in Jenners' window after arriving off the train, she had felt intimidated by the glamour and wealth displayed there. She felt more at home in the millinery department of Patrick Thomson's on the North Bridge. Her new hat cost only ten shillings, a quarter of the price of one in Jenners. She was very pleased.

After they finished shopping they enjoyed tea and scones in the tea room on the first floor of the store. It felt good sitting with other Edinburgh gentlemen and their wives, instead of serving them. She was amazed at the prices charged.

'It's a disgrace, Alfonso, a shilling each! If only I could charge that in my shop.' She had to admit to herself, though, that she couldn't have had such fun if they were still in Fontitune. Sometimes the hardship and worry were worthwhile.

About thirty of the Italian ex-servicemen were also swept up by the rhetoric. Tronchetti had kept in touch. Gradually he enrolled them all in the movement. It was even better than Alfonso had hoped. Once they had enough supporters they would receive substantial funds from the Italian government. They could rent a hall and they could organise themselves.

There would be Italian lessons for the children, funds for widows and orphans and money to organise dances and *feste*. On Ferragosto, 15 August, the Consul was going to organise a big picnic for all the immigrants in Scotland and have a sports day for the children and a dance at night. Mussolini himself was even going to send them a silver cup to present to the winners!

'At last,' Alfonso thought, 'at last, a government that looks after its people.'

They were both invited to the Blessing of the Fascist Flag on 4 February. Alfonso was surprised that Maria agreed to come. He put on his corporal's uniform with his new black shirt and pinned his war service medals proudly on his jacket.

Maria dressed elegantly in a long black dress with a dark shawl to hide her pregnancy. She felt very up to date with her new black felt cloche hat pulled down over her eyes. They walked down Easter Road arm in arm to the Queen's Hall in Leith. After the speeches and blessings, the crowd of two hundred, made up of dignitaries and representatives of the churches and both governments, saluted the flag and then clapped enthusiastically to celebrate the new working relationship between the British and Italian governments. The Church of Scotland Moderator Graham of St Andrew's applauded when the Catholic Archbishop Mackintosh spoke.

'My dear friends, this is a great day for our two countries. Scotland and Italy have so much in common to celebrate. Our values and goals are alike. We just need to look at our common proverbs to see how close our cultures are.

'Just like the Scotsman, the fundamental quality in the Italian is his attachment to his family and the home. We all agree, women must be at home, must keep away from politics and the workplace. You know the proverb, "Sad is the house where the hen sings and the cook is silent!"'

At this everyone laughed and clapped, including Maria, who agreed wholeheartedly with the Archbishop that a woman's place was in the home.

The Archbishop, enjoying his new popularity, continued 'And we Scots and Italians are gallant and value a good woman, "A man without a wife is without a head."'

More laughter and clapping from the audience.

'And of course we are two races who are prudent with money. Look at the proverb "Money saved is money twice gained."'

Maria whispered to Alfonso, 'See, I told you it was better to go to Patrick Thomson's.'

'Members of the Fascismo, look to our proverbs for guidance. Il Duce will only accept into the movement those of outstanding moral character, those who are models in the practice of the Christian and civil virtues, those who are upstanding in the Community.

'Mussolini demands that you honour your family, your God and your country. What better message than that? But he also demands an effort, an added talent if you are to be good Italians, good Scottish citizens. His is the most inspiring proverb:

"*Meglio vivere un giorno da leone, che cent'anni da pecora!*"

"Better to live one day as a lion than a hundred years as a sheep!"'

The whole audience rose in applause, not a single sheep among them.

After two minutes' solemn silence for the fallen comrades in both armies, the Fascists and Italians sang D'Annunzio's rousing song from the First World War that had been deliberately adopted as the Fascists' theme.

Giovinezza, giovinezza, primavera di belezza,
Nel fascismo è la salvezza, della nostra libertà!

Young People. Young people. Springtime of beauty,
Fascism is the saviour of our liberty!

Alfonso's heart filled with immense national pride. He remembered each of the men who had fallen alongside him in the war. They had died for this. They had died for this true vision of peace and co-operation between countries. They had died for love.

Maria looked up at him when he joined with the other soldiers and raised his arm in the ancient Roman salute. There were tears rolling down his cheeks. He was swept away by the humanity of the moment, desperate to relate to and be a part of the future of his beloved Italy.

He had no idea that Toscanini, his musical hero of the battle at Monte Santo, was refusing to play 'Giovinezza' at La Scala in Milan and was publicly opposing Mussolini and all that he stood for.

Fulfilling the prophecy of La Madonna in Maria's dream, their baby girl was born on 30 March 1924, two years to the day on which Olivia had died. Alfonso and Maria wept together. Their sad memories of their lost child intensified their joy at the new birth. Alfonso could see only hope for their future.

'We'll call her Olivia Benita. Mussolini will protect this child and

Anna, Alex, Lena and Johnny

secure peace in her lifetime.' Alfonso proudly made the decree and no one dared argue against it.

Marietta and Cesidio had also had a new baby boy called Alessandro. It was with a sense of elation that Alfonso and Maria took the tram to go down the coast to visit their friends with their new baby girl.

The women hugged each other warmly. Their lives were really starting to look good.

When Alfonso was out of earshot, Maria quizzed Marietta about this Fascist club.

'Marietta, I didn't see you and Cesidio at the ceremony last month. Did you know about it?'

'Oh yes, Maria, Cesidio got an invitation from his old army unit. I don't want him to get involved. Alfonso and some of the other men have been trying to convince him, but I really think it's best to keep out of it.'

'That's what I said to Alfonso, but he is so fired up with it. I've never seen him so happy and contented so I am afraid to say anything else.'

'I understand that it's different for you, living in town. Down here it is so much easier; we are part of the Scottish community. They call Cesidio "Sis", and me "Mary Coppola", if you don't mind.'

Maria laughed. Alfonso was called Mr Crolla in the shop, or "Tally bastard" depending on the time of night. 'What about London? Are your relatives there joining up?'

'Yes, some of them are very keen. They already have a Fascist club and they have an Italian school, hospital, free holidays for the children. It sounds really good.

'To tell you the truth, Maria, down here in this small community we're more troubled with religion than politics. The Presbyterian Church and the Free Church of Scotland are against us opening on Sundays. They think we're a bad influence on the young.'

'How can they say that? We do everything for our children? Is that not true?   Are Lena and Giovanni going to school yet? What age are they now?'

'Six and five. They go on the tram to Musselburgh, Our Lady of Loretto. It's a lovely school. Giovanni can read three words already! But the tram fare up and down every day is quite a lot. I'm not sure if we'll be able to send them every year. We'll see.'

They took the children for a walk up School Lane and across the Edinburgh Road to see Inglis' farm, which was at the edge of the village. The farmer grew crops of barley, wheat and kale, but Marietta wanted the children to see the horses and the pigs. They loved the big black pig that snorted and farted and rolled in the mud. The little pink piglets scrambled for a teat and suckled as long as they could before a bigger, stronger sibling nudged them out of the way.

'Maria, Mr Inglis has two piglets for us, one for you and one for me.'

'Oh, what a treat! *Grazie*, Marietta. Alfonso will love that. How are you going to cook it?'

Maria found the prospect of stuffing the piglet with rosemary and garlic and roasting it in the oven even more exciting than her new hat, and certainly more interesting than Alfonso's antics with big boys playing at soldiers or politics.

Alfonso didn't see it like that at all. He saw a real opportunity to bind his relatives and compatriots together and to take responsibility for making their community successful in Edinburgh. He attended meetings regularly with the Scoto-Italian Society and enjoyed increasing his knowledge of both countries.

He marched with the Fascio in the Armistice Day celebrations in November, marching with the ex-servicemen from the Scottish regiments and playing their Italian marches and 'Giovinezza' alongside the 'Flowers of the Forest' and 'Scotland the Brave'.

1926

Life was good. The business was doing well. They had moved into a new top flat on Brunton Place, a lovely bright home with plenty of space and a beautiful large kitchen. It had a bath and electricity, two luxuries Maria enjoyed immensely.

After school and at the weekends the older children started to work in the shop. It was a great help; it saved paying wages, and the children could speak English, which really helped their mother. Maria had never made any effort to learn to speak English. She still could not read and write, although Alfonso had insisted she learn to sign her name so that when her new Italian passport was issued she didn't mark it with her thumb print and a cross as she had done before, but scrolled her name clumsily across the bottom.

The shop did especially well when the Hibernian football team were playing at home. Then Mrs Glen and the girls couldn't get the queue served fast enough. Maria and Alfonso were working all hours saving every penny they could. They wanted to open a bigger shop, nearer the football ground.

When the football was on, Alfonso, Domenico and Vittorio stood at the gates of the stadium and sold warm Scottish mince pies from a tray. Margherita ran up and down Easter Road with boxes of more pies as fast as they would heat up in the oven. After a few months the organisers allowed the likeable Italian lads to come into the grounds and sell at half-time, which did more trade in a few hours than the shop did all week.

Alfonso's scheme with Pietro was paying off as *pacco* after *pacco* arrived from Italy. Pietro wrote regularly and reported on the great changes that were happening in Italy with Mussolini's plans. Mussolini was building roads and draining marshes, giving work to thousands. The trains were running on time and were much safer and more efficient, so the parcels that Pietro was sending were taking three days to arrive instead of five.

Alfonso paid attention to this news and it reassured him that he was right about Mussolini. The man was a saviour for Italy.

When the sausages and cheeses arrived, Alfonso packed them into two old suitcases he had bought in a second-hand shop in the Grassmarket and he made his way around the Italian shops. This meant that not only did he earn a bit of extra money but he enjoyed keeping up with all the families.

He was always keen to pick up snippets of information or report positive news about Italy and Mussolini. Valvona and De Marco, who both had Italian grocer's shops, were not too happy that Alfonso was selling direct to their customers, so now and then he'd talk to them and sell them some sausages or cheese at wholesale prices to keep them happy.

There appeared to be plenty of business. Valvona had opened an Italian produce wholesale business in Merchant Street, in the heart of the old town near Candlemaker Row, on the way down to the Grassmarket. There were plenty of Italian businesses in Edinburgh and the east of Scotland who bought from him. A lot of them were dependent on Valvona for ingredients they couldn't buy elsewhere. It became a place where Alfonso could meet other Italians and keep an ear to the ground.

Visiting the Grassmarket area he became aware of another side of the Italian community. The first wave of immigrants had managed to get a hold in business and most were fairly successful. Some families, however, hadn't been so lucky and were struggling to survive. In some of the outlying villages, Italians were working as farm labourers, their wives and daughters cleaning or sewing to make a living. In some shops, too many family members had come across from Italy and there was not enough work for them all. Few Scottish businesses would employ unskilled Italians.

After the immigration law of 1920 restricting immigration, a loop-hole allowed young children to come into the country under the umbrella of adoption or education. Some arrived off transport ships with labels round their necks asking directions to the Italian family they were going to. Some families were unscrupulous, not offering them education but making them work in their shops up to eighteen hours a day, with board and lodgings their only reward.

In the Grassmarket, in the dark, damp tenement buildings overshadowed by Edinburgh Castle, there were some Italian soldiers who had been wounded in the war and had returned to a life of poverty. If a husband died in the war, Italian wives found themselves without income, feeding five or six children living in a squalid room and kitchen with shared outside toilets. Any income would be from cleaning or ironing. The children didn't attend school but scraped a living doing errands for shopkeepers or delivering messages.

Scottish families living in this area were also scraping a living. Abject poverty is a great leveller and the mixture of Jewish, Irish, Italian and Scots produced an exotic, vibrant community. With ingenuity they used every skill they could to survive. Some grew herbs and funghi in window boxes balanced precariously on their window-sills. One old soldier even had a mousetrap on his window-ledge in which he caught unsuspecting sparrows and roasted them over a brazier to eat.

Alfonso often took the children to the Grassmarket on Thursdays. The tree-lined square had a weekly market with lots of colourful stalls selling fresh produce, clothes and nick-nacks. Irish dancing, an Italian with a barrel organ and a monkey, and the children running barefoot around the square made Alfonso feel he was almost at home in the piazza in Picinisco.

There was also an Italian ice cream barrow at the market, pushed along on two wheels. The Hokey Pokey man sold penny cones in the summer and enterprisingly used his barrow to sell hot chestnuts in the winter, keeping the customers happy all year round.

A gypsy with a tamed parrot sat at the water fountain. 'Fortune telling! Threepence to know your future!'

She put two cards in front of the parrot. If it picked up the pink one, you would have a girl, the blue one, a boy. Margherita believed completely in the gypsy's powers. When Mamma had visited the gypsy just after Olivia had been born the parrot had picked up two pink cards at once and the gypsy had predicted that Maria would have another two baby girls. Maria had been very excited about this news and there had been great talk about whether the prediction would come true or not.

Sure as fate, Maria did eventually have another two girls, Gloria Italia was born in January 1926 and almost a year to the day, Maria's final daughter, Filomena, was born!

Alfonso kept an eye out for the more vulnerable families and often, without letting on to Maria, he would bring them some cheese or bread, lend them some money or just give a handful of sweets for their children. He gained a reputation for being very kind and willing to help out. He often solved one person's problem by helping another.

It became apparent to the Consul and the officials in the town that Alfonso had built up a name for being fair and good. He was charismatic and naturally took the lead. So when the funds became available to open the Edinburgh Fascio hall, Consul Nicol Bruce approached Alfonso to inform him that he had been 'selected' to be the secretary of the club. Alfonso was flattered and accepted the honour without hesitation. When he went home and told Maria, all hell broke loose.

'*Madonna mia!* Alfonso, how could you? Why do you want to take on all that responsibility? You'll just get involved and be running after everyone, wasting your time.'

'But, Maria. I have been chosen! In a way, I have no choice. It is an honour but also it will be good for us. I will be more respected in the community. Domenico leaves school soon. He'll be able to help you and we will be able to open another shop.'

'And who'll look after the first shop if you are out doing the Fascist Party business and I am left here again with the girls?'

At that, as if they realised their father was up to something, Olivia (no one, not even Alfonso, could bring themselves to call her Benita) and Gloria burst out crying.

Maria picked up Filomena, still a baby, and tried a different tack with her husband.

'Alfonso, please. Say no! I have these three girls to look after.

Filomena, Maria, Olivia and Gloria, c. 1926

I've six children to wash for. We have eight mouths to feed. We need you around *us*, not around other families.'

'Maria, I have been selected, I didn't volunteer. I have no choice. It's an honour to serve our community. Look on the bright side. I have to go round the families in the outlying districts to recruit more members. I can get more orders for the *salsiccie* and pecorino at the same time. Pietro will get more business as well. And the children will get free Italian classes, and there are going to be free holidays for them in Italy.'

Maria knew that a holiday in Italy could cost as much as ten pounds. She went quiet. She dreamt of letting her children go back to visit their homeland.

Alfonso waited a moment and then, just as Maria was about to say something, he picked up Olivia and sat her on the table.

'And Olivia, my beautiful little girl, my first job is to organise a party for you and your brothers and sisters', and just as Maria was going to pull Olivia away from him, 'and for Mamma and Papà to go and dance and have a lovely time.'

Maria gave in. There was no use arguing with Alfonso. His heart was set on it, and anyway what was wrong with them all having a little bit of fun?

17

The Lawnmarket, Edinburgh
October 1926

There was nothing Alfonso enjoyed better than spending a Wednesday evening in the back shop of Ferdinando Crolla's with his friends. It was a small shop on the Lawnmarket, the road leading up to the esplanade of Edinburgh Castle, so there was plenty of passing trade. Solicitors and lawyers from the courts came in for a chat and a packet of cigarettes; shoppers and stall-holders from the regular markets and all the Italians in the area knew Ferdinando.

The Deacon Brodie public house was across the road but Alfonso and his friends would never have dared enter a Scottish pub. Firstly they hardly drank spirits and beer, preferring a glass or two of red wine. Secondly, they were in the habit of playing cards together, a round of *scopa*. This would be forbidden in public places.

More to the point, their wives would forbid it. Sitting talking with the other men, out from under their feet, was one thing. Spending money in a pub, boozing and flirting with loose women, was quite another.

On this evening Alfonso was glad to have his friends all together; he had some good news.

'Boys, I've heard from the Consul. They've finally put down a deposit on the two floors at 20 Picardy Place. We'll have our own *dopolavoro*, after-work club. There's a good-sized hall, big enough for dances. We'll have an after-school club, a bit like the Brownies and Guides, to keep the kids busy. Better still, we're getting an Italian chaplain!'

'Does that mean that I can go to confession and the priest will know what I'm saying? That's not a good idea, Alfonso!' Emidio was quick to knock his brother's enthusiasm. 'And it's round the

176

corner from your fish and chip shop, Giovanni. You'll be pleased. You can go to confession more often!'

Giovanni laughed. His fish and chip shop on Union Place was doing very well.

Achille Crolla, one of Alfonso's young nephews, was very interested. 'It sounds great. What a man this Mussolini is! Who'd have thought an Italian government would look after us emigrants and give money to help us!'

Zio Benny was against any involvement with the *Fascisti*. 'I've never had anything from any government but bills, taxes and calling-up papers. What's so different about this one?'

'You are very cynical, Zio Benny. There's good news all over the place. Pietro in Italy is cock-a-hoop. They're getting roads built in the South, and there are new regulations that help young families. Mussolini says if you have more than seven children you don't pay any taxes.'

'Pietro never pays any taxes anyway!' Emidio chipped in.

'How much will it cost us, that's more to the point?' Giovanni Crolla was the most astute businessman of them all. Like Zio Benny he owned a lot of their shops and they paid him rent, and if not, they often owed him money.

Alfonso had all the details. 'Its not a lot: ten pounds a year, less for the women. For five pounds the children can join the Balilla and get Italian lessons, sports, dancing and a trip to Italy, all free.'

Giovanni snorted. 'How can paying five pounds be free?'

Alfonso's brother was becoming notoriously cautious with money as he got older. To save repairing his shoes, he lined them with folded newspaper. He even put newspaper under his semmit to keep him warm in the winter. Rumour had it that it was he who started wrapping fish suppers in newspaper to avoid paying for wrapping paper. He never bought new clothes; his torn trousers were patched and he kept his hair and beard long to keep his head warm. A customer complained in his shop to the boy serving behind the fryer that an old tramp was annoying him. The old tramp was Zio Giovanni, and he owned the shop!

Alfonso was not worried about Giovanni's doubts. Everyone had to make up their own minds about the Fascio.

'Anyway, the hall will not be ready in time for the Armistice Day march so we have to choose another venue for the dance.'

'Now you're talking, Alfonso!' Joseph, one of the younger men, wasn't married yet and the Italian dances were a great stomping ground for finding a girl. The young Italian girls were not allowed to go to any other social events. If you didn't snap up the prettiest girl at school, at church or behind her father's shop counter, you were left with the plain ones. Marriage to Scots girls who set their sights on the brooding dark Italian boys was greatly discouraged.

'Alfonso, now that you are our *Duce* will you be laying the wreath again this year?' Emidio was a bit sarcastic. He was finding business difficult. He hadn't managed to make a go of the shop in Elm Row. It wasn't a very good site for an ice cream shop.

'You can lay the wreath if you like, Emidio. I don't mind.' In fact Alfonso did mind. It was the highlight of his year when he marched up the Mound to the Mercat Cross leading the *ex-combattenti*, following the Colonel from the Royal Scots Greys and the Royal Artillery. When Alfonso took his turn with each official to lay the wreath at the cenotaph he felt immensely proud.

'Do you remember last year? What a laugh!' Emidio got a dirty look from Alfonso.

'It wasn't funny, Emidio. You never know when to take something seriously.'

'Oh, Alfonso, get off your high horse. It *was* funny! We were strutting our stuff up the Mound when some daft man in the crowd shouted that we were out of order being at the front of the march.'

'I had been told to lead the march, Emidio. It wasn't my choice.'

'I know, but the crowd didn't know. So what do you do? Reverse us down the hill to the back of the procession, like a bunch of dafties.'

The men in the room were all laughing. It had been a fiasco.

Joseph stood up and mimicked the Mayor in charge of the march. He hung a rope of garlic bulbs round his neck to represent the gold chain of office. In a posh Edinburgh accent with a strong Italian lilt, he pronounced:

'Halt! These honourable Italians are guests in our country and should be treated with respect. Corporal Crolla, with respect, please lead your men back to the front of the march.'

Joseph marched round the table, everyone shouting in turn, '*Uno, due. Uno, due.*'

Zio Benny was not amused. 'Boys, it's all very well to laugh. But if you remember correctly, the crowd was objecting to you as Fascists at the front, with your black shirts on, not as ex-soldiers of the Italian army.'

'I know, Zio, you have a point. But they were confusing us with the British Union of Fascists, run by a chap Mosley. He's a thug.'

'I know that, Alfonso. But be careful. You'll be tarred with the same brush.'

This was all getting too serious; Joseph preferred to talk about dances. He had his eye on the D'Agostino girl and knew she would be going.

'Let's concentrate on the job in hand. Let's organise the dance. What about music? Can we get something more modern. How about a big band like Rowland Powell's Broadway Dance Band? They're playing in the Caledonian Hotel for their Hallowe'en Ball. Maybe they'll do a session for us on the sly. We could get Zia Maria doing the Charleston.'

That got a laugh and turned the conversation back to lighter topics.

They chatted away for an hour or so, deciding in the end that Alfonso should book the same hall as last year and the proceeds from the raffle should go to the Italian Widows and Orphans fund. When Joseph said he would look after any widow who was under twenty-five and had blue eyes and a nice figure, Alfonso scolded him.

'That's enough Joseph! You're going too far!'

'Oh, Zio. I was only trying to be patriotic!'

They all laughed. The young boys enjoyed their popularity in the community. With not many of them to go round, they were always being fêted and charmed by all the women, young and old.

Ferdinando put a straw *fiasco* of wine on the table and brought out the cards.

'Enough talk of wreaths and widows. You'll have me watering down my *vino* with tears. Who wants to deal the cards?'

He had taken the eights, nines and tens out of the pack and divided out fifty spent matchsticks to each of the men to play with.

He put a packet of ten Capstan Full Strength cigarettes in the middle of the table as the prize.

'Shall we play to twenty-one? I'll tell you, boys, it's just as well we're not in Cockenzie. I've heard Marietta likes a game of *scopa* and she's a fierce opponent!'

Alfonso burst out laughing. 'I've heard she cheats. Cesidio says she keeps a spare *sette bello* under the table and whisks it out when she's losing.' He looked over at Zio Benny, 'Never trust the Government, Zio Benny? Never trust a woman!'

That got the biggest laugh of the night. That's what they all loved about Alfonso. He was happy to make fun of himself. They all knew Maria gave him a hard time, but so did all their wives!

After a few games, not on a winning streak, Zio Benny got up to go.

'I'm off, lads. Thanks for your company.'

Alfonso stood up as well. It was past eleven and Maria would be looking for him. 'I'm off too, boys. See you next week. I'll go ahead and book the hall.'

As they left the shop to walk together down the Royal Mile and on home, Benny noticed three constables standing across the road from the shop.

'Evening, officers.'

'Evening.'

As they moved out of earshot past Deacon Brodie's, Zio Benny spoke in a low voice. 'Strange, three policemen up here at this time of night. They must be watching for something.'

The next morning news flew round the Italian community that seven police officers had raided Ferdinando's shop in the Lawnmarket and arrested eleven Italians for gambling. Alfonso was lucky he hadn't been arrested. Those policemen that they had seen when they left must have been watching the shop.

He was angry that the men had been arrested. He'd been there. They weren't doing anything wrong. Now he was even more convinced that they needed the Fascio hall. Then the men could play *scopa* in peace among their own, without this harassment. It was Alfonso's job to keep talking to the police and other officials to make sure they understood the Italians and didn't make rash judgements about them that would end in disaster.

Some of the Italians had been in court before on gambling charges. They saw nothing wrong in having a game of cards after work. They weren't gambling. They were pretty taken aback that they had been raided by the police.

On the day of the trial, Alfonso and Benny sat anxiously watching in the courtroom.

Mr Macpherson, the prosecuting officer, began the proceedings on a serious note.

'I would like to remind you all that you are aliens in this country. You men are strangers here. Our laws are different from those in the country you have left. I remind my right honourable friend that the 1845 Gaming Act declares it illegal to open, keep or use a house, office, room or place for the purposes of betting with persons thereof.

'I therefore ask your client, Ferdinando Crolla, Mr Gibb, were he and his compatriots playing the game *scopa* for the purposes of betting?'

Poor Ferdinando was in a state of shock. He had been released on bail but was terrified he would be jailed or, worse still, deported. The courts were very strict.

'Mr Macpherson,' – Alfonso had primed Ferdinando to be very polite and address everyone by name – '*scopa* is a pastime. It's a traditional game we play, just for fun. We played for cigarettes, not for money.'

'Did you and your compatriots drink alcohol on your premises after hours?'

'We drank lemonade or Bovril; some of us had a glass of wine. The back of the shop is my home, where I live. We were not in the shop.'

'Some of you are known members of the Fascist group in Edinburgh. Were you conducting a Fascist meeting?'

Ferdinando started to sweat. Why were they mentioning the Fascio? They had just been having a drink and a game of cards.

'Yes I am a member of the Italian *Fascisti* club, but this was not an organised meeting.'

'Why were so many of you – mmm, eleven in all, I believe – why were eleven men present together so late in the evening?'

'We were organising the dance for the Armistice Day celebration

181

and we meet after work as our shops all open till eight. It's the only time we are all off work together.'

'Mr Ferdinando Crolla, can I ask you why you remove the eights, nines and tens from the pack of cards? Why?' Mr Macpherson was raising his voice and becoming almost aggressive.

'Objection!' Mr Gibb knew Ferdinando. He was in Ferdinando's shop at least twice a week. 'My lord, if my right honourable friend, Mr Macpherson, had done any basic research into this case, he would have found out that the game of cards referred to, *scopa*, is played with an Italian pack of cards,' and here he turned to the prosecutor and sneered, 'which does not contain any cards to the value of eight, nine or ten!'

After two days in court, Councillor Spears declared his verdict.

'Mr Macpherson, I am sorry to say to you that I do not understand the game of *scopa*. What I can say is that I cannot find anything illegal in the evidence.'

He banged his hammer with a flourish. 'I therefore find Mr Ferdinando Crolla Not Guilty. I find the other ten accused Not Guily! Court Dismissed!'

Next week, when he popped into Ferdinando's for his cigarettes, Councillor Spears asked if they would teach him to play *scopa*. It seemed to be a very interesting game.

18

Cockenzie
1933

The front of Di Ciacca's Café in Cockenzie became the village's meeting place.

On Sunday mornings, after the eleven o'clock service, the parishioners of the Auld Kirk would drift into the shop for Sunday treats: jugs of ice cream, sweeties and chocolates.

On Sunday evenings, the Plymouth Brethren walked around the village and stopped at 5.30 exactly to preach and sing Christian songs. They sang outside the Thorntree Inn to offer Salvation to the fishermen and then outside Di Ciacca's to preach their take on the Bible to the Catholics.

When the Orange Order marched through the High Street on the Twelfth of July in celebration of the historic Battle of the Boyne, they whistled their way past the shop. It was apparent to everyone that they beat their drums louder and more enthusiastically as they passed the shop. They were excited to have real Italian Catholics in the village who would know they were prepared to 'kick the Pope'.

Immediately after their walk, they would all pour into the shop for fish and chips and a bottle of Dunn's ginger beer, unabashed by their religious bigotry.

'Nae offence, Sis. I dinnae even ken the Pope.'

'There's a picture on the wall in the back shop, Tam, if you want to have a look at him.'

The Fisherman's Box Walk took place every September. Marking the end of the summer fishing season, this was a celebration of survival over the elements and was as significant to the fisher folk as the feast days were to the Italians in the Fontitune. The fishermen marched through the village with their ancient banners

Cesidio and men from the village outside the shop in Cockenzie c. 1933

displaying the traditions of the sea followed by their womenfolk and a lively village band.

Since the Italian family had now been in the village for almost fifteen years the fishermen added an honorary stop at Di Ciacca's to their traditional route. This was a great honour to 'Sis' and 'Mary', who stood outside their shop proudly to listen to the music. It was a colourful affair. The fishwives, dressed in traditional costume, danced and sang.

In the evening after they had all gone home for their supper an old boat was burned in a huge bonfire on the Boat Shore, an event to which Cesidio and Marietta were invited.

The 'Box' was a social fund organised by the skippers of the boats to help the widows and families of their neighbours in times of need. In those days, the fledgling Social Security, the 'brew' or the dole, was means tested. The real poor often fell neglected between its bureaucracies. It was common knowledge that Sis did his part in helping those who were down on their luck in the community.

During the years that the miners from Prestongrange were on strike, or when demand for coal was low, they often had no money to buy food. Real poverty and hunger raised their ugly heads. The children and the miners would go down to the shore and pick up the 'sea coal' that was washed from the bing at Prestonpans into the sea and back up onto the shore. In the summer and autumn the poorer miners had an unwritten rule with the farmers that they would 'glean' the fields after the harvest and pick up any damaged potatoes, cabbages or sprouts that had been left by the pickers.

Many a fisherman or miner down on his luck would hang about the shop at the tail end of the night. 'Sis, hae ye any scratchings?'

The crispy bits of batter and small crispy chips that were left at the end of the night were given away to whoever needed them. If he could, Cesidio would throw in a free 'haddie' or a haggis with the scratchings, offering a helping hand discreetly, with no thanks asked for.

The fishermen's association owned the flats above the shop. When one room came up for rent, Cesidio and Marietta took it and moved in above their shop

Starting with one room, a shared toilet and no running water, they gradually bought it, then a second and third room as they came up for sale. They modernised them, adding plumbing, gas and electricity when they could. Eventually Marietta had a good-sized kitchen, with a gas range with two rings, and electric lights

When, after many years of living in Cockenzie, she had a bathroom installed, Marietta was thrilled. A sink, a flushing toilet and a big white porcelain bath with running hot water from the hot-water tank in the roof was the lap of luxury.

Even so, they spent most of their time downstairs in the shop. The children had been working since they were little, helping behind the counter, sweeping and mopping the floor, cleaning the potatoes for the chips, counting the piles of farthings, ha'pennies and pennies every night that their mother took out of the drawer in the shop.

Giovanni, known affectionately by everyone as 'Johnny', was now a young, good-looking boy of fourteen. He and his brothers and sisters had half-heartedly attended Loretto Catholic School in Musselburgh, off and on, when his parents could afford the fees. A shilling a week, plus the bus fare, a penny up and a penny back,

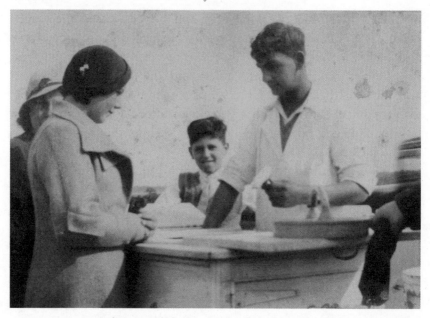

Johnny with his ice cream barrow c. 1934

was a lot of money to find. He and Lena had left school and were now working in the shop full time. It was standard practice among the Italains that the children left school as early as possible to help build up the family business.

Johnny's job was to sell cones from a barrow, which contained a freezer with chilled inserts filled with freshly made ice cream. When the Port Seton swimming pool opened in the summer of 1933, he was a fixture at the door of the pool selling ha'penny cones and sliders. The outdoor fresh-water pool was a great attraction. Built to the east of Port Seton harbour, ten minutes from the café, it had an Olympic high dive and a 30-foot deep end. The problem was you had to pay to get in so, as often as not, Johnny and his friends still swam at the back of the rocks, free of charge.

One morning in late September there was great excitement in the village. Round the corner, along from the Boat Shore, an automobile was heard sputtering and splattering in jerking jumps along the untarred road. Children poured out of alleys and doorways into the street, running barefoot, following the glossy new black car.

At that time there were only about four cars in the whole village, apart from the van that 'the Store', the Co-op, used to deliver groceries to the surrounding farmhouses. At the weekend, if the weather was good, big open-topped charabancs came down from Edinburgh and discharged smart families from the town onto the Links for a Sunday stroll. With their fancy hats and parasols, the families made rich pickings for Johnny.

But this was a Wednesday. Whose car was this? It must be someone important.

The shiny black Ford 8, chunky at the front with a squat fat rear, looked very smart. The windows were rolled down and the driver had a dark jacket, dark hat and a big sweeping moustache. He looked like a foreigner.

The children ran ahead and shouted to Cesidio to come out of the shop.

'Sis, Mary, Johnny, come and see! It's one of your Tally pals in a big fancy car!'

Cesidio and Marietta came out of the shop door, Cesidio in a spotless white cotton coat over his waistcoat and tie. Marietta had a long white apron over her dark skirt, three inches from floor level. Her sleeves were rolled up and she was wiping her hands, which were covered with flour, on a dish cloth.

'Anna, Lena, come and see. Zio Alfonso is coming along the High Street in a fancy new car.'

The girls appeared at the front of the shop, and the boys, hearing the commotion from the street, put their heads out of the window of their upstairs bedroom.

'Look at that, Alex. What a cracker!'

Alessandro, Marietta's youngest, should have gone to school but was ten now and often stayed off school if there was work to be done at home.

Both boys' heads disappeared from the window as they ran down the outside stair of the house to see Zio Alfonso's new car.

The car came to a shuddering halt about two feet from the pavement in the middle of the street. Within seconds it was surrounded by men and boys, all fascinated by the newness of the car. It was an aspiration of every man and boy to own an automobile.

'Marietta, darling!' Alfonso got down from the car and went over

187

to greet Marietta. He looked like a very prosperous man in his tailored dark suit, crisp white collar and short, fashionable dark spotted tie. He still sported a waistcoat and watch fob, but Marietta noticed the buttons were straining a bit over his belly. His ubiquitous white handkerchief in his top pocket was ironed to crisp perfection. As he removed his trilby hat, she also noticed an ever so slightly receding hairline, giving him a distinguished look.

Alfonso was in his prime.

'*Cesidio, compare, come stai?*'

The men greeted each other as *compare* as a mark of respect. Alfonso kissed the girls on each cheek and held each of them away from him, looking them up and down and giving them a low whistle under his breath. '*Bellezze!* Anna you're looking lovely! *Cara*, can you fetch the children out of the car for me.'

In the back of the car, clambering to get out, were Alfonso's young daughters, Olivia, Gloria and Filomena. At seven, five and four, these three were like a second family to Alfonso. His oldest children were all teenagers now and working in the shops.

The girls were dark-skinned with thick black hair all cut short with a straight fringe over their brown eyes. They were all dressed in the same cream knitted suits with pleated skirts and sturdy black

Anna with her father, Cesidio, c. 1932

188

shoes, white ankle socks folded over with a cuff. Their pretty round faces were beaming.

It was a lovely warm morning, a typical Indian summer. Alfonso took a deep breath, enjoying the sea air.

'Anna, take the girls down to the Boat Shore to play on the sand for a bit. Take Alex with you. Come back at one. I'll have your dinner ready.' Marietta helped Anna take the girls' socks and shoes off and tucked their skirts into their knickers. 'Let them have a paddle but don't get their clothes wet. Zia Maria won't be pleased.'

'Don't worry about that, Anna, darling. Let the girls enjoy themselves. Cesidio, come and have a look at the car. Do you want to have a drive?'

Cesidio gave an appreciative whistle. This was Alfonso's first car. He let Cesidio drive it for a turn round the village, showing him how to start and stop it. Cesidio couldn't resist pumping the horn and waving every time he saw one of his customers.

'By tonight the whole village will be thinking I have a new car and they'll all be in to have a look. I'll have to cook extra fish!'

When they got back to the shop, the local boys had congregated to hang around the car. Cesidio took Alfonso round to the back of the shop and down onto the foreshore. They walked along to Bell's Rocks so that they could look over to see the children playing. It was such a clear day Alfonso could see the Forth Railway Bridge away in the distance.

The girls were sitting in the sand making a shop out of rocks and happily selling each other pretend ice creams on cone-shaped shells.

Alfonso took his jacket off and rolled up his sleeves. He patted his friend on the back.

'Well done, Cesidio. You've done a great job here. Who would believe you would have your own business, home and family, and all doing so well?'

'It's thanks to Zio Benny.'

'Zio Benny's been wise for us all. When I travel round the villages there are so many families now that he has helped, working hard and making a good living.'

'Alfonso, congratulations. I hear you have been honoured as Cavaliere from the Italian Government. What an honour! Marietta was wondering if we should all bow when we see you now that you're Cavaliere *and* Vice Consul. I'm surprised you still want to visit your cousins out here in the sticks!'

Alfonso laughed. 'Marietta can take all the mickey she likes. If her pasta isn't up to scratch I'll have her arrested! Now, Cesidio, a bit of business.'

They stood at the water's edge looking out over the calm sea. A few fishing boats anchored offshore were waiting for the tide to allow them to come in to harbour.

'This must do you good, this fresh air, *compare*. I have here the Census Form from the Italian Consulate. The Government wants to register all emigrants. This census will help them make sure all their records are up to date.'

'That's fine. What do they want to know?'

'Just your family members: wife, children, place of birth, that sort of thing. You wouldn't consider joining the Fascio yet, Cesidio? At the moment we're up to 50 per cent membership. I need to get my numbers up so that we get our grants from Italy.'

'No, Alfonso, *mi dispiace*. Marietta's dead set against it. The children want to join though. They've been going up to the dances and really enjoying it. Marietta doesn't want the girls to mix with the Scots boys, and yet she doesn't want us to join the Fascio Club. I told her she can't have her cake and eat it.'

'Don't worry, Cesidio. If the children want to put their names on the Balilla list they can go to the meetings and the Italian lessons. My Vittorio and Domenico go and are speaking beautiful Italian. You'd never know they were brought up in Scotland when you hear them speak. Tell Marietta we have an Italian Mass on Sundays. That might sway her.'

'I've heard there's a chance the children can get a holiday in Italy.'

'Yes, young Joe Pia runs the Cubs at the church so he's taking over as our children's leader to organise the trips. I'm hoping to send the girls when they get a bit older. Would Lena and Giovanni like to go with Margherita? Maybe next year?'

'I think they'd love that. There's no way I can afford to send them myself. You're right, Alfonso. It's important they learn about their heritage. They were both born in Italy after all. They are Italians. Do you have news from Picinisco?'

As they walked back up to the shop Alfonso told Cesidio all the news. He corresponded regularly with Pietro. Alfonso's father had died a few months before. Alfonso had found it devastating that he had not been with his father when he had died. He felt as if there was something unfinished between them. Alfonso's dream of going back to see his father settled and successful was not to be. The saddest thing was that his father had never seen his youngest children.

Thinking of Tadon Michele now with Cesidio, Alfonso was overcome with homesickness and longing for his family in Fontitune.

He stopped and looked at Cesidio. He put his hand on his friend's shoulder. There were tears in his eyes.

'*Sai*, Cesidio, the youngsters will never understand the sacrifice we have made, this longing for home that is deep in our souls.'

'*La lontananza*. I know what you mean, Alfonso.'

'They do feel a passion and excitement for Italian things, especially Vittorio, he's mad for Italy. He's mad about Italian football! But this agony, this tearing inside, they'll never understand that. When I think of Tadon, living his life away from us all, not knowing his grandchildren, I . . .' Alfonso stopped, not wanting to cry in front of his friend.

'You know, Cesidio, sometimes I am desperate to go back home!'

Cesidio was shocked at the strength of Alfonso's emotions. He understood completely. Often he would sit on the rocks alone and look out to sea, thinking of the life they had left behind. Always he wondered if the sacrifice had been worth it. Was it a better life here? Sometimes he wondered.

As if to pull them from their melancholy the children came squealing across the rocks, balancing on the stones in bare feet, screeching with fright for fear they would fall, and laughing joyously when they slipped into a rock pool and wet all their clothes.

They shouted to their father. '*Papà! Aiuto!* Help!'

The men went to help Gloria and Filomena, who were drenched, and carried them back to the shop.

Anna followed, holding Olivia's hand. 'Zio Alfonso. You should send them down here for their holidays. Look what a good time they've had.'

Marietta had a steaming ashet of pasta laid out ready with a rich

191

Alfonso (far left) and Maria Crolla (second from the right)
with friends, c. 1934

red *sugo* and pieces of pork and fillet of beef studded with garlic and parsley.

'Wash your hands, *ragazze*. Come and eat with us, Alfonso. Everything is ready.'

As they ate, Cesidio poured a glass of wine and added a drop to the children's glasses, which were filled with Dunn's lemonade. Alfonso tucked a serviette at the children's necks and then tied one round his own.

'*Buono, Zia Marietta, grazie.*' Olivia was very polite and, as the oldest child, had been warned by her mother to tell Zia Marietta that her cooking was good.

'*Grazie*, Olivia. How are you enjoying school?'

'I like it sometimes. But the children laugh at my pepperoni *panini* and tease me for smelling of garlic.'

'Who's in your class?'

Olivia knew this question referred to other Italians, children whose parents Zia Marietta would know.

'Eduardo Paolozzi. We call him Eddie!'

192

'Olivia, tell Zia Marietta what the teacher said to you on the first day.'

'Miss Wilson went round the class with her pointer and asked us all what our names were. When I said Benita Olivia Crolla, she said "I've never heard such a silly name. We can't have that! Olive is fine. We'll call you Olive." I don't like being called Olive. The children call me Olive Oil, Popeye's wife!'

'They don't mean anything by it, Olivia. Here all the women call me Mary Coppola because that was the name of the Italian lady who had the shop before me.'

Alfonso was concerned that some of the immigrants wanted to anglicise their names.

'It's not right, Marietta. It's OK for a bit of fun but I have heard that a few of the Italians are applying for naturalisation. We have talked about it in the Fascio. I think it's all wrong. We are Italians first and foremost. We can't deny our roots.'

Cesidio didn't approve either.

'One of my cousins is applying. I don't understand. We've fought for our country alongside the British. We're allies after all. Look at Marietta here. She was born in London but she's still Italian.'

Alfonso asked Marietta, 'You don't want to change your name, do you?'

'No, why would I? But I do worry. Your Mussolini is strong, but he could make a wrong move. There is a lot of prejudice around. Here we're part of the community but I get the impression in town it's not as simple.'

'You're right, Marietta. That's exactly why we need to keep in touch with our Government in Italy. It needs to know the problems we still face. But there is really nothing to worry about. Mussolini is well respected in British Government circles and, you know, we've been working here for twenty years now. The locals all know us and trust us. There's many a man been glad of our fish and chips!'

They were eating in the back shop and talking in Italian. Anna jumped up and down to serve the customers as they came in. She ate quickly. Then she called the girls through to the shop and sat them on the wooden counter, playing with them. They licked ice cream cones with raspberry sauce dripping down the side.

'Cesidio,' Alfonso thought this was a good time to talk some more business, 'Olivieri from the Italian Bank has asked me to encourage you to open an account with it. He wants as many Italians as possible to support it so that it can become well established.'

Marietta had gone to the front shop to get some ice cream but she kept her ears open. At the mention of Olivieri she came back in. She was quite sharp.

'Alfonso, don't talk about Olivieri to Cesidio. Your own wife doesn't like the man and I know she is not happy that you have put her savings into the bank.'

'Now, Marietta, don't be so suspicious. Olivieri is a good man and the bank is doing really well. If we Italians don't support each other's enterprises we won't be able to reap the benefits.'

'Well, Alfonso, Olivieri is very unlikely to come out here to buy a fish supper from me, so I think we'll keep our money in the Bank of Scotland. Anyway, I don't want Italians knowing my business.

'Now, did you bring down my pecorino and *salsiccie*? Are they still in the car?'

Alfonso was secretly a bit scared of Marietta and wasn't going to argue with her. She was very strong, and a bit cunning, he thought. Look how well they had done down here, out in the sticks. He knew Cesidio; he was a great chap but not as ambitious as his wife.

He brought in the *pacco*, which was warm from being in the back of the car. He left the car doors open because the car was now stinking like a barnyard.

'Marietta, have you been to Valvona's new premises on St John's Hill?'

'No, not yet, but I've heard it's very good shop.'

'Oh it is. It's quite big, the shop's on the first floor, the warehouse in the basement. He has good produce from the London suppliers, Donatantonio, Parmigiani and the like.'

'Does he have ice cream makers? We need to get a new machine.'

'I don't think he has, but he should, shouldn't he?'

'I know a supplier in Eyre's Hill in London. He had a business right next door to my father's.'

'Good, Marietta. Give me the name and I'll get in touch.' Alfonso liked to be the middle man, make a few extra pennies here and there.

'We'll have to go and have a look at Valvona's. I'll see if his

194

salsiccie are better than yours, Alfonso.' Marietta always liked to tease Alfonso. She knew just how to keep him from being too bossy, coming down from Edinburgh trying to put ideas in their heads.

Alfonso liked to leave a good impression at these encounters. He was a Cavaliere after all. He had been honoured because he was well known for helping the Italians. He liked to pass information to them that would be mutually advantageous.

But this woman was a challenge. He'd gained no ground all afternoon with Marietta, although he had eaten a marvellous lunch.

It was time to collect the girls and get ready to go home.

'Thank you for lunch, Marietta. Look at the children. They've had a wonderful day. They look like *scugnizzi*, Neapolitan ragamuffins.'

'Don't blame me, Zio Alfonso.' Anna didn't want to get into trouble from Zia Maria. 'When you get them home you'd better have plenty of soap and water.'

'That reminds me, Marietta, Antonelli told me if you take the old cooking fat from the fish range to the soap works in Prestonpans they'll make it into soap for you.'

'Oh, we'll do that. You can see from the girls we need plenty of soap down here!' Marietta had been doing that for the past ten years but she didn't want to hurt Alfonso's pride any more than she already had.

Johnny cranked the car so that the engine would start and, with Olivia sitting in the front and the two younger girls already fast asleep in the back, Alfonso pumped his horn and drove up School Lane and on to the Edinburgh Road to drive home.

Marietta was a tough cookie. No new business for the Fascio or the bank. But, with luck, she would let the children put their names down for the Balilla. He felt it had been worthwhile, a good day out.

Alfonso felt a bit sleepy on the way home but Olivia kept up a constant chatter telling him excitedly all about the games they had played and what a lovely time they'd had at the beach. He looked over at her lovingly. What a gift from God she was, this precious child who had saved his broken heart.

When they got home an hour and a half later he drew up against the pavement and, slightly tipsy still from the red wine and the fresh air, pulled up the brake just a fraction too late and bumped his shiny new car with a thump into the pillar box on the corner!

Cesidio had been right. That night they were extra busy in the shop. Everyone came in to see if he really did have a new car. He had to send Alex running along to Marshall Street at the harbour to get young Nellie Knight to help out. Alfonso should come down more often.

19

1934

Addolorata was very excited. She had been up since five-thirty, cleaning out the grate for her mother, scrubbing the table and sorting the clothes for her younger siblings. As soon as the fire was lit, she put the kettle on to boil. She stirred the porridge oats with water and balanced the pot on the fire. She would just have time to run to the dairy to get some milk before they were all up.

When she got back, the house was like bedlam, youngsters crying, boys fighting, mother screaming '*Madonna mia!*' in exasperation. Addolorata dumped the warm jug of milk on the table and, before her mother could ask her to do anything else, she ran into the bedroom.

By a quarter to seven she was scrubbed clean, her long raven black hair pleated and tied round her head, covered by a black woollen scarf. Her black cotton overall was nipped in at her slender waist, tied tightly with a belt. Her dark wool stockings and brown brogues made her look older than she was.

'How do I look, ma?'

'Let me see you. Ah, Dora, darling, you look a picture. Go on, you'd better hurry or you'll be late. You don't want Miss Garland to sack you on the first day.'

Addolorata always wished she had been called something else. Who would want to call their child after our Lady of Sorrows! Perhaps it had been a prediction. Addolorata had suffered quite a bit of pain so far in her first fourteen years. But things were going to change. This was going to be the start of a new life.

As she came out of the stair, her eyes squinting in the morning sun, she ran quickly past Dirty Boab's in case he opened his door. She hated the way he always tried to hug her when he saw her.

The Grassmarket always looked beautiful at this time of day, with the castle towering above and the dark tenement buildings lit up by the morning sunlight.

She turned left and ran along the Cowgate, crossing at St Patrick's Church, shouting good morning to Father Mario.

'Where are you off to so early in the morning, Dora?'

'I'm off to work, Father. My first job. Wish me luck!'

She crossed to St John's Hill and, catching the scent of the pungent smell of roasting coffee, she followed her nose. The wooden door of the warehouse was open. She thought it best just to go in. There were two flights of stairs in front of her. No one was around so she made her way up. At the top of the stair was a frosted glass door with a sign embossed in gold lettering.

B. Valvona & Sons
Italian Produce and Wine Merchants
Telegrams: Chianti Edinburgh
Telephone 31410
UFFICIO

Addolorata blessed herself and said a quick prayer. Now that her chance had come, she had lost all courage and stood stricken with fear at the door.

'Who's that? Who's that at the door?'

Miss Garland's Morningside accent ripped through Addolorata's nerves like pencils on the slate at school.

'It's me, Miss Garland: Dora.' She pushed the door open and, taking a deep breath, stepped into the office.

'Addolorata, what time is this to start work on your first day? I expect all employees of Valvona & Sons to arrive at least fifteen minutes early.' Miss Garland was mis-named. She was slender, austere and mean spirited, thin lipped and short-sighted with a pale washed-out complexion. Her dull brown hair was pulled severely back from her face in a tight bun. 'Is that clear, young lady?' she looked at Addolorata over the rim of her glasses. 'Is that clear?'

'Yes, Miss Garland. I'm sorry, Miss Garland.'

'Sorry is not a word in my vocabulary. If you are going to keep your job you had better never be tempted to use the word again.'

Miss Garland, sly as she was, was well aware of this young Italian girl's circumstances. The girl was the oldest of six children living with her widowed mother in a room and kitchen in one of the slums in the Grassmarket. Miss Garland knew that she needed the job. Her mother relied on a cleaning job, and clothes for the children came from the police fund. If she kept a tight rein on her, wee Addolorata would be a good worker. Now that Mr Valvona had opened this new warehouse the workload had almost doubled, but according to Miss Dennison, the accounts clerk, the takings hadn't. Addolorata would earn ten shillings a week, a quarter of what a grown man would want for the same work.

When Addolorata went downstairs to the first floor she walked into paradise. To a young girl used to hunger and hardship this long narrow room, full from floor to ceiling, stacked with food and wine, looked like an Aladdin's cave. The smell overpowered her and made her stomach lurch with hunger.

Innumerable cheeses were stacked on high shelves. Most she had never seen before: huge, golden round cheeses and small wrinkled grey ones – all pungent and sweaty. Soft white cheeses wrapped in greaseproof paper dripped milky water onto a tray underneath. Flat, round white cheese oozed a juicy cream from the cracks in its chalky rind. Addolorata found it almost impossible to resist putting her finger into it and greedily licking it.

Salamis hung from hooks in the ceiling, arranged like soldiers, the biggest ones at the back, the smaller crinkly ones at the front. Next were the prosciuttos, wrapped majestically in royal blue shiny paper and stamped with red and gold stars, to declare their superiority. Then rows of sausages – mottled, pink and cream, fat and juicy, thin and gnarled – tied together in links, shiny and appetising.

A huge pink pistachio-studded mortadella lay on a counter beside a red slicing machine. When the girl behind the counter sliced it, layering each slice like gold leaf between sheets of white paper, Addolorata nearly fainted with desire to taste it. Once she got to know the girls, they cut her a sly slice which she ate behind the coffee sacks, tapping her foot gently to stop the mice coming forward to join her.

A wide wooden counter stretched the length of the room. The front of the counter had tall, brass-lined glass windows displaying different shapes of macaroni like diamonds in a jeweller's shop: long, thin, short, fat, ridged, smooth; tiny star-shaped pastina and broad sheets of pasta for lasagne and tortellini, little baubles stuffed with sweet pork and herbs.

Addolorata soon learned how to open the drawer for the customer, take the pasta out with white-gloved hands and weigh it before wrapping it in huge sheets of delicate white tissue paper.

The shelves stretched high, right up to the ceiling, packed with gold and red tins of tomatoes, tuna, beans and sardines. There was a section for smelly salt cod, and brown jute sacks full of dried beans and peas, prunes and dried fruits. She loved to slip these under her tongue when Miss Garland wasn't looking and suck on the sweet dried fruit.

At the far end of the store were flagons of olive oil and vinegar. The bags of chillies, pepper, fennel and coriander, as well as countless other spices, made Addolorata sneeze and her eyes water when she spent hour after hour weighing them into brown paper bags.

The wine was stacked downstairs. Addolorata was not allowed to touch the wine and was constantly reminded by Miss Garland, a staunch member of the temperance society, of the evils of drink. In her office upstairs, with her ledgers and pencils, Miss Garland struggled to avoid the foreign assault to her senses that took place every day.

As she got to know her way around, Addolorata became indispensable to Miss Garland. Mr Valvona and his son Ralph came in daily, usually around nine-thirty, dressed in suits with their bowler hats and walking sticks, looking nothing like a pair of grocers. Addolorata made them a coffee in the Neapolitan coffee maker on the stove in the office. As she spoke dialect Italian and English she had a good idea of what was going on.

Miss Dennison was not pleased with the sales figures. A tall slender woman with a thin face and sharp eyes, her demeanour betrayed a cautious nature, incongruous in such a colourful environment.

'With all due respect, Mr Valvona, it's all very well getting all these wonderful products up from London, but the Italians here aren't quite as well off. They are just buying the same stuff: Chianti, rigatoni and pecorino. Even the sausages are not selling so well. I think Mr Crolla is cutting into your sales when he goes round with his suitcase.'

'Miss Dennison, don't you worry. We have an idea how to handle Mr Crolla, haven't we Ralph?'

Ralph was a delicate young man, mildly asthmatic, more interested in books and cars than sausages. Unusual among the Italians, he had been to university and really wanted to be a lawyer. Addolorata thought he was a snob. He could never remember her name and called her missy if he wanted her to do anything.

The warehouse was busiest at the end of the week. On Thursdays and Fridays all the deliverers arrived from Italy and London. Most of the vans stopped off at Manchester, supplying the grocery shops in Ancoats, then came on up to Edinburgh, then across to Glasgow.

The 'Big Italians' came in on those days as well, travelling in their new fancy cars from as far as Dundee and Fife, the Borders and East Lothian. They all had businesses of their own and, although they were Italian like her, Addolorata thought they were way above her and her likes that lived in the Grassmarket.

Some of their sons were very handsome and her mother told her to be especially nice to these young men.

'Dora, if you marry one of them you'll get a business of your own. How about Ralph Valvona? Do you not fancy him?'

'Ma, I wouldn't marry him if he was the last man on earth. I like Victor Crolla, though; he's always nice to me.'

'Don't mix with the Crollas, Dora. They're in the "Blackshirts" and they're too big for the likes of us.'

Addolorata thought her mother was silly. Mr Crolla was always really nice to her. The next day when he came in with Vittorio and his three wee girls he gave her a handful of liquorice allsorts and asked her to watch the girls while he talked with Mr Valvona.

She was surprised when Miss Garland said it would be all right. She took the girls to the delivery chute and they spent a lovely hour sliding down from the open window on the first floor to the pavement below. They ran up the stairs again laughing and joking, waiting in line to slide down the chute again.

Miss Garland showed the two men upstairs to the office. Mr Valvona and Ralph stood up and shook hands with their guests.

'Mr Crolla, thank you for coming. May I introduce you to Mr Pretsel, the company's auditor?'

Mr Pretsel looked like an auditor, if an auditor has a look.

'Cavaliere Crolla, Vittorio, how nice to meet you.' They all shook hands and sat down. 'Shall I begin? As you know, Mr Valvona has recently invested heavily in expanding his business, opening this new warehouse in this prime area of the city and he has increased his product lines to over three hundred.'

The two sons, Ralph and Vittorio, sat opposite each other, eyeing one another suspiciously.

Mr Pretsel continued. 'I have here the copies of all the accounts over the last three years. It is apparent that the business is growing; it increased 6 per cent last year. It is clear that there is a real need for a good supply of continental produce for the Italian community in the city.'

Alfonso said nothing; his bank manager had approached him and told him that Valvona was desperate to get out of the business and that his expansion had backfired. His son Ralph was not a natural businessman. Alfonso thought he had been over-educated, which in his view made the young soft.

'Now, I understand, Cavaliere, that you have already built up a substantial business yourself in this field, supplying direct from Italy to your relations.'

Vittorio tried not to snigger. His father's substantial business consisted of packs of cheese and sausages from Zio Pietro sold from the back of his car.

Alfonso cleared his throat. 'Yes, I am aware from talking to my clients, the likes of Benedetto Crolla, Donato Crolla and Marietta Di Ciacca in Cockenzie, that they prefer the quality of my authentic product. No offence, Signor Valvona.'

'Well, that is exactly why we are talking, my friend.' Mr Pretsel was relieved that Mr Crolla had spoken at last.

Valvona spoke up, 'We, in the Company of B. Valvona & Sons, think that you have an intimate, more personal relationship with our mutual clients. We would like to put it to you that, in the interests of both families, it may be advantageous if we work together.'

Afterwards in the car, with the girls in the back, Alfonso discussed the meeting with Vittorio.

'You see, Vittorio. They approached us for help. That puts them in the weaker position. They are showing us their accounts, but we show them nothing.'

'But, Papà, you don't have any accounts! You just get cash from Zio Benny for the *salsiccie* and put it in your pocket!'

'They don't know that. They're jealous of us. That makes them think we're better off than we really are. Let them think we have a big importing business. Let them think that, because we have two shops now, and maybe three if Zio Emidio doesn't get his act together, we are not desperate. You've not to let them know the truth. Never let them know what you're thinking.'

Vittorio had heard his father's business mantra over and over again.

'Papà, you haven't saved any money. Mamma has saved up plenty. But you have nothing.'

'You know that. I know that. But they don't know that. Mamma is like Zio Giovanni, she likes to save. A good way to make money is not to spend it. But remember, Vittorio, to move forward, sometimes you have to take a risk.'

When they got back home to 8 Brunton Place, Maria was waiting. She ushered the girls in.

'Come in girls. Go and wash your hands. The dinner has been ready for ages. Alfonso, Vittorio, where have you been? It's after one-thirty.'

Alfonso waited till they had eaten, a thick plate of *zuppa di lenticchie* and a piece of fried lemon sole, before he had the courage to tell Maria what he was up to.

'You're going into business with Valvona! Alfonso are you mad! *Dio mio!* Vittorio, in God's name, what are you and your father up to?'

'Mamma, don't say "*Dio*".' Olivia was still at the table listening to everything, ready to defend her father.

'Olivia, leave the table.'

'Now, Maria. *Calma! Calma!* It makes sense. Valvona wants out. The son wants to take over but he doesn't keep good health. We'll buy up most of the shares but keep the name so that we get all their business. They've opened this wonderful new place but they aren't doing any good selling. They are too intellectual. *Loro non capiscono!*'

'Alfonso, we are just getting on our feet. With Margherita, Domenico and Vittorio all working now we're turning a corner.

You're forty-seven now, you're not a young man. Why do you want to take a risk again?'

Maria was devastated. She had transferred her savings to the Italian Bank to please Alfonso and his grand designs, and she had been pleasantly surprised to see that she had saved up nearly one and a half thousand pounds. Secretly she had been harbouring the dream that, once Margherita got married – she was twenty now – the two boys would run the shops, and she and Alfonso and the girls would go back to Italy. She would leave the boys behind. They would choose wives of their own one day, and she wasn't keen on the idea of being a mother-in-law. But if Alfonso was going to take on another hair-brained business risk it might never happen.

Alfonso put his arm round her.

'Maria, darling. We have to do this. It's a big chance for Vittorio. Trust me.'

Maria went straight to the point.

'How much have you borrowed?'

Alfonso made a fatal mistake. He told her the truth. He forgot his own rule not to let her know what he was thinking. 'Two thousand pounds.'

'Oh, God!' Vittorio groaned. Now his dad had done it.

'Right girls, let's get out of here.' Vittorio made a fast exit with the girls and took them down to the ice cream shop. He was keeping well out of his mother's way while she was in this mood. They stayed away until late. Margherita gave them pie and peas for their tea and they waited till past eight o'clock before going home.

None of them liked to be in the house when Mamma was giving their father a piece of her mind. It was best to keep out of the way and let their father sweat it out.

'Why's Mamma upset? What's Papà up to?' Margherita was keen to know the details.

'Margherita, you really need to trust Papà more. He's taking risks now so that our future will be secure. You'll see, the new company will be called Valvona & Crolla, but Papà says within a few years we'll buy them out and it will just be Crolla's. We'll have a business that all the Italians will depend on, a business that will link us right back to Italy and pave our way home.'

*

Even before the ink on the new partnership was dry, Addolorata noticed changes in the warehouse. Without wasting a moment Vittorio got to work and within days every free space on the walls was plastered with advertising posters and sales offers. A crucifix and a lovely picture of La Madonna di Canneto were put up on the wall beside a photograph of a fat Italian in uniform with a smooth baby face that Addolorata thought was quite handsome. There were bright-coloured posters for Barilla pasta and Strega liqueur. There was also a poster of the Football World Cup, which Italy had just won, much to the delight of every customer who came in.

Somehow everything was more exciting, more irresistible. Music rang out from a scratchy gramophone player: Verdi, Puccini, Caruso and the *inni dei Fascisti*, the rousing marching hymns of the Fascists.

Vittorio and Domenico were in at seven every morning, smart in black cotton aprons with sleeves rolled up, passionately selling all the wonderful produce to anyone who came in. They sliced the mortadella and offered it to everyone in the shop to taste. They sold more in a day than the Valvonas had sold in a week. They opened the pecorino and grated it in front of the Italian women so that the smell assuaged their nostrils and they bought, not one cheese, but two, just in case the Crollas sold out.

Poor Ralph Valvona didn't know what had hit him. The Company was swamped with an avalanche of enthusiasm and good will. What an energy these Crollas had. He started to feel just a bit over-whelmed.

Gossip got round and everyone came to see what was going on. Business was booming. Everything was exciting! Everything was Italian!

In Germany, however, another deal had been done, a sinister, evil deal that would impact on all their lives, impact on the world and make Maria's worse nightmares come true.

On Hitler's order over two hundred officers and soldiers of the SA, the stormtroopers of the German Nazi Party, had been arrested and shot in cold blood on Saturday 30 June 1934. 'The Night of the Long Knives' secured Hitler's power and set him on his road to destruction.

If Alfonso had had any idea of the allegiances that would form between this murderer and Alfonso's hero, Mussolini, he would have been devastated. Like thousands of others he was hoodwinked by the positive propaganda that Mussolini generated. Innocently he encouraged many others to follow suit.

At that moment they were all oblivious to the dangers ahead, seeing only good fortune and prosperity.

20

'Are you ready, girls?' Alfonso was getting agitated. The bus was leaving in half an hour and he didn't want to miss it. 'Maria, are you ready?'

At this rate they would miss the whole thing. 'Maria!'

He stood in the hall dressed in his Sunday suit, ready to go. It had been a busy day, the second day of the Roman Catholic Eucharistic Conference. Priests and parishioners from all over Scotland had been attending meetings and Masses celebrating the feast of Corpus Christi.

Alfonso had been at the Cathedral helping with the arrangements. Now he was taking Maria and the girls to St Andrew's Priory in Morningside where the Solemn Procession of the Blessed Sacrament was taking place that evening followed by High Mass. Domenico, Margherita and Vittorio were staying back to work. The shops were all busy with the extra people in town.

As he called again, Olivia and Gloria came giggling from their bedroom, full of beans. They were smartly dressed in their St Mary's primary school uniform.

'Let me see you, girls. Stand straight.'

They looked all spick and span, hair pulled back in pony tails.

'You look lovely, girls! Now where's your mother, and Filomena?'

'Here we are, Alfonso. Don't fret so much.'

Maria looked very fetching in a straw bonnet with a bunch of yellow silk flowers pinned to a ribbon round the brim. She presented her youngest for approval.

Alfonso smiled.

Filomena looked like a little bride, a picture of innocence, in a white lace dress stretching down to her ankles, skimming her new white Start-Rite shoes. Her long white lace veil had a ringlet of white flowers on top. She wore her new gold crucifix on its heavy gold chain round her neck. She held her rosary beads and prayer book in her white-gloved hands.

'*Carissima. Bellezza di Papà!*' Alfonso kissed his youngest daughter and gave her a hug.

Filomena pushed him off. 'Papà, don't. You'll knock my veil off.'

She took her sisters' hands and the three of them trotted out into the fresh air.

It was just as well they hadn't missed the bus. By the time they got to the Priory there were already thousands of people there, in long queues at the gates stretching down Canaan Lane. The meticulous checking of entrance passes was taking a long time.

The grounds were beautiful: manicured green lawns, colourful summer bedding and full canopies of thickly leaved trees. The altar was built up on a high plinth, guarded by four tall pillars dressed with swathes of red, black and gold. The spotless white linen, gold candlesticks, monstrance and chalices arranged majestically on top created a powerful image.

Filomena saw her classmates and ran off to join them without a by-your-leave. Alfonso, Maria and the other two girls climbed the steep natural embankment so that they could get a better view of the service. The morning had been dull and misty but now the clouds had dispersed leaving a bright, warm summer's evening.

By the time the white-and-red gowned altar boys had lit all the candles, the numbers in the park had swollen to at least ten thousand. The senior acolyte announced, with the aid of a microphone that screeched across the park, 'The solemn procession is about to begin. Please put out all cigarettes and refrain from talking.'

Looking down at the crowd Alfonso whispered to Maria, 'It looks like every Catholic in Scotland is here. We could be in Rome itself. Look at all the bishops and priests.'

As he spoke, the first hymn started. The choir's voices soared magnificently over the congregation.

The procession moved forward slowly. Held aloft by eight altar boys was the statue of the Sacred Heart of Jesus. Following behind were the First Communicants, girls in their pretty white dresses, then the boys in white shirts and shorts with scarlet ties and sashes.

Holy Communion c. 1934

'Papà, Papà, there's Filomena.' Olivia waved enthusiastically at her sister. Maria grabbed her hand and pulled it down. 'Shh.'

Alfonso waved instead.

Behind the children came the Holy Sisters of Charity, with their long black robes and winged white head-dresses. Walking straight-backed, they looked severe, their beady eyes grinding into the back of every child should they dare take a step wrong.

Twenty altar boys followed on, then forty priests and three bishops from all over the country. Monsignor Salza represented the Italian community. Jesuits, the monks from Newbattle and the Irish Passionist Order from Prestonpans all took their place. Finally Monsignor McGettigan and Archbishop MacDonald took up the rear.

As the Archbishop passed, the congregation genuflected and crossed themselves in a wave of obedience and respect. Scotland's Catholics only made up 7 per cent of the population and it looked as if most of them were present.

Olivia and Gloria thought the two-hour service was far too long and boring. Maria thought is was far too short and was disappointed when it drew to a close as the final Benediction was sung. The Blessed Sacrament was held high in the jewel-encrusted monstrance to a climax of singing, clouds of incense and the splashing of holy water.

At the end, Alfonso felt quite overcome. 'What a magnificent service. Wasn't it wonderful! And Filomena had her First Holy Communion. Wait here, I'll go and find her.'

As he left, the senior acolyte took the microphone again. 'Attention Please. Attention Please!'

It took an age to silence the crowd who, to give them their due, had behaved impeccably throughout the service but were now desperate to talk.

'Attention Please!' He sounded very agitated. The crowd eventually quietened. 'The Archbishop has requested that you remove your yellow conference badges before leaving the Priory.'

This information was received with even more discussion and noise. Why on earth would the Archbishop ask them to do that?

Alfonso returned with Filomena, who was delirious with excitement now that she had actually tasted the host. She pushed her sister.

'Gloria, you were kidding me on. You said it tasted of chocolate. It does not.'

Their father was in a hurry. 'Maria, take off your badge. Filomena, take off your veil, *cara*, we need to go home.'

'Oh, Papà!'

Alfonso turned to his wife. 'They're worried there's going to be trouble. Anti-Catholic protesters are outside. Come on. You keep hold of Filomena, I'll keep hold of Olivia and Gloria. Don't let go of her hand. In this crowd we'll lose them. The bus is waiting; if we move quickly we'll get away before any trouble starts.'

They were lucky. The buses were waiting at the rear of the Priory, clearly marked with the Parish destinations. They all climbed on and as soon as the bus was full it moved away slowly, following a line of buses making their way through the crowds.

As they drove onto the main road they heard loud speakers and a lot of shouting.

'Is it a football match, Papà?' Olivia was used to the racket of the crowd on a Saturday afternoon at Easter Road.

Alfonso had no time to answer.

Gangs of young men and women waving orange and blue scarves ran alongside the buses banging on the side and shouting anti-Catholic slogans. Without warning, a brick smashed through the back of the bus splintering glass all over the passengers on the back seats. The children all started to scream.

A bottle smashed in the street.

The bus conductor shouted out. 'Get down! Get down under the seats. Cover your heads.'

As he spoke, another brick smashed at the side of the bus, bouncing off with a great thud.

Alfonso pushed Maria and the girls down. Looking out of the window he saw a black motor car with written cards on it, 'No Popery! No Popery!'

Loudspeakers called out incessant messages, 'No Priest but Christ', 'For God and Freedom.'

Ahead were mounted policemen with batons, charging forward to disperse the crowds.

The bus took an hour to get out of the area, an hour in which they lay terrified under the seats. The women and children were crying, huddled together, frightened of the next brick coming through the window.

Alfonso looked at Maria. 'What's all this?' He couldn't understand the force of anger against them.

The next day they heard that the Protestant Action Leaders and Councillor John Cormack had been on the scene. Rioting and clashes with police had gone on all night. Some priests were attacked on Princes Street and had to get help from police officers to get into a taxi cab and make their escape.

Alfonso spoke to the police in his shop the next day. 'What's all this about? Our celebrations were entirely peaceful.'

'We did our best. The cells are full. Cormack rouses the mobs then stands back and tells them not to react. He's a dangerous one. But don't worry, Mr Crolla. We have everything under control. This kind of thing won't happen again.'

On Sunday, Alfonso spoke to the priests in the Cathedral. They had been shocked by the rioting but saw it as a minority pushing against their presence.

The reaction in the press was against the antagonists, with plenty of support for the Catholics from all walks of life. It had been a frightful experience but it looked to all concerned as if it would not be repeated.

Alfonso thought of the unrest that had gripped Italy ten years ago. Mussolini had put a stop to it all, clamped down on rioting and strikes, kept control of the situation. World leaders had reason to be thankful to him for stopping Italy descending into anarchism or ending under the control of the Communists. People needed strong firm leadership. Otherwise, this was what happened.

Britain had built up good relations with Italy through the popular Consul, Count Grandi, and Mussolini's son-in-law, Count Ciano. They were both excellent diplomats and highly respected.

By sheer force of his personality and charisma, Mussolini had also won the respect of other statesman such as Churchill and Eden. Indeed, in 1934, Churchill remarked that, if he was Italian, he too would choose Fascism.

Mussolini wanted to re-create the Roman Empire in the twentieth century, entwining Fascism with the traditions of the Church. He adopted the ancient Roman salute. He took the symbol of the *fascie*, reeds bundled around an axe, the same symbol that lectors carried in ancient Rome as a symbol of authority. This same *fascie* symbol was also respected by the USA and used on the reverse of the mercury dime, on the statue of Lincoln, even on the floor of the House of Representatives.

Mussolini instituted a new calendar. The year 1922, when he marched on Rome, became Anno 1, Year One. (He had in fact taken the train from Naples, and had simply been handed the premiership by the King, but he liked and promoted the image of a march!)

In a masterstroke of modern propaganda he carefully marketed his image as a figure of fitness and health and athletic physique. Clean shaven and well dressed, he looked every part the modern movie star.

It was forbidden to discuss his health, though he had symptoms of a stomach ulcer. And, because his birthday was never celebrated, Mussolini's image remained eternally young. He posed bare-chested in the fields, working man to man with the peasants, encouraging increased production of food. He was a hands-on dictator of the people.

His relationship with the Catholic Church was insidious. He opposed its control and spoke out against it until it dawned on him that its power was too great to ignore. His deal with Pius XI resulted in the Lateran Pact of 1929 ending a generation-long quarrel between the Church and the Italian state.

Between Pope and Dictator they colluded to control the female population. Laws were introduced, from the sensible and well received, such as increased tax allowances for families and better child care and schooling, to regulations that went too far on the use of contraception and abolition of abortion. Mussolini introduced a tax on single men, and rewarded families with increasing allowances for every child. It was true. In Italy, families with seven children or more paid no tax at all.

Mussolini's plan was to increase the population of Italy. Falling birth rates since the 1880s, followed by mass emigration plus a world war, had reduced Italy's population drastically. Mussolini needed higher birth rates to build up his armies of the future. The Catholic Church's theology was simply to respect all life.

The absurd became ridiculous. Mussolini decreed that women should not wear trousers as they were unflattering, that skirts should be worn two inches below the knee, his personal preference, and that women should be encouraged to be slovenly because such women were more proliferate.

He created new holy feasts to reinforce his influence over the predominantly Catholic population: 23 March, the advent of Fascism; 21 April, the birth of the city of Rome; 24 December, National day of the Mother.

Religion and state gradually became one voice.

On the walls of towns and villages all over Italy he decreed that 'Mussolini is always Right!' If the Pope was infallible then so was he!

Mussolini was voted Man of the Year 1927, in *Time* magazine. He was admired as the 'Roman Genius' by Churchill and as the 'Saviour of the Italian Nation' by the Pope, Pius XI.

The up-and-coming Hilter was fascinated by him and fashioned the Nazi Party on the Fascist Party of Italy. When they met for the first time in 1934, Hilter came away impressed and inspired. Mussolini turned to his aid and whispered, '*Non mi piace.*' He referred to him as a 'silly little monkey'.

Mussolini looked abroad to increase his control. Those who had emigrated were also subject to his genius for propaganda. Funding to support Italians abroad was substantial. In Britain, London, Liverpool, Manchester, Cardiff, Glasgow all had Consular Offices and Fascio halls.

In Edinburgh, the Italian Consulate's Office was in the premises of the Italian Bank, on the ground floor of the Fascio in Picardy Place. It was not clear who paid the rent or whether the bank was independent of the Consular's office, but they did each other no harm. Directly across the road was St Mary's Roman Catholic Cathedral and, across from that, the Playhouse Supper and Picture Theatre. The Palais de Danse Ballroom was in Leith Street, a stone's throw away. Giovanni Crolla's chip shop was on the corner, and a two-minute stroll down Leith Walk took you to the new 'Continental Produce' shop that Alfonso had opened in Elm Row.

In effect all Italian registrations of births and deaths, banking, dealings, religious ceremonies, eating, gossiping, dating and dancing could be done within a golden triangle at the top of Leith Walk.

Relations with the local authorities and local churches were positive. When the Italians were invited by the Lord Provost of Edinburgh to represent the Italian Allied Army and participate each year in Armistice Day marches or support charity rallies, Picardy Place became the natural assembly point.

In the large, high-ceilinged double room on the first floor of the Fascio hall, the sign above the Georgian marble fireplace stated in gold scrolled letters 'Respect the country that offers you hospitality'. On the opposite wall was the maxim '*Onore, Famiglia e Patria*', similarly scrolled.

Like that of a Holywood film star, a full-size picture of Il Duce dominated the room, with a smaller picture of the Italian king, Vittorio Emanuele, below him. A crucifix was respectfully hung in every room.

Despite Mussolini's Government's grand designs, the Fascio became in effect a social club. None of the Italians were interested in politics, in fact involvement in local politics was expressly forbidden. This was a family social club. They were interested in getting on in business and being respected in their adoptive country.

In the absence of a piazza, the *dopolavoro*, the after-work club, became a meeting place for the older generations. The Ballila and Piccolo Balilla were clubs for the youngsters.

The golf club, football club, Italian conversation club, the dance committee and fundraising committee all proved popular, providing much-needed social contact for the families who by now had lived in Scotland for many years. Every meeting or class began with a prayer, the Roman Salute and a rendition of the Fascist song, 'Giovinezza'.

For the teenagers in the community, some who had been born in Italy like Domenico, Lena and Johnny, and most born in Scotland like Margherita, Vittorio, Olivia, Alex, Anna, Gloria and Filomena, dances and family picnics were arranged.

Under the watchful eye of the aunties and *nonnas*, they could mix and match, maintaining the traditions of their parents' youth, resisting the tide of modernity and assimilation. Pressure was strong to marry within the Italian community. Those who chose not to found themselves and their new partners ostracised.

A few joined the Fascist Party entranced by the cult of Mussolini. Most joined to satisfy nostalgia and replace a sense of belonging and nationality that they had lost in the early years of immigration. The leaders in the groups, people like Alfonso, saw great advantage in the whole community being bound together. Others used it only as an occasional social club, never signing allegiance, but were welcomed just the same.

To participate in holiday trips to Italy the youth had to sign up as members of the young Fascist club, the equivalent of the Boy Scouts or Guides, which almost all did. The chance of a free holiday in Italy was too good to miss. They all wanted to go; it was such a treat.

Johnny, aged 12, in uniform of Avanguardisti, c. 1932

For the immigrant community, in

215

general, things were looking good. Dreams were beginning to come true. Italy had a strong leader that both the Catholic Church and the British Government approved of, *Grazie a Dio*.

As Alfonso liked to say, things were on the up and up!

The only cloud on the horizon was that Emidio had run into bad times and, with his every move scrutinised by enthusiastic policing, had eventually returned to Italy, leaving his wife and family behind. Alfonso had been upset, but they corresponded regularly, and Emidio now helped Pietro maintain the supply of sausage and cheese coming from Fontitune.

Despite Maria's misgivings, Alfonso had made a good deal with Valvona. Fired up by the enthusiastic response from his compatriots, by the end of the year he and Valvona had decided to open a second retail shop in the premises Emidio had vacated at 19 Elm Row. On 29 November 1935 the second branch of Valvona & Crolla was opened.

Maria felt overwhelmed. She remembered the meagre supper of *salsiccie* and pecorino she had shared with Giovanni and Alfonso that first night she had arrived in Edinburgh. Now her husband and son were importing the produce and selling it to the substantial Italian community in the very same place.

Back then she could never have imagined that Alfonso's vision would come true.

21

Cockenzie
1935

It was a warm sunny morning. Everyone had been up since dawn. Cesidio and Johnny had been making ice cream for hours. The new boiler and electric freezer were saving a lot of time. Now as many as six ten-gallon cans of milk were delivered to the back door every morning.

Marietta and the girls had been cleaning the shop and getting it stocked up with chocolates, cigarettes and sweets. Jimmy Caulder and Tommy Dougal had peeled and chipped five sacks of potatoes and were now gutting fish, slick and efficient as they layered row upon row of fillets of haddocks on top of each other.

Alex had left school. For his eleventh birthday he had been given a pair of long trousers and a white coat. He had started work. This morning he was busy cleaning and scrubbing the ice cream tricycles that he, Johnny, and another two lads would cycle down the coast.

He really hoped he would get to go to Seton Links. A madman had started selling five-bob aeroplane flights from the sands and he wanted to see the plane go up in the air and fly over the Forth with its single passenger in the back.

This was the first week of the Edinburgh Trades Holiday fortnight. They would all be working flat out right through the Glasgow Fair in the second fortnight in July and until the September holiday weekend.

It was as if the whole of the Central Belt of Scotland moved east. Boarding houses filled up, front rooms were let out, and along the coast makeshift camps grew up where holiday homes were made out of ramshackle huts, tents and even old railway carriages.

With the long bright summer evenings and the cramped space of the holiday accommodation, the holiday-makers spent their time on

The Di Ciacca family on the beach

the beaches and walking up and down the promenade. The men hung around the local taverns, drinking with the fishermen.

During the day Johnny and Alex took ice cream barrows all the way down the coast and at night they all stood in the shop selling fish suppers and chips from five o'clock until well past two in the morning. With no other competition in the village, except the Grant family's Wemyss Café, they could hardly keep up.

The housework also had to be done. Marietta employed a young local girl, Margaret Davidson, whose mother had come every year to Cockenzie as a herring packer.

As a youngster, Mrs Davidson had travelled, working with two other girls, gutting and packing the herring into coopers, working from morning until night and getting about a shilling a barrel between them – about fourpence per hour. If the catch was good over the twelve weeks, the girls could earn twelve shillings, a fortune. Then the work ended for the winter, leaving them unemployed.

It was a harsh way of life, and one that was declining. Before the war the herring had been prolific in the Scottish waters, providing livelihoods for many communities. Most of the herring were sold to Germany and northern countries. This market closed over the war years but, worse than that, fishing had been banned in the Firth of Forth because of the imminent dangers of enemy attack. The fishing industry collapsed.

Margaret's mother was glad to find her a job with the Italian family. A friend from school, Jeannie Heriot, from a fisherman's family, also came to work there.

Margaret and Jeannie had arrived at the house as usual at seven in the morning and cleaned and dusted the rooms. Today was wash-day. Marietta insisted that everyone wore a starched white cotton apron. That meant that the girls had to wash about thirty aprons every week, as well as all the sheets, shop cloths, towels and the boys' white shirts and collars.

Everything was done by hand. The girls would wash all day. Outside the back of the shop was a small washhouse: a stone-flagged room with a large sink and a cold-water tap. After filling the large brass pot with water, Jeannie lit the range under the boiler. First everything was scrubbed with carbolic soap against the washboard in the big ceramic white sink. Then the water was boiled again and all the whites were added in batches, and boiled for half an hour or so to get all the stains and grease from the frying out of them. Then the girls had to rinse everything twice in changes of cold water poured into a big steel tub. Finally they wrung out the clothes and put them through the mangle.

The weather was good so everything was hung out to dry, arranged tidily and evenly on the washing line strung between big poles in the back green. It was long hard work.

There was so much to do that Marietta was helping the girls, her sleeves rolled up, her white apron damp with soap suds.

'Marietta!' Cesidio called through. 'Do you want to talk to this man?'

'Who is it, Cesidio? We're busy here. We still have a load of washing to do.'

'Talk to him. He says he can help you.'

At that Cesidio pushed a thin, wiry man in a dark jacket with his tie loose at his opened shirt, into the back green.

'Who are you? I'm too busy to talk to anyone.'

'Mrs Deechacka, please give me five minutes. It'll be worth your while. I can save you a lot of time.' He had his sales patter down to a fine art.

219

Marietta and the girls kept on working. If they stopped they'd never get finished.

'Mrs Deechacka, I would like to compliment you on the wonderful white of your apron, if you don't mind me saying so. But I can see that you will take the rest of the day to finish. You are also, if you don't mind me pointing out, paying these young girls at least ten shillings each a week; half the time they will be doing the laundry. Am I right? Am I right?'

Before Marietta could open her mouth he went on.

'I have in my car the very newest model, a Bendix automatic washing machine, just arrived off the boat from none other than the United States of America. I am happy to inform you that, if you sign up today, Mrs Deeeechacka, I can offer you the latest Bendix electric or gas-powered automatic washing machine for the offer price of a deposit of eighteen shillings and a repayment of only one pound a month for eighteen months. What do you girls think of that?'

The girls would not dare say a word. By the sound of it, this cheeky man was trying to take their job from them. Much as they hated doing the washing it was a job after all.

Marietta did a quick calculation in her mind and worked out that it would cost the best part of the girls' wages for a year to pay off the washing machine. Not a bad investment, if it worked.

'I'm sorry, my man, I am not interested. It is not at all worth the risk of paying a deposit and taking a debt for a machine that I don't need.'

Jeannie and Margaret listened carefully.

'But, Mrs Deechacka, it is such a good price and a wonderful labour-saving device.'

Marietta was not interested. She turned to leave the room. 'Good day.'

'Mrs Deeeechacka, if you don't mind, I can offer you a free trial for a day to see how wonderful this appliance is. It would be unfortunate to see these poor girls work so hard when they could be employed elsewhere and leave you with free time.'

That was a thought. There was so much work to do. If this machine saved two days' work a week it would be well worth it.

'Girls, what do you think? Would you prefer to go out and sell ice cream rather than do the washing?'

This idea appealed to the girls.

'Ok, you've got a chance. You can give us a free trial.'

'Done.' The traveller took his chance. He'd driven all the way from Edinburgh and not sold one machine in two weeks.

The following week the machine arrived and, plugged in and plumbed with wires and hose pipes, the washing was put into the top of the machine. It churned and rattled, swishing the soapy water backwards and forwards for the best part of two hours. Jeannie, Margaret and the man watched in admiration. Everything was going according to plan until it started its spin cycle. Then all hell broke loose.

Upstairs Cesidio heard screams from the girls. He ran out the front door, down the stairs and into the shop. He joined Marietta, Anna and Lena hurrying through to the back. They all stopped in their tracks.

The salesman was alarmed: shirt sleeves rolled up, sweat pouring down his brow, hanging on to a contraption that appeared to be spewing white foam and jumping with speed across the floor.

'O, *Mamma mia!*' Marietta watched in dismay.

The machine shuddered again, jumped forward, pulling the electric plug from the wall and continued to shudder and shake for a further five minutes until the central drum stopped revolving.

When it finally stopped, the salesman stood back and, wiping his brow, straightened his tie.

'Well, Mrs Deechacka, what do you think? Is this not the most marvellous invention?'

The clothes were all crumpled and creased. Many of the greasy stains were still showing. Some of Marietta's fine linen was torn.

'What? Money, noise, disruption and damage – just to prove a point? I don't think so! Go on! Sling yer hook!'

The unfortunate salesman was shown the door. The poor girls were left to dry the floor and wash the clothes by hand all over again. So much for convenience!

The room at the back of the chip shop had been converted into a sitting room. With the addition of a wireless, a coal fire in the

221

Anna in the shop c. 1939

winter and the two lovely Italian girls serving, it became a magnet for the youngsters in the village.

The young fishermen hung out in the shop when they came back at night from the fishing. Auld Coolie, Hammer, Dingle and Shipmate all vied for the attentions of the girls. Tommy Horne and John Bryan were almost inseparable. Village tittle-tattle had it that Big Paul had a soft spot for Lena, who was now eighteen. Coolie was Anna's favourite. She was still only thirteen but well aware of her charms.

The local Cockenzie girls were forbidden by their parents to hang out in the shop and were less than happy with the attention the Italian girls were getting. Of course it was an unspoken understanding that the Roman Catholics girls would never be allowed to marry a Scots lad, let alone go winching with one, so in fact it looked like there was no serious competition.

At night the sitting room filled up with smoke and noise as the boys lingered over a Barr's Irn Bru with a ball of ice cream or a Macallum dripping with scarlet raspberry sauce. They often ate their evening meal there, mushy peas and chips, tea and bread and butter, a bargain for sixpence with as much hot water added to the pot as necessary to make it last as long as the night.

In November Cesidio got a letter from Alfonso asking him to come to a special Mass that was being held in Edinburgh.

'What's it about, Cesidio?' Marietta was always suspicious of letters from Alfonso when they were marked with the official stamp of the Fascio.

'I don't know. Something about *La Giornata della Fede,* the "Day of Faith".'

'Ignore it. If he asks us we'll tell him we didn't get the letter.'

A few weeks later two of the Italian women from Edinburgh arrived in Cockenzie. Marietta was surprised to see them. It was very unusual for any of them to travel without their husbands, and especially not all the way down to Cockenzie in the winter.

'Hello, Carmela. Hello, Peggy.' Marietta came round from the counter to kiss the women. 'You're looking well, both of you. What are you doing all the way down here?'

'We wanted to talk to you and Cesidio about something.'

Marietta brought them through to the sitting room. She told Anna to find her father. Over a cup of tea, the women told Cesidio and Marietta why they had called.

'Cesidio, do you remember if you received a letter from the Fascio recently?'

Marietta nudged Cesidio under the table.

Marietta, Lena, Anna and Cesidio outside the shop in Cockenzie

'Eh, no, not that I can remember. We filled in the census that Alfonso asked us to. And Johnny and Alex have put their names down for the summer camps.'

Peggy ventured 'Yes, isn't it marvellous what Il Duce has done for us. Look how much we have gained from standing together as a group.'

Marietta spoke up; she wasn't shy of saying what she was thinking. 'That's all very well, Peggy, but this Abyssinian affair, Mussolini going to war in Africa, it doesn't do any of us any good.'

'Oh, but it does. Il Duce says we have to be strong as a nation. We have to make sure that in Europe we can stand up and be counted with the same respect as all the others.'

Carmela added: 'The thing is, the League of Nations has imposed sanctions on Italy. After all that he has done for us, all the good that he has done, for the first time Mussolini needs us to support him. For the first time he is asking for something in return.'

Here we go, thought Marietta.

Peggy took over the argument. They had obviously handled this double act a few times already because they had all the answers ready.

'In Italy, only last month on *La Giornata della Fede*, the Holy Father, the cardinals and bishops stood up in their pulpits and asked the congregation to donate gold for the good of Italy.'

'What do you mean, gold?' This was a new one on Marietta.

'They asked the women of Italy to give their wedding rings for the cause. Priests and bishops set an example; they gave the church bells so that they could be made into guns, gold statues that could be melted down for the funds of Il Duce.'

Marietta snorted in disdain. 'I'm sorry, girls, I've never heard anything so ridiculous. Why is Mussolini going to war when we are at peace and he can't afford it. I'll not give anything. It will just encourage him.'

Peggy showed Marietta a steel ring she had on her wedding finger. 'Look, here's the steel ring I got in return for my humble offering. Inside, look, it is engraved with the name of Il Duce. It's a small price to pay, Marietta.'

Marietta was not interested in war nor in funding Mussolini's hair-brained schemes. Just like the washing machine salesman, the women left Cockenzie empty handed and with Marietta's reputation of being *furba* intact. Nonetheless, they had successfully collected a lot of gold from other Italian women in Edinburgh who were happy to give their support.

That night Marietta lay awake worrying. She nudged Cesidio awake.

'Cesidio, Sis. These women are mad. If they encourage Mussolini to like the taste of war, their sons will be called up to fight.'

Alfonso Crolla c. 1936

'Let's hope it doesn't come to that. It'll be a flash in the pan. You'll see. Thank God our boys live in Britain. They are far safer here than if we were still in Italy. Go to sleep. It's nothing to worry about.'

He couldn't have been more wrong.

Although the war in Africa was short and successful the feeling of relief that swept over the Italian community was delusional.

Newspaper reports that planes and tanks had knocked over mud huts and that poison gas had been used on starving people were dismissed as evil propaganda. Mussolini was a good man. He would never allow any such actions to be committed in the name of Italy.

In Africa, a new country was opened up to Fascism and to the Catholic Church. The Fascist army was followed by a Catholic army of priests, missionaries and nuns ready to save the souls of the Abyssinians and offer them Catholicism and 'civilisation'.

The episode rocked the world. The British and French Governments became wary of the Italian dictator and reacted to Mussolini's warmongering by imposing sanctions. Italy had failed in Africa before and had been frustrated after the First World War. In the Treaty of Versailles, Italy felt it had been shabbily treated, its heroic efforts not respected enough. The British and French failed to give Mussolini a clear enough message that his actions were unacceptable.

In his own opinion Mussolini had successfully out-manoeuvred governments, Church and enemies. He had won his African war and got away with it. Unfortunately, he began to believe his own propaganda and his own infallibility. Ominously he started to be impressed by his German neighbour.

Not only that, General Francisco Franco took courage from Mussolini's bravado, and the Spanish Civil War broke out in July 1936.

Many Italians began to realise that the powers of the state were too strong and they mistrusted its relationship with the Church. They started to speak up against the regime and to disassociate themselves from it.

Many others, Alfonso among them, were still deceived by its guile and carried on regardless.

22

Edinburgh
1937

The Italian community all over Britain felt the backlash of the Abyssinian affair. In Edinburgh the excellent relations that the Consul and Alfonso had built up with the local authorities became decidedly chilly. There was increasing hostility in the press. It gave ammunition to anti-Catholics like Cormack, who held rallies and talks, and were now classing the Italians with the Irish Catholics, as a threat to the Protestant Faith.

News spread round the community that all was not well with the Italian Bank. For people unused to handling money or giving it to a stranger to look after for them, this seemed not surprising at all. Rumours spread that Olivieri from the bank had disappeared.

Within hours a crowd had formed at the bank's premises in Union Place. The door was locked, the office empty. By the time Alfonso arrived, everyone was agitated. They turned on him, shouting questions in a state of panic. Alfonso knew no more about the situation than they did, but they didn't believe him. He didn't even know where Olivieri was. He had heard that there had been a meeting in Glasgow but he didn't know what had happened.

Achille Crolla arrived, agitated and flustered. He pulled Alfonso aside. 'We're in trouble now, Zio. Look at this.'

He had a sheet of the *Scotsman* newspaper. Alfonso took time to read it. Oh, dear. They *were* in trouble. He called upon everyone, about forty men by now, to be quiet. He stood on an upturned lemonade box, speaking in Italian, anxious to prevent anyone in the street understanding what he was saying.

'*Senti, amici. Non vi preoccupate.* Look, here is a report in the newspaper. Olivieri is in Glasgow. He has applied to put the bank into liquidation.'

227

They didn't understand the word or how this could be something that they didn't have to worry about. The bank was locked up. Their money was inside, all their savings. How could that be nothing to worry about?

'What do you mean "liquidation", Alfonso?' Donato, one of the younger men called out angrily. 'Do you not mean "bankrupt"?'

They all knew what that meant. They had heard radio reports about bankruptcies in America and were well aware of what it meant. If Olivieri was bankrupt then they were all bankrupt.

Alfonso felt extremely uncomfortable. It was he who had advised most of these men to deal with Olivieri in the first place. It had all looked good at the time.

'Look, boys. Don't panic. It says here that it is only a technical hitch. It's something to do with the sanctions. Olivieri has funds in Italy but they are frozen because of restrictions on money moving out of the country. It says here that everyone will get their money. Everyone will be paid.'

It took all morning to calm everyone down but, unfortunately for Alfonso, they moved away from the bank down to Elm Row and hung around his shop all day discussing their finances and their chances of getting their money back.

Giovanni listened and waited till he had assessed their main worries. It dawned on him that it maybe wasn't as bad as it sounded.

'Boys, calm down. Calm down. Think about it. Yes, you've all got savings in accounts with the bank but most of you also have debts. If you think about it, most of us probably owe Olivieri more than he owes us. The best thing is to get back to work. Wait and see what happens. Open accounts with other banks and start putting your money into them. Keep quiet and don't cause panic.'

A lot of the men went quiet. It was true. Most of them used the bank to get loans to buy their shops or pay for their stock. Many of them had accounts with other banks already. A lot of them had money under the bed. Gradually they left the shop. Best not to let anyone know what their financial situation was. If some of them were in trouble, best not to look too flush.

At the end of the day, Alfonso sat with Vittorio and Domenico discussing the situation.

Domenico was not too concerned. 'It looks OK, doesn't it, Papà? We've borrowed a ton of money from Olivieri.'

Alfonso wasn't listening. He had just had a dreadful thought. He went as white as a sheet and had to wipe the sweat from his brow, smudging his white handkerchief with dirty streaks.

'Papà, what's wrong? What is it?' Vittorio was worried. His father looked ill.

'*Oh Dio! Oh Dio!*'

'What?'

'How am I going to tell your mother?'

They decided it was best not to say anything until they saw what was going to happen. What she didn't know wouldn't hurt her.

When they got home that night they realised there was no chance of that. As soon as she heard their feet on the stairs Maria was at the door shouting in Italian at her husband. The neighbours all opened their doors to find out what was going on and were frustrated that they couldn't understand a word.

While the men had all been at Elm Row thrashing out their concerns, their wives had turned up at Easter Road. Poor Maria had had an afternoon of grief from them.

Later that night, Olivia crept out of bed. She had listened to everything and, though she didn't understand, she realised Papà was in big trouble with her mother. She found him sitting by the fire, his cigar in the corner of his mouth, looking very worried. She stood and watched him for a while, to make sure he wasn't crying.

He looked up. 'Olivia, *cara*, are you not sleeping?'

She came over, put her arms round him and sat on his knee, not saying a word. She smelled his cigar and cologne and snuggled into his chest, secure.

'I'll give you my pocket money, Papà. Don't worry about a thing.'

He kissed her forehead and ruffled her thick black hair to reassure her. '*Capa nera, capa nera!* You'll look after me, won't you?'

They sat together until she fell asleep, then he carried her back to bed and tucked her in.

Valvona & Crolla was showing signs of strain as well. In order to raise the two thousand pounds he had needed to do the deal with Valvona Alfonso had persuaded his wife to deposit her hard-earned savings into the Italian Bank. With her cash up front, Olivieri was then prepared to lend him far more money than was prudent.

In effect Alfonso owed far more to the bank than Maria had put in, though she didn't see it that way. He was waiting to see what was going to happen. Meanwhile he felt he owed some help to the ones who were struggling. He felt responsible for involving them with Olivieri. He lent money to those who asked him and extended credit for those who needed it. He couldn't really afford it but he felt he had no choice. Domenico was running the ice cream shops in Easter Road, and Vittorio and Alfonso were trying everything to get the new business at Elm Row to do well.

The narrow entrance and high ceilings in the shop at Elm Row were a problem for displaying food. There was no substantial storage space so the shelves were used to pack all the stock, right up to the roof. Every space was crammed with food and wine. Salamis, cheeses, garlic and herbs hung on strings from hooks in the ceiling.

The scarlet coffee roaster in the front of the shop was surrounded by jute sacks filled with green raw coffee beans. Every morning Vittorio lit the machine and, after pouring the beans into the coffer, stood shaking the large shallow roasting pan, checking the beans as they coloured. He rubbed the beans between his fingers, judging their oiliness and bit them, crunching them and smacking his lips to check that they had not burnt.

The aroma of roasting coffee was everywhere; it clung to your clothes, your skin and your hair. The caffeine in the air filled your senses and uplifted your spirits so that by the end of the roasting everyone was laughing and joking, teasing the customers and generally animated.

The intense smell invaded the air and drifted out into the street. From the top of Leith Walk a wonderful aroma of exotic promises drew customers in. They hung around, chatting and talking business, buying more than they intended to, captivated by the exuberance of it all. As people went in and did not leave, a queue built up, spilling out into the street and up Elm Row.

With no refrigeration, cheeses became ripe and pungent, melting over slabs of cold marble, adding a stinky smell to the atmosphere. Chillies and pepper nudged shoulders with vanilla pods and cinnamon, sacks of chick peas propped up sides of fishy *baccalà*. All the flavours and smells of the warehouse were transferred to Elm Row, but the smaller space and larger number of customers added the final magic.

Maria found herself back in the old basement where she had spent her first few months in Edinburgh. Now she was busy baking bread in the old bread oven under the stair. As soon as it was ready she brought it up to the shop, warm and steaming, piling it high at the door to tempt every customer to buy some.

Vittorio and Alfonso were men; order and tidiness were not their forte. The floor was packed with boxes, cases and tea caddies. Customers tripped over tins of tomatoes and packets of pasta. Flagons of wine and sherry dripped forbidden liquids into glass bottles that were filled to order. The place was chaotic.

They sold with enthusiasm. They naturally flattered and charmed, talked and laughed, selling cheeses and slicing salami. It was the news and gossip that were really interesting. No. 19 Elm Row became the second centre of the Italian community. As much lending and borrowing, winching and wooing, settling of quarrels and property transactions was done in the back shop as in the Consular offices in Picardy Place.

A few Scottish customers would timidly attempt to come in to the shop. Although they were entranced by the bustle and the range of produce, they found the smells overpowering and the babble of Italian so intimidating that they hardly ever came back.

Even though the shop seemed busy the business was still not making money. Valvona blamed Crolla, and Crolla felt it was Valvona's fault. Soon the strain on the new partnership began to show. The costs of opening the shop, sanctions on goods coming from Italy and the Italians' reluctance to pay their bills were putting pressure on cash flow. Hard work was not the only thing needed to run a business.

'Mr Crolla, I am sorry to report that our Profit and Loss Account to date shows a net loss of £490. It is very disappointing that opening the premises at 19 Elm Row has not substantially increased our turnover and has in effect simply added to our overheads.' Ralph Valvona was secretly pleased that the books were not looking good. He was not keeping well and found the energy and exuberance of the Crollas overwhelming. He had worked in this dreaded grocery business for over ten years. It was a mug's game. You bought beautiful fresh produce, worked hard to sell it to the Italians, who complained constantly about the price.

They had no idea of the costs of transport from Italy and the overheads of a food shop. After they bargained the price down to the bare bones they refused to buy the whole thing and so left you with the crust of the cheese or the ends of the salami. Then, to top it all, Domenico gave some away, Vittorio offered discounts to his aunts and Alfonso ate whatever took his fancy. What a fiasco!

Alfonso felt ill at ease with this young man whose family had arrived in Edinburgh a generation before his. Ralph had a university education and knew far more about importing continental produce than all three of them put together. Alfonso felt intimidated, a sensation he was not familiar with.

But he was not put down by this young lad.

'I take your point, Ralph, my boy, but if we examine the underlying causes, we can see that there are circumstances beyond our control. Trading is very difficult. The Italians are not spending; they are waiting to see what is going to happen with the bank. The strict sanctions have limited the importing of so many goods. At least there are no restrictions on macaroni.'

'That's true, Mr Crolla, but we need to look after ourselves. I see here that we are offering high discounts to Crollas and other family members. Is this good business to favour one set of customers?'

Alfonso thought this remark was impertinent. 'Ralph, I have certain responsibilities within the family you know.'

Vittorio was sitting quietly; this was his very first board meeting in the small office at the back of the shop with Ralph Valvona. A small window in the door let him keep an eye on the shop. Vittorio felt proud. They had been doing rather well. The shop was nearly always busy and there was a queue outside the shop most of the day. Yes they'd made a loss, but profit wasn't everything at this stage of the game.

He did not enjoy working with Ralph, who came to work dressed as a lawyer with his pin-striped suit and bowler hat. He was a grocer, for heaven's sake. Yet he sat in the office all day and left

Vittorio to do all the work. They had to bring Addolorata from the warehouse to help. His father was out most of the day, going round to call on the Italians in the van loaded with produce. He didn't see what was going on. To top it all, Miss Dennison kept an eye on them all the time, counting the stock and checking the takings. It was as if she owned the company, not them.

He sat and listened to Ralph droning on. He was so negative all the time. Everything was doom and gloom. He couldn't see the bright side. When Ralph started complaining that the wage bill was too high, Vittorio could keep quiet no longer.

Valvona & Crolla minutes, 28 Nov. 1936

'Surely, Signor Valvona, it's merely a point of view. With respect, look at Addolorata. She works for forty hours a week for less than ten shillings. That helps feed her mother and her brothers. She's worried about what she'll eat tomorrow. Here we are worried about wage costs, complaining about a book loss on our accounts, but we have a full stomach, and, look,' he picked up the *fiasco* of Chianti that was already half-empty, 'a bottle of wine in front of us.'

Ralph was just about to swallow a mouthful of the very same Chianti. Indignant at Vittorio's cheek, he splurted it all over his crisp white shirt. When he finished coughing and choking he was thoroughly annoyed. What an impudent young man! Calls himself a businessman? He didn't have a clue. 'Really, Vittorio, you should have a little respect for your elders.' He looked at Alfonso and raised his eyebrows, shocked. 'You are very naïve to think that the wages you pay your staff are slight. In business you must learn to treat every expense with care. Every outgoing comes off the bottom line.'

Alfonso was incensed that Ralph was talking to his son like this. 'Signor Valvona, I did not want to bring the matter up, but you are aware, are you not, that £100 of our losses are directly account-able to a former employee of your esteemed father, who was em-bezzling funds from him.'

So they were going to blame his father! It was too much! Ralph stood up, pushing his chair over and taking a step back from the table. He had drunk two glasses of Chianti Ruffino which gave him the courage to give vent to his frustrations.

'Mr Crolla, I would like to express my doubts that this working relationship will ever actually work. In my estimation it does not have a glimmer of hope of succeeding. Young Vittorio here has a lot to learn, he is hardly educated and is not at all sophisticated in the world of commerce. And you, Mr Crolla? With all due respect, you either give the profits away to your friends and relations or you eat them!'

Whether it was Valvona's original intention to get rid of the busi-ness or whether Alfonso engineered the split, by January of the following year, Valvona had gone. Valvona & Crolla as a partner-ship had lasted barely two years.

Maria had warned them it would never work.

She had no chance to dwell on it. There were other things she was more worried about. The British Union of Fascists, an organ-isation completely independent of the Italian Fascist Party, was gaining notoriety. When its members held rallies or talks there was great public interest. Mosley, their much reviled leader, had held a rally in the Usher Hall in Edinburgh, which had resulted in a lot of trouble.

The Italians would never consider attending any of these meetings, nor were they even interested in them. Their world revolved around their family, Church and shop, not politics and unions. Nevertheless Alfonso was shocked at the violence that was generated by Mosley's latest meeting, which was attended by over six thousand people.

There was a great clash between the British Union of Fascists and their opponents. Crowds gathered and shouted for the death of Mosley. Police had to be called out to control them and, after street brawls and fights, three men were arrested. The newspapers were full of anti-fascist talk.

In the ice cream shops in Easter Road, Maria felt uncomfortable. Some customers were quite aggressive to her and Margherita, especially if Domenico wasn't there. She became nervous and wanted Alfonso to resign from the Fascio Club.

'But, Maria, these British Fascists have nothing to do with us. They have nothing to do with the Italians, not even in Italy. We are just a social community looking after our families and protecting our businesses.'

'Alfonso, please. Please. There's going to be trouble. You weren't here during the last war. I was here on my own. Sometimes I felt afraid to go out of the door. I don't want to go through that again. Why are you involved with all this? You need to look after us. You're away all the time in the van as it is. I'm exhausted looking after the house and the family. I just want a bit of peace and quiet.'

She started to cry. She loved Alfonso and admired all that he had achieved. She admitted that because of him her position within the Italian community was elevated and she enjoyed the respect the other women gave her. But somehow she felt that things could not go on as they were. The mood from her customers had changed since the Abyssinian affair. She felt the old suspicions and prejudices of the past raising their ugly head again.

'*Cara*, I only want peace as well. These people rioting are not against us. They are against Mosley. Maria, I can't stand aside and back away from my duty. With this unrest it is even more important that I keep working for the Italians. A lot of them are struggling with debts. It's not easy. I'll look after you. Don't be frightened.'

Maria was uncomfortable. She always wondered why some families kept out of it all, kept their heads down and never came to the Fascio. Cesidio and Marietta would not join. They hadn't put any money into the Italian Bank. Marietta had been shrewd enough not even to give up her wedding ring. Maria had had no choice, married to the secretary; she had to set an example. She fingered the steel ring that had replaced her gold one. She hated it.

'Alfonso, I *am* afraid. Things are not going to go well. I can see it coming. Mussolini is too big for his boots. He is a fool. He'll make friends with Hitler and then we'll all be lost. We will have no friends here and no friends in Italy. We'll be enemies to everyone.'

When Alfonso next talked to Consul Trudu he explained his concerns. Trudu convinced him the Abyssinian affair was done now. Il Duce wanted peace, as all Italians did. Alfonso spoke to Father Guido, the Italian Chaplain, and asked his advice. He was advised to pray for peace. When Alfonso met Cesidio and Benny for their walk from Corstorphine village into town, a habit they had recently started, just to get away from everything, they discussed the situation at length. They could only hope the leaders would make the right decisions and take everyone's needs into account.

On Armistice Day that November they attended Mass in St Mary's Cathedral. Alfonso, Consul Trudu and members of the Italian

Alfonso laying a wreath

community took a car up to the City Chambers. A crowd of well-wishers gathered as two young Italian men removed their heavy overcoats and in their black shirts and headgear of the Italian Fascist Party stepped forward at the Stone of Remembrance, laid a wreath, saluted smartly and bowed. The wreath was inscribed 'To our Scottish comrades who fell while fighting in Italy'.

As he stood and looked at the small, peaceful crowd Alfonso felt

236

no animosity from the Scottish veterans beside him. A soldier under-stands the unconditional loyalty you feel to each other, not the king or the government, but the man fighting alongside you, fighting for his family as you fight for yours.

As he listened to the haunting lament of the Last Post Alfonso wept for the men he had seen die beside him in those horrific years of war. Italian, Scottish, French, German, Austrian men, all men just like him. As he wept he prayed to God that Maria was wrong and another war would never come.

Alfonso escaped the disaster of the bank closure with the luck of the Devil. Valvona & Crolla owed a massive £1,062 16s 0d. The liquidators agreed to settle for the sum of £600, which was all Alfonso could raise. The manager of the Clydesdale Bank in Easter Road had known the family since they had their first shop round the corner and offered them an unsecured overdraft.

Other Italians also came out better than they hoped, and so by default Alfonso gained the status of folk hero. Only Maria was not pleased.

'All my savings! Alfonso, I worked so hard and now I've lost all my savings.'

The shop was still not making a profit and even Miss Dennison was giving Alfonso a hard time. He began to make himself scarce and, taking to the wheel of the shop's delivery van, made his way round the Italians, stopping off and selling a little produce, giving credit for a lot more and collecting even more gossip. In the next village he gave a little gossip and picked up an order in return.

It reminded him of the days when they brought the sheep back up the mountain – sell a little cheese, collect a little gossip.

Miss Dennison was a clever businesswoman. While Alfonso was away, she sacked half the staff, including the salesmen and poor Addolorata. Vittorio argued fiercely with Miss Dennison but couldn't persuade her to change her mind. She understood that, unless they cut costs drastically, the business would fold.

Now that the Valvonas were out of the business they were dependent on Miss Dennison for her knowledge of the suppliers and other contacts. They knew that without her the whole thing would collapse.

Vittorio and Domenico

When Alfonso came back from his run he met Addolorata leaving the shop. She was not in her black uniform and had obviously been crying.

'What's the matter, darling? Don't cry.'

'Miss Dennison has sacked me.'

'Why? You're a good girl. You work hard.'

'She says you can't afford to pay me.'

'Oh.'

Alfonso realised they had no choice. He patted Addolorata on the head and she looked up at him. He was crying himself. He put his hand in his pocket and gave her a pound note and some liquorice allsorts.

'I'm sorry, darling. *Non c'è niente da fare.* There's nothing I can do.'

It took two years' hard work to get over the bank crash. Olivieri was eventually jailed for fraud and embezzlement. It transpired he had never had any associations with any bank in Italy and had just been a conman on the make.

Alfonso was shocked by the whole episode. How had he been taken in? And, apart from that, how had the Italian authorities and the Fascio been taken in as well?

He took Father Guido's advice and prayed more. Maybe God would help him understand.

23

Summer 1938

Even although it was barely half-past seven and it was pouring with rain, a bustling crowd had already assembled on platform 1 of Waverley Station. It appeared to onlookers that the Italians were moving out en masse. The place was full of them: whole families, all dressed up, laughing and shouting, making a horrendous commotion.

Families had come from all over the east of Scotland bringing their sons and daughters to join the annual holiday trip to Italy. The youngsters all knew each other. Many of them were cousins or school friends. The reputation of the holiday induced an air of frenzied excitement and expectation. Most of their older brothers and sisters had already been on previous trips and had returned full of stories of great adventures. The consensus was that in Italy the sun shone constantly.

It was Olivia's turn to go. Over the last few years Margherita, Johnny and Alex had all been on the holiday and she had waited patiently for her turn. She had been up since the crack of dawn sitting fully dressed at the side of her bed. Gloria and Filomena had got dressed as well, annoying her by asking endless questions.

Now she ran around looking for her cousins Vera and Wefa. At fourteen years old they were in the top group of the Piccole Italiane so would be in charge of the younger children. They were going to enjoy that. Vera's father, Achille Crolla, was Alfonso's cousin.

The children were all dressed in the black uniform of the Opera Nazionale Balilla, the Italian youth group, fashioned on the principles of Baden Powell's Scouts and Guides. The boys wore black shorts and shirts, long grey socks with a double yellow stripe round the top, pulled up to attention. A yellow tie and black fez hat with smart badges and ribbons completed their ensemble. The girls wore

239

black skirts, white blouses and yellow cravats, with black felt cloaks pinned over their shoulders.

When they were spotted by some of their Scottish friends from school they turned round and stuck out their tongues. These lads made a fool of them for stinking of garlic or eating worms. Now they looked on, enviously watching them leave for a holiday abroad. Their reputation in school would go sky high.

As the clock struck eight, the train's whistle gave a piercing squeal. Steam escaped noisily from the funnel, the brakes screeched and the engine started to strain and snort, desperate to go.

'*Ragazzi! Ragazzi! Attenzione!*' The *Capo*, Joe Pia, whistled twice, the noise piercing above the hubbub of mothers and fathers, brothers and sisters, aunts and uncles. Everyone was caught up in the excitement of the trip. No one was the least bit anxious. After all, they were visiting home.

'Olivia, Olivia.' Maria shouted to her daughter to say goodbye. Olivia left her friends and ran over to give her mother a big hug.

'*Fai la brava*. Be good! Say your prayers every day. And remember to eat everything.'

There was no worry that the children would not eat well. When Margherita had been on the trip two years ago, she had sent a three-page letter describing the wonderful meals that they had eaten. Four a day!

'*Mamma, il cibo qui è cosi buono.*'

'Pasta, vegetables, omelettes, meat. And we get a cup of coffee every morning with the biggest doughnut in the world!'

Maria had been so happy when Alfonso had read that out to her. Her mind had filled with the aroma of the food she remembered in her youth, the pasta her mother used to make with the rich oxtail sugo; the vegetables; pepperoni, courgettes and *melanzane*, the bitter greens sautéed in *olio, aglio e peperoncino*. Somehow the memories of the smells and the flavours were always more intense, more satisfying than the food she cooked here.

She held Olivia tightly. Olivia was going to have such a wonderful experience. Maria gave her a final squeeze and watched as Gloria and Filomena hugged their sister. They felt uncomfortable that she was going without them.

'I'll bring you a present. I'll bring you something nice.'

Alfonso bent down to face his daughter and pulled her to him. Her face was squashed into his chest. She breathed in deeply, imprinting the smell of her father in her mind.

Her Papà was the greatest ally in her life. If she was in trouble with her mother, which was not unusual, he would pretend to give her a row but wink at her when her Mamma turned her back. If the boys were annoying her, he would shout at them to leave her alone. She trusted him with everything and would do anything to please him. She hugged him.

His heart was full of pride. Look at her. Beautiful child.

'*Capa Nera!*' He held her away from him and looked at her. '*Capa Nera!*' He kissed her on both cheeks.

'*Papà, grazie.* Thank you for letting me go.'

Alfonso straightened himself, held her shoulders and looked down into her eyes. 'Olivia, this is the most important thing in your life. You are going to step on Italian soil. You are going to see Il Duce. You are going to salute the greatest man on earth!'

He put his hand into her pocket and pushed something inside.

The train whistled again, louder and longer than before.

'*Ragazzi! Ragazzi! Attenzione! Uno, duo . . .*'

In a final flurry of excitement the children all lined up in order

Avanguardisti, Italian children from Scotland on holiday in Italy

as they had practised over and over again in the Fascio hall. Their rucksacks and food parcels were balanced on their backs. They stood to face their parents and raised their right arm in Roman salute.

> *Amore, Dio, Parenti e Patria!*
> pa pa pum pum, pa pa pum pum,
> *Giovinezza, Giovinezza*

Then, singing with gusto, they turned with a military stamp of their feet and marched onto the train.

As soon as they were all on board, discipline broke down as they scrabbled to the windows to wave goodbye. They pulled the windows down and hung out precariously, pushing forward to catch sight of their families as they waved and shouted their goodbyes.

About fifty children in all, aged from twelve to sixteen, dressed like miniature soldiers, left Edinburgh for Italy to visit their homeland for the first time.

Olivia shouted from the window.

'*Ciao! Ciao! Papà! Mamma! Ciao!*'

Her sisters waved and shouted, jumping up and down.

There wasn't a tear shed. Neither the youngsters nor anyone on the platform had a single doubt about the adventure. To give the children the chance of a holiday in Italy was wonderful. For the children the adventure was almost too exciting to contemplate and the feeling of privilege and trust that had been given to them only compounded their confidence.

Once the train had moved out of the station and into the long dark tunnel that separated the countryside from the city, Olivia settled down into a seat by the window, opposite her friends. She looked out of the window at the houses and fields rushing past. The weather was dull and grey, rain splattering on the window.

As the train disappeared from view, Alfonso put his arm round his wife. The girls looked up, waiting for his reaction. Olivia was his favourite after all.

'Papà?'

They waited. Was he going to cry? Sometimes Papà cried.

'Right! What shall we do? Olivia's having a holiday in Italy so why don't we have a little holiday here? We'll go to Patrick Thomson's for tea and scones, and then go to see *Snow White and the Seven Dwarfs.*'

How the girls loved their father! Who cares about Olivia! They were going to the pictures!

On the train, once the excitement of the parting had passed, Olivia pulled out the present her Papà had given her. Nestled in the folds of a white cotton handkerchief that smelled of her Papà was a five-lire note, a string of brown wooden rosary beads and a little paper note.

'*Cara Olivia, ti amo tantissimo. Prega ogni mattina per Mamma e Papà, la tua famiglia e anche per Il Duce. Fai la brava. Papà.*'

Olivia took a deep breath and tucked her gift back into her pocket. She laid her head against the cold glass of the window and closed her eyes. 'God Bless Mamma and Papà, my Family and God Bless Il Duce.'

The journey took three days and two nights. The girls were entranced. They saw the steep drop down to the sea at Dunbar, the land flattening out as they travelled down through England and then the white cliffs of Dover.

Crossing the channel by ferry was exciting. The sea was calm and they could run around the ship, looking at all the passengers.

It was night time when they boarded the train in France and they slept most of the way. When the train climbed up and through the Alps they felt they were going to Heaven. They couldn't believe the snow glistening on the tops of the mountains.

When the train crossed into Italy they all had to get out to be counted against the communal passport that the *Capo* had brought. When they heard the guards talking Italian, they all burst out laughing. They understood it, but it was different from the Italian that they spoke at home. It was more like the Italian they tried to learn in the *scuola* in Picardy Place.

They all lined up to use the toilet. Wefa came out screeching 'Olivia, it's a hole in the ground! Hold your nose and don't fall in!'

In the station café trays of milky coffee and brioches were lined up for them. The ladies in charge were clucking round them like mother ducks, blabbering away, laughing and joking.

'Taste the coffee, Vera, taste the coffee.'

Olivia had never tasted anything so delicious in her life. She dipped her brioche into the warm coffee and sucked it. It tasted of a mixture of vanilla and butter with an intense coffee flavour. It gave her a feeling of well-being.

The lady behind the bar had seen her reaction. '*Ti piace?*'

'*Si, grazie, Signora.*'

The woman was thrilled that these children from England (she didn't know a country called Scotland existed) could speak Italian, were dressed in the costume of the Balilla – and enjoyed her brioche.

The following day, by the time they reached the camp site on the Adriatic coast, the youngsters were completely immersed in Italy. They found things familiar and truly felt at home for the first time in their lives. The camp site had over 150 canvas tents, split into groups for girls and boys of different ages. There were children from all over Italy, from France, Holland and Abyssinia. They all spoke Italian, different groups with different accents, but all in Italian.

The big tent at the top of the camp was the mess camp where they ate, four times a day. Just as Margherita had said, the food was wonderful. To Olivia it tasted familiar but not at all like Mamma cooked at home. There was much more variety, different pastas, meats and fish. Vegetables she had never seen before, fried or sautéed, in salads or raw, in pasta or in *frittata*. The bread was thick and chewy with a dark crust. They smeared it with thick cherry jam or chunks of pecorino cheese.

There was fruit in abundance, bigger and juicier than anything she had ever tasted. Huge soft peaches that dribbled juice down her cheeks when she bit into them, soft yellow apricots that tasted like jam inside, and green, seedy sweet figs that her Papà had often told her about but she had never seen.

During the meals, the officials walked around to inspect the youngsters.

Olivia put her head down as three men approached her table, guided by one of the teachers. They looked impressive in their uniforms – medals and badges glistening in the light. They stopped right in front of her. Wefa nudged her and, nervously, Olivia looked up.

One man asked her if she was enjoying her holiday '*Ti diverti qui?*'

She replied '*Dieci giorni, Signor.*'

In her eagerness to reply, Olivia had misunderstood the question. She thought he had asked how long they were staying here.

The sergeant and his comrades burst out laughing. He patted her encouragingly on the shoulder.

'*Brava, Inglese!* You must keep learning Italian. Keep coming to visit us and we'll teach you.'

The girls would have put on weight if it hadn't been for the strict regime of the day. Woken early in the morning by a blast of martial music from loudspeakers, they all had to march for half an hour to the booming of military tunes.

Then, after listening to a recorded message from Il Duce, they had to stand to attention and answer the call from the teachers.

'*Ragazzi d'Italia!* What do you believe?'

'In the name of God and Italy I swear to carry out the order of Il Duce and to serve with all my strength and offer my blood in the cause of the Fascist Revolution.'

'*Soldati d'Italia*! Who must you obey?'

'We must obey Il Duce!'

'Why must you obey?'

'I must obey because I must.

My first duty as a child is obedience.

The second, obedience.

The third, obedience!'

After a Fascist song, the day would proceed with sports and competitions, more singing and meals. For the girls there were separate times for sewing and playing with dolls, learning about being good mothers. For the boys, there were more strenuous games,

Patriotic Italian songbook

harsher drills and more military-style training; they marched with wooden replica guns and thrilled at playing soldiers and war games.

The most exhilarating thing for all the children was the continuous hot sunny weather. They ran around in shorts, swam in the sea and enjoyed the feeling of freedom that the Italian climate provides. They never felt that it was too hot or too sunny. It was as if their bodies had craved the sun all their lives. Even though it was sunny sometimes in Scotland, it wasn't a clear, bright translucent sun as it was here.

'Olivia, Wefa, the *Capo* says that we are going to see Il Duce the day after tomorrow.'

'When?' Olivia was so excited. Her Papà had told her if they were good Il Duce would come to see them. She felt as confident and excited as if her own father were coming.

Finally the day came. They were all issued with new uniforms, spotless and clean. Women sat in the mess hall sewing up trouser hems and adjusting skirt lengths so that every child was dressed exactly to specifications.

This was an impossible task because no sooner had one child been sorted than the next came in with a torn shirt from falling off a tree. Nevertheless, after lunch and their hour siesta, which had become a natural habit to them all, the music rang out over the loudspeaker to call them into their positions.

What a scrabble of seven hundred excitable children and a hundred terrified teachers and helpers all running, bumping into each other, knocking the smaller ones over, to get to their positions on time.

When they were all lined up they stood silently in anticipation. The sun was still high in the sky, beating down on them. Their fez hats were warm, sweat was dripping down under the rim. The sweat poured out under their shirts, the boys in the black shirts suffering worst as the airless claustrophobic atmosphere made them feel faint and dizzy.

'I can't stand this,' Wefa whispered to Vera.

'Sh!! Sh!!' Olivia was furious. They weren't allowed to talk.

'You shush!' Wefa was feeling decidedly cross.

Just as Olivia was going to whack her with the side of her hand they all nearly jumped out of their skin as the music started up over the loudspeaker. As the Italian National Anthem blared out over their heads they automatically in unison raised their right hands, straight in a Roman Salute.

Then, on a magnificent, tall white Austrian stallion, towering high over their heads, rode Mussolini, resplendent in a white Navy uniform, straight back, chin jutting forward, one hand holding the reins above the other, seemingly oblivious of the army of youths below him.

He dismounted and climbed up onto a podium that dominated the camp, an absurd contraption that looked like the end of a battle-ship.

The music stopped.

Everything was silent.

Mussolini strode over to the very edge of the platform and stood, feet wide apart, head up and hands clasped behind his back. Without moving his head he looked down at them, as if he was inspecting every single child's appearance and demeanour.

He waited.

They trembled.

Then he thundered out, shouting over their heads:

'*Gioventù d'Italia! A chi la vittoria?*'

In unison, enthusiastic and completely without prompting the children shouted out to their leader.

'*A noi, Duce! A noi!*'

The music started up, and to the rendering of the 'Faccetta Nera', song of the Abyssinian victory, the young future army of Italy marched past Il Duce.

Olivia, Wefa and Vera kept in line as they had been drilled.

'*Uno, Due, Uno, Due!*' Arms stretched out high, as far as the shoulder of the person in front, higher if the person in front was barely three feet tall.

'*Uno, Due! Uno, Due! Passo!*'

On cue, Olivia turned her head with a sharp jerk to the right and looked up, up, straight into the mesmerising, deep cornflower-blue eyes of the most beautiful man she had ever seen in her life.

In the tent that night, the girls talked non-stop.

'Olivia, wasn't he really handsome? Even more handsome than Cary Grant and Errol Flynn rolled into one.' Vera couldn't get over

247

how stunning Mussolini looked. Tanned and smooth-skinned with a strong nose and jaw, he looked like a film star.

'Did you see him look at me?' Wefa was convinced that Mussolini had especially looked at her, somehow noticed her among all the other children.

'What do you mean, Wefa? How did he look at you? He looked at me. I've never seen eyes as blue as his. He looked right into my eyes and I'm sure he saw right into my mind.'

Olivia's outburst shocked the girls. They fell silent and lay quietly with their thoughts. Each felt a curious mixture of pleasure and guilt.

A disconcerting thought crossed Olivia's mind. Was this feeling what falling in love was? He was magnificent. Papà was right. How could any other man compare?

That night Olivia forgot to say her prayers or to dream of her father.

When the girls got back to Edinburgh they were full of Italy: the food, the music, the swimming and the sea; everything about it was wonderful.

But they were all quite reticent about speaking about their experience with Il Duce. Somehow those feelings were private and special and perhaps even a little shameful.

When Alfonso asked Olivia how she had felt when she had seen Mussolini, she blushed.

'He was nice, Papà. But not as nice as you.'

While the girls were away, the political crisis with Germany had reached fever pitch. On 15 August Hitler had mobilised the army strictly against all agreements and post-war pacts. His intentions were to take Czechoslovakia, having earlier in the year annexed Austria, without much opposition from the Austrian people.

To people all over Europe it looked like another life-threatening cliff edge. They waited to see, this time around, how the politicians – elderly gentlemen in pin-striped suits, with bowler hats and umbrellas – would deal with this medal-bedecked, gun-toting uniformed leader of Germany.

On 30 September 1938, just weeks after Olivia had returned from Italy, it appeared that the umbrella was mightier than the gun.

Chamberlain, the British Prime Minister, stepped down from an aircraft courtesy of Adolf Hitler, with a Swastika emblazoned on its wings, clutching a piece of paper in his hands. The ink was hardly dry. It bore evidence of the peaceful resolution he had negotiated.

That evening people gathered in each other's homes and cafés to hear the BBC radio news bulletin at nine o'clock. Chamberlain assured the nation that ". . . this paper is symbolic of the desire of our two peoples never to go to war with each other again'.

All round the country everyone cheered. It looked as if at last there was a leadership in Europe that would put an end to threats of war.

For his annual Armistice Day speech, Mussolini stood on the balcony at the Piazza Venezia in Rome in front of an assembly of one hundred thousand *ex-combattenti*. Forceful and domineering, he delivered his speech. More than ever, he felt power was in his hands. A friend of both Britain and Germany, he was intoxicated with himself. He intended to dominate both Britain and Germany. His message of peace had a sinister tone.

'The blue patch on the horizon of the political sky is spreading. Responsible men are working towards this end, but it would be imprudent and unlike Fascists to give way to exaggerated and premature optimism.

'There are men, who, feeling themselves particularly beaten by the peaceful European and human policy followed by the Axis, dream with their eyes open of impossible retaliation.

'For this reason, comrades, it is still necessary to sleep with our heads on our knapsacks as we used to do in the trenches.'

The crowd cheered as he reaffirmed his goal to maintain peace, claiming it was due to him that this crisis had passed.

Alfonso read the speech with trepidation. There was something ominous about Mussolini's words. The mood in Britain was more optimistic. People here felt that peace was more secure. Perhaps Il Duce knew of things the British were still to find out.

In his heart Alfonso was afraid that the chance for peace was dying. His faith in his leader assuaged his doubts and he clung desperately to hope.

24

15 August 1939

It was the kind of morning that makes you glad to be alive: clear blue skies, a perfect morning for a picnic. Five open-topped charabancs and three Scottish Motor Traction Co. double-decker buses waited in line at the bottom of the steps of St Mary's.

On cue, as the church bells started to ring, the doors of the cathedral opened and a handful of men slipped out and immediately lit up cigarettes. They looked very up to date, dressed in light, loose-fitting tailored suits with wide trousers with turn-ups. After the first deep inhalation of smoke, as if pre-rehearsed, they loosened their ties and pushed their trilby hats to the back of their heads. Now they could relax.

The open doors revealed the closing procession. The senior acolyte led the procession enthusiastically, swinging the thurible, filling the atmosphere with clouds of incense. Several altar boys in long white surplices with full white ruffs led the procession followed by the cathedral choir, men and boys dressed in long cream robes with gold bands round their waists. They sang the verses of the Ave Maria in Italian, accompanied by the women in the congregation.

Four priests, Monsignor McGettigan and finally the Archbishop, resplendent in floor-length gold and white vestments, mitre perched high on his head, slowly followed the procession down the aisle. With his hands hidden under his stole, he held the spectacular gold monstrance high, exhibiting the Holy Host. As he passed, the congregation genuflected, made the sign of the cross and placed their thumb and first two fingers on their lips.

The first four pews of the church disgorged four brigades of the Piccole Italiane choir, all dressed smartly in their black *fascisti* outfits. Marching proudly like little soldiers they each managed to sneak a look sideways as they passed their families, exchanging a wink or suppressing a giggle.

At the end of the aisle they moved to the left and as the last of the singing died down, the congregation stood up en masse, genu-flecting, and then busily made their way out into the warm summer sun.

The young women were dressed in elegant day dresses of silk and linen, belted at the waist and fashionably three inches below the knee. Their light overcoats were loose and comfortable, slightly shorter than their dresses, swinging gracefully from the shoulders. Their chunky high-heeled shoes, white cotton gloves and summer hats jauntily perched on their curled hair completed the impression of Greta Garbo glamour.

The more mature women, Maria and Marietta included, were dressed more staidly with longer dark-blue and black dresses with white lace collars. Their hats were darker and pulled down over their faces; their large black handbags displayed power and control, holding promises of intrigue and treats.

The bus drivers whistled to each other. This was going to be chaos. After much kissing and shaking of hands among the crowd, Vittorio and Domenico started to usher the crowd onto the buses. Once the Archbishop and priests had changed into black suits and white Roman collars, they were ready to go.

The Mass of the Assumption of Our Lady had been very moving. Cavaliere Tronchetti had read out a message from Il Duce himself, directed especially to all Italians living abroad. He implored them to pray for peace, to maintain good relations with their neighbours and to behave with honour and honesty in the name of their Italian citizenship. 'Do not fear for war. I, Il Duce, will sue for peace in Europe. Peace in the World.'

In the congregation some had been captivated, reassured by the message; some had reacted with scepticism – they had heard it all before. None were indifferent. The threat of war was still real.

Marietta looked across at Cesidio and made a sign of dismissal. She pushed her chin up, her mouth down and whipped the back of her hand under her chin then whispered under her breath, 'What can he do? The baboon!'

The previous day, the *Scotsman* newspaper had reported that

Mussolini was indeed against any war and was convinced, twenty-five years after the outbreak of the last war, that extreme caution was necessary to avoid conflict.

The newspaper had not yet reported that Winston Churchill was on that very day standing on the banks of the Rhine with General Spears and General George, the Commander in Chief of the Supreme Allied Command, watching the French build up defences against the Germans troops amassing on the other side.

Europe was on holiday but its armies were on alert.

The motorcade of charabancs and buses moved out of the city, making their way steadily towards Stirling. Everyone was in high spirits. As they approached the small villages along the way, locals, hearing the singing and laughter, came out of their houses to wave. Occasionally the whole shebang ground to a halt as they stopped at an ice cream shop or fish and chip shop to pick up some Italians who had not made it to the Mass.

As they approached the King's Park a huge shout went out. '*Aaaahhhh! Mannàggia!*'

The Glasgow Italian contingent had arrived before them. The buses pulled up outside the park. As they all climbed down Vittorio

Scampagnata, Alva Glen, c. 1939

and Johnny went up and down rallying everyone. 'That's it, boys. The Glaswegians have arrived before us but that's the only thing they'll beat us at today.'

With great hilarity and excitement, the baskets of food, tartan rugs and lemonade boxes filled with bottles of Chianti were carried into the park.

'Marietta,' Maria caught sight of her friend, 'come over and sit with us. We can see everything that's going on from here.'

The women settled down, laying out the rugs and unpacking the food.

Of course it was not like in Italy. At Ferragosto in Italy, 15 August, they had processions and feasts and fireworks for a whole week. The streets would fill with women making pasta, roasting *porchetta and* frying vegetables. Stalls would be piled with *crostata* and *crespelle, creustella* and *biscotti di finocchio*, all the treats that were associated with the Feast of the Assumption.

But the tradition had been maintained in its own way here: Mass, a trip to a park, somewhere central so that Italians from all over Scotland could make it, and an afternoon of sports and games with a dance afterwards. This was the biggest get-together of the year and the one most looked forward to.

The children were already running around the park, too excited to eat.

The men joined the women on the rug, taking off their jackets, rolling up their shirt sleeves but leaving their hats perched on the back of their heads. The *Ruffino* in the straw flasks was warm and it was making them sweat in the sun.

'Maria, your *frittata* is really lovely, *grazie*.'

'It's best when you make it with yesterday's left-over pasta, isn't it? Perfect for a picnic. Have another slice, here. You see, I prefer your *pastone* with the ricotta and *salsiccie*. This is very nice. Alfonso, Cesidio, have some pizza.'

Alfonso bit into a thin slice of pizza that was stuffed with *scarola*, sautéed greens. The oil dripped down his chin and he wiped it with the back of his hand.

Alfonso felt he had to clear the air. He felt he had misjudged Marietta.

'Marietta, you know, you were right not to get involved with

Olivieri. I am mortified. I really didn't have a clue that he was a crook, and a big crook at that. To tell you the truth, I'm quite shaken by it all.'

Cesidio felt embarrassed for his friend.

'How could you know, Alfonso? A wolf in sheep's clothing, that was what he was.'

'I should have understood. It seemed to me the right thing to support Italy, but his bank wasn't anything to do with Italy! I am a fool, Cesidio, a fool. And Maria's still not pleased with me.' He looked over at his wife. 'She warned me. She was right after all. I don't know when I'll get back into her good books.'

He pulled a look of mock sorrow.

'Not for a long time, Alfonso. You're quite right. You're still in my bad books.'

Alfonso moved over and kissed her cheek.

'I see your Margherita is friendly with the Conetta boy. They look pretty chummy over there.' Marietta had heard rumours that Margherita was going to marry Tony Conetta, one of her nephews from Glasgow.

Maria looked over at her oldest daughter. She had turned out to be a very beautiful young woman. She was slight, and today, in her pale blue-and-white spotted summer dress with a straw hat perched on top of her dark hair, she looked a picture. 'Well, she's twenty-five now. It's past time. You and I were married with three children by then.'

'Maria, can you imagine that? At her age we had already come over here, following our husbands, almost penniless, babes in arms. We had no idea what was ahead of us.'

'I know. I know.'

Maria was thoughtful. Things had been quite hard for her and Alfonso recently. She worried about the future. What if there was a war? What if the boys are called up to fight? She tried not to dwell on that today. The sun lifted her spirits.

'Look how lucky we've been, thank God. I know it's been hard. *Speriamo*. Please God our children have it easier. You and I, Marietta, our job was to make the change. They'll never really understand the worry, and I don't want them to.'

'You know, we can't complain. We've got good men, hard-

The Crollas and the Di Ciaccas c. 1939

working and faithful. They love their children first, that's how it should be.'

They looked over at their husbands and laughed. The two men had fallen asleep, flat-out on the grass, hats pulled over their foreheads, snoring loudly. The Chianti had got the better of them.

'Anyway, Margherita *is* getting married in October. He's a good boy. Nice-looking.'

'Where will she live?'

'Glasgow. Tony has a fish and chip shop there. I'll miss her. But I think she'll be happy. It's a bit more glamorous than Edinburgh.'

'It's a lot more glamorous than Cockenzie!'

The women laughed again.

Vittorio and Domenico came over with Johnny. They ate standing up, sharing some pizza and beer.

Vittorio tried to waken his father. 'Papà, come on, it's nearly three o'clock, time to organise the races.'

Alfonso groaned. At fifty-one, he was definitely not fit for races. He had put on a bit of weight over the last few years and would much prefer to lie in the sun.

'Come on, Papà. We need to get a move on.'

Once he was up, Alfonso felt better for his sleep. They walked to the centre of the park, encouraging the youngsters from all the family groups to follow them.

'Right, boys. Get the rope ready. Let's start.'

He took a whistle from his top pocket and gave a shrill blow. Everyone looked up from their picnics. Here we go. Alfonso's in charge. All the youngsters and children rushed forward. This was the best part of the day.

They went through the races: hundred yards, five hundred yards, sprints for the youngsters, egg-and-spoon race for the mothers, fifty yards each for the Balilla and the Giovanni Ragazzi. Vittorio kept the score, whipping up a frenzy of competition between the east- and west-coast Italians.

As the heat of the day cooled, everyone gradually joined in so that, by the time the Glasgow versus Edinburgh football match began, the whole crowd, of almost three thousand, was crammed along the sidelines, cheering and shouting, clapping and whistling.

'*Forza Glasgow, Vai, Vai!*'

'*Oh! Dio!*'

'*Oh! Madonna!*'

'No . . . !'

'Goooooooooooooooooal!'

With a final push in the closing seconds of the match, Glasgow won by three goals to two. The Conetta boys were fierce competition, beating the Edinburgh lads into submission.

To much hullabaloo, Tony was presented with the Fascio Football Cup by Alfonso's eldest daughter, his new bride to be. Everyone cheered and whistled. A wedding in the autumn was a great thing to look forward to. Most families in the park were related to each other one way or another; many of them would be involved.

With the help of his young sister, Domenico got the heavy rope from the basket and laid it on the ground.

Alfonso stood on an overturned lemonade box and, after blowing the whistle to call for quiet, shouted through the megaphone: '*Ragazzi e Ragazze*, for the Seventeenth Annual Ferragosto Celebration for Il Fascio della Scozia, *avanti*! Step forward for the tug-of-war and the top prize of the day, Il Duce Mussolini Silver Cup!'

This was the big moment of the day. It was a fight to the last.

Edinburgh Italians, c. 1939

Never mind the football, it was the show of strength that mattered.

'Team leaders, step forward.'

Tony Conetta stepped forward for Glasgow.

Everyone cheered.

Domenico Crolla stepped forward for Edinburgh.

Hurrah!

A hush fell over the crowd. Glasgow had won the football. Would they win the tug-of-war as well?

'Call your team, one at a time.'

'Glasgow, Frank Conetta!' A cheer from the crowd.

'Edinburgh, Achille Crolla!' Cheers from the right.

'Glasgow, Aristide Di Ciacca!' Johnny's first cousin, Cesidio's brother Louis' son. More cheers.

'Edinburgh, Johnny Di Ciacca!' Cheers from both sides; the Di Ciaccas had many more relatives in Glasgow than Edinburgh.

'Glasgow, Landy Conetta!' The Conettas would be a force to reckon with, all tall strong men.

'Edinburgh, Alfonso Crolla!' The young ones in Glasgow burst out laughing. Alfonso was not exactly in his prime.

Maria whispered to Marietta. 'He'll add weight to the back. They'd better not laugh at my Alfonso.'

'Glasgow, Hughie Hilly!' Hugh was an Irish footballer who had married one of the Glasgow Italian girls. He was a wiry, strong man and would be a good opponent.

'Edinburgh, Monsignor McGettigan!' Edinburgh would have the Church on its side.

'Glasgow, Father Rossi.' So would Glasgow, albeit a younger, fitter Church!

Father Gaetano Rossi was a young Italian priest who had arrived in Glasgow the previous year to complete his ecclesiastical studies.

And so it went on until there were ten on each side, men and boys, fired up to win the cup.

Olivia was given the whistle. She had been primed by her father. She was to wink at him just before she blew it to give the Edinburgh team a head start. Vera and Wefa were her cheerleaders.

Tony had primed Margherita to keep an eye on her father to give the Glasgow team a head start!

They lined up: shortest and smallest at the middle, heaviest and oldest at the back. They were all strong men, used to carrying hundredweights of potatoes, boxes of fish and cases of lemonade. They shouted at each other to make each other laugh. This was a serious competition; any tricks were allowed.

Olivia stood to attention on the lemonade box. She straightened her back and jutted out her chin, then put the whistle to her lips.

Both teams stared ahead, eyeballing the opposition.

Alfonso kept an eye on Olivia.

Margherita kept an eye on Alfonso.

Margherita, c. 1939

Tony kept an eye on Margherita.

Olivia winked to Alfonso. Margherita winked to Tony. Everyone burst out laughing. Olivia blew the whistle and they were off!

Edinburgh pulled. Glasgow lurched forward.

Glasgow pulled back. Edinburgh held their ground.

A huge roar went up from the crowd. Everyone yelled, each side shouting louder than the other.

The youngsters went wild, jumping up and down, ecstatic with excitement.

The Glasgow boys pulled with added strength. They crouched down near the ground and dug in their heels, pulling the Edinburgh boys nearer to the line, now ragged and in disarray.

The Edinburgh crowd groaned. They were going to lose.

The Glasgow boys concentrated. '*Tira! Tira!*'

The Edinburgh boys slackened a little and Achille fell over. Everyone laughed. That's it. They edged towards the line.

The crowd groaned more loudly.

Jumping up and down on the lemonade box, Olivia was beside herself with excitement and the fear of losing. She needed to help her Papà. As loud as she could manage she yelled out over the microphone:

'*Gioventù d'Edimburgo!. . . A chi la vittoria?*'

Hearing her take on Mussolini, everyone burst out laughing. The Edinburgh team, inspired by her spirit, all yelled back in unison while they gave a final superhuman heave of the rope:

'*A noi, la vittoria. A noi!*'

They pulled and pulled until they all fell on their backs and, keeping the rope taught, they pulled the Glasgow boys over the line and on top of them.

Alfonso eventually pulled himself from the rummage that had tumbled on top of him. Olivia called again through the megaphone, beside herself with joy.

'*A chi la vittoria?*'

Good humoured in defeat the Glasgow contingent gave an almightily roar:

'*A voi! A voi!*'

Olivia, Wefa and Vera ran round the park shouting praise to Il Duce and enthusiastically shaking hands with all the winners.

Anna and Alex hadn't been to the picnic because the shop had been really busy. But now they closed the shop half an hour earlier than usual, keen to go to the dance. Margaret, who was by now part of the family, and Alex had cleaned up. They just had time to get changed before Willie Lees came to collect them in the taxi at eleven o'clock.

Johnny, Marietta, Anna, Alex, Cesidio, Lena, c. 1938

Marietta had taken Lena, Anna and Margaret into Edinburgh the week before to buy them new dance dresses from Jenners. She had treated them all to afternoon tea in the North British Station Hotel. Now they were all excited at the thought of joining the revellers at the dance. They had worked since seven that morning but were still full of energy.

When they arrived at the Assembly Rooms in George Street, almost at midnight, the dance was in full swing. The stunning chandeliers glittered in the main ballroom reflecting the colours of the girls' dresses. The men were in evening suits, one or two in British army uniform. There were three or four young American Italians in uniform as well, billeted in Glasgow and scooped up by the Glasgow Italians to enjoy a bit of local hospitality. They were much in demand by all the girls.

The Big Band was playing 'When the Saints Go Marching in' and it looked as if everyone was up on the dance floor, dipping and diving, having a wonderful time.

Anna immediately found Johnny and Olivia, who were sitting at a table with the Conetta boys. The music was intoxicating, the atmosphere in the room electric. Having recovered from losing the tug-of-war, the Glasgow boys were making sure they got more dances from the Edinburgh girls.

Alfonso went to take Maria up to dance. She laughed.

'It's too fast Alfonso. Wait until a slow dance comes on.'

Alfonso sat down beside her. 'Do you know, *cara,* this has been one of the happiest days of my life. Just to see everyone enjoying themselves, all together, hasn't it been just perfect?'

Maria took his hand.

The music stopped and as everyone hung around on the dance floor waiting for the next tune, Vittorio took the microphone.

'*Signore e Signori,* thank you all for making the effort to join the seventeenth Ferragosto Celebrations. I think we can all agree that it has been a spectacular day!'

Applause filled the room.

'I have three announcements to make. Firstly I'd like to announce that next year's Ferragosto will be held in King's Park, Alva Glen, Stirling.'

'Hurrah!'

'The second is that after many years of hardship I am happy, no, thrilled, to announce that, finally, the convenience of modern appliances has reached the outskirts of society. Cesidio Di Ciacca has finally purchased a meat slicer for his shop in Cockenzie!'

This ribbing was followed by a huge roar of laughter. There was enormous rivalry between the families, especially among the young.

'And finally, the top presentation of the evening, after a tremendous competition and, for once, no cheating . . .', a groan from the crowd, '. . . the prize of the Il Duce Silver Cup for the Tug of War goes, for the fifth consecutive time, to . . . Edimburgo!'

This was accompanied by more rapturous applause and much stamping of feet.

'And, if you please, Cavaliere Signor Alfonso Crolla as Secretary, could you please step forward.'

Alfonso loved nothing better than taking the stage. Not to be outdone by his son, he went to the microphone.

'*Amici,* thank you for this honour and for your support. We are living in dangerous times but I am confident good will prevail; Il Duce will not let us down. We are Italians, an honourable nation. As representatives of Italy, in this our adopted home country, we have a unique job to do, to continue to support the cordial relations that have built up between our two peoples. Keep your faith and you can't go wrong. God will not let us down either.'

Applause greeted this and a groan from the young ones. They didn't want any serious war talk to spoil their evening.

'No speeches, Zio Alfonso, let's dance!'

'Well, why not.' Alfonso got the message; these youngsters just wanted a good time. He'd show them a good time.

He turned to the band leader, 'Maestro, La Ballarella.'

The older couples in the five hundred strong crowd cheered and stood up. This was the dance of their youth; forget the jitter bug and Charleston.

'*Andiamo*,' Alfonso called on his friends, 'let's show these young-sters how to dance!'

He pulled Maria onto the dance floor, Cesidio took Marietta and Benny and Giovanni stood up with their wives. The other older couples followed and, as the familiar Italian music started, they automatically fell into line.

With rhythmic clapping and encouragement from the youngsters standing around, they danced the traditional courting dance of *la cioceria*.

Throughout the evening, family after family lined up proudly in front of a hurriedly pinned-up black tablecloth to get their photo-graph taken. Husband standing proudly behind wife, brothers and sisters staring modestly into the camera, backs straight, chins out, eyes strong and determined.

Today of all days was the result of long hours of hard work and was an achievement as important and satisfying to the young people as if they had just been awarded a university degree.

Well after three in the morning they all stood and sang the National Anthem of Italy, then of Britain, and finally with most enthusiasm, because they loved the tune the best, 'La Giovinezza'.

Finally the lights went down and the band played the last waltz, 'The Moonlight Serenade'.

Alfonso went over to Maria again. 'Is this slow enough for you?'

Maria was happy. Margherita was dancing with her *fidanzato*; Vittorio was dancing with Margaret from Cockenzie; Johnny had taken Olivia up, and Domenico was with one of the D'Agostino girls. Gloria and Filomena were dancing with each other.

Alfonso held Maria close. He pressed his cheek against hers, his skin rough with stubble. He smelled of his usual cologne. She relaxed in his arms. She felt safe when she was close to him like this. The music seduced her and she closed her eyes. She felt like a girl again; all the emotions of that day they spent alone on La Meta all those years ago came flooding back.

As if Alfonso also sensed it, he pressed her towards him.

'*Ti amo per sempre, carissima,*' he whispered in her ear, sending a thrill down her spine. 'I'll love you always. Everything is going to be all right.' .

25

For over a year the British Government had been making preparations for the impending war. Air-raid shelters were built, gas masks issued, black-out rules and air-raid procedures practised. Even although all twenty-year-olds had been conscripted and over a quarter of a million children had already been evacuated from the major cities, the population as a whole still had a perception that war would never come. The gathering show of preparation made them generally feel secure instead of threatened.

It was with this mentality that, when Olivia pleaded to go with her friends to Italy again, Alfonso gave in. Bruce Nicol and Signor Trudu, the Consul at the time, had assured him that there was no risk. The girls had enjoyed themselves so much last time, and what harm would it do?

So it was that, a few days after Ferragosto, with her friends Vera and Wefa, Olivia joined half a dozen other youngsters from Edinburgh, and many more from all over the country, to holiday in the Fascio camp. They were even more exited than they had been the year before. Now fifteen, the girls were promoted to the Avanguardisti, the Italian army youth group. They would get extra privileges, the chance to visit Rome, perhaps even hear Mass with the new pope, Pius XII.

As they stood waving their daughters goodbye, Alfonso and Vera's father, Achille, were oblivious to the plans the Home Office were drawing up for the future use of camps here in Britain.

'Alfonso, do you think they'll be all right? This war isn't going to blow up, is it?'

'Achille, I've spoken to everyone I know. The mood is that it's all posturing, they're just trying to move up the pecking order, look better in their own countries by looking strong abroad.'

'I hope you're right, Alfonso. I am a bit worried.'

Alfonso patted Achille on the back. 'Let them have a good time. They're young. There's plenty of time for them to grow up, take on responsibilities. Let them enjoy themselves before they choose men and get married! Then they'll have no chance!'

Both men laughed. They admitted that their poor wives put up with a lot from them at times.

When the usual *pacco* arrived from Fontitune, news was good. Emidio had decided to come back to Scotland and was on his way. They also had great hopes in Italy that lasting peace was on the cards. The propaganda of Il Duce was as effective as ever.

The business seemed to be faring better. Vittorio was doing a great job in the shop and Alfonso had been travelling in his Ford V8 all over Scotland. He had customers as far north as Dingwall and as far south as Galashiels. Valvona & Crolla was now supplying almost every Italian family in the country.

Miss Dennison, ever vigilant, was still concerned that Alfonso was too lenient with his customers. Most families were still a month or two in arrears with payments; the debtors' balance was uncomfortably high.

'Mr Crolla, the turnover and profit have increased but I have to warn you that we do have a perilously high level of debt on the books.'

'I know, Miss Dennison, and I appreciate your concern. I am in a very difficult situation. Many of our customers are still recovering from the collapse of the Italian Bank. You know, they hold me partly responsible.'

'I understand, Mr Crolla. But we are not running the "Next Italian Bank". At the moment we are in effect financing many interest-free loans.'

'You are quite right, Miss Dennison. I hadn't looked at it like that.' Alfonso still felt dependent on this good woman but how could she understand the psychology of the Italian? Everything relied on goodwill. A favour was repaid with loyalty, a valuable asset to any business. 'I'll make sure I collect as much debt as possible. Please send out the orders as usual.'

But Alfonso still returned with too little cash. The excuses varied. The cigarette traveller had just been. The doctor's bill was overdue.

Or, if the account was very overdrawn, the customer might threaten to buy from the opposition, Fazzi's van from Glasgow. That in itself was enough to persuade Alfonso to supply more goods on credit. One way or another, Alfonso succumbed to the wiliness of his fellow compatriots, who sensed an inherent soft spot in him and were happy to exploit it.

Despite this cash-flow crisis, the company finally made a profit, £650 14s 9½d: the biggest profit in its history. Alfonso felt justified. His policy of building customer loyalty was paying off.

He was happy to put Miss Dennison's concerns aside. He had more pressing worries at home. Margherita's wedding preparations were in full swing. The date was set and the house was in turmoil. The groom's mother was a force to be reckoned with. Every time Alfonso got home there was another catalogue of problems to solve. Guest lists, church rehearsals, dress fittings, venue selection, menu planning, the list was endless.

Life was generally so frantically busy that the Soviet–Nazi pact on 23 August went by with little discussion. But the news on 1 September that Germany had attacked Poland could not be ignored. This would mean war. What sane person would choose war?

In Rome the group of 384 British children on holiday at the expense of the Italian Government were having a ball. The weather had been glorious and the camp was a tremendous success. The high spirits of the group were not suppressed when they were taken to Rome to join in one of the many Fascist parades in honour of Il Duce. Kitted out in the uniform of the Avanguardisti, Olivia, Wefa and Vera joined their group.

The older boys were all issued with real rifles,some loaded with live ammunition. The younger groups, the 'Figli e Figlie della Lupa', some as young as four and five, were given wooden rifles to parade with. They held them straight-faced and serious, mimicking the older boys.

When they paraded in the afternoon down the Via Del Corso towards the Piazza Venezia, crowds lined the streets and hung out of windows, waving Italian flags and shouting and cheering. Like a miniature army, the youngsters looked straight ahead, legs kicking out in the Fascist march.

At the Piazza, they lined up, over a thousand in all. When Mussolini appeared on the balcony he looked god-like, in a bright white uniform, laden with medals. They cheered crazily and shouted as he saluted them. After songs and recitals that they had rehearsed for days, he called out to them, his voice powerful and hypnotising, '*Figli e Figlie della Lupa, a chi la Vittoria?*'

To which each youngster replied with conviction:

'*A noi! A noi! Viva Il Duce!*'

The crowd of young people cheered with as much conviction and enthusiasm as if it had been a famous football team or Mickey Mouse.

When Count Ciano took his turn to speak it almost looked as though a cartoon character had arrived. The contrast to Mussolini could not have been greater. Ciano was short, balding and frail-looking, lacking in charisma. His voice was high and squeaky; after the bombastic gravitas of Il Duce, he seemed like a puppet. Instead of inspiring them to cheer, the girls found they had to nip each other to stop giggling.

He was calling them to thank Mussolini for his efforts in maintaining peace in Europe. Olivia sensed unease about the man, a nervousness and insincerity; it was as if he didn't believe what he was telling them.

Three days later, on the morning of Sunday, 3 September 1939, her misgivings made sense. Their camp leader called them together and informed them all that Hitler had declared war.

In Cockenzie, most of the village was in the café or spilling out into the street. Although it was Sunday, the church was empty. Cesidio switched on the wireless. No one made a sound. They all expected the news to be bad.

At 11.15 the Prime Minister's very English voice was heard, formal and sombre. Hitler had ignored Chamberlain's ultimatum.

'. . . consequently this country is now at war with Germany.'

He spoke of the evil that they would be fighting, the Nazi injustice. When he had finished speaking, the National Anthem sounded around the shop and into the street. Everyone stood silently, tears in many eyes, children hanging on to their parents' hands.

Cesidio, Marietta, Johnny and Alex stood among the crowd.

Lena, Anna, Margaret and Jeannie were behind the counter. They burst into tears. When the music finished, Cesidio switched off the wireless. He spoke very quietly, deeply shocked at what he had heard:

'God help us', and then, louder so they could all hear, 'God Save the King!'

Everyone answered in agreement. Not one person thought it odd that he spoke up, nor questioned his sentiments. He was one of them after all.

In Edinburgh the Italian ice cream shops and cafés were open as usual but were all empty. In the city, few chose to hear the news in the company of Italians. Mussolini was in cahoots with Hitler. Who knew what he would do next?

When Vittorio translated the announcement for his mother, Maria was distraught.

'Olivia is in Italy alone! Vittorio, how will she get home? What will happen to her? *Oh Dio!*' she cried out in anguish.

Maria lived her life expecting God to let her down. No matter that she prayed incessantly, no matter that she obeyed all the fasts and abstinences without fail, somehow she had an inner premonition that God could not save her from her fate. She was terrified. She remembered the nights she cried alone with her babies when Alfonso was fighting in the war, tortured nights of uncertainty. Nights that stretched her faith to the limits. The same terror engulfed her now.

Mussolini was well away from Rome by the time Olivia and her friends were assembled in the dining hall and told the news. They were told not to be concerned. It might be difficult for them to get back to Britain, but Italy was not entering the war, so they would be safe here.

Olivia didn't feel safe. She felt a cold fear in the pit of her stomach. Everyone assured them that they would get home safely but she was not convinced. Many of the children panicked as a wave of shock swept over them.

Irrational fears took over. Petty things started to worry them. Would Olivia miss being a bridesmaid at her sister's wedding? Wefa was worried that the Germans might bomb her bedroom at home and she would not have any clothes left. Vera was terrified of leaving the safety of the camp. Surely it would be better to stay here? What they were all afraid to acknowledge was the fear that really haunted them: would they ever see their parents again?

Alfonso and his sons went immediately to Picardy Place. Achille was already there with the other parents, anxious for news.

'Alfonso, you said it was safe!' Achille was angry.

'I didn't know. I didn't know. Do you think I would have let them go if I thought this would happen?'

'Have they closed the borders?'

'I think so. I'm trying to find out. I think they've organised transport for some of the children to stay with their relatives in Italy.'

'Do you mean they'll end up in Fontitune?'

'I don't know, man. I don't know!' Alfonso was close to despair.

They telephoned the Consul's office in London; it took hours to get a connection. They couldn't help. They tried hopelessly to contact Italy. It was impossible. Alfonso tried to get help from the local police but they had more pressing concerns. In Edinburgh the streets had an air of menace about them: armoured cars, soldiers in uniform, men with suitcases, women crying. The war had already affected everyone. The Italians' problem was not a priority.

Vittorio and Domenico had all but made up their minds that they would just get on a train and go and get the girls themselves. They didn't even know where the girls were but they could surely find out. If they could get news to Pietro they could at least get to Rome and take them up to Fontitune.

Returning home with no news, Alfonso found his wife lying on the bed, her eyes swollen with crying. She pulled herself up.

'Have you found her? Is there any news?'

'Nothing. The telephone lines are all busy. It's impossible to get through. The boys are still trying. It will calm down soon.'

He stepped over to help her up. She pushed him away. She couldn't take any more. Years of trying to make sacrifices, being alone, working hard and coping beyond her endurance crashed around her. If anything happened to Olivia she could not go on, she could not endure any more.

'*Cara*, try not to worry. The authorities will look after them all. Of course they will.'

'The authorities! The authorities!' Maria pummelled Alfonso's chest with her fists. 'This is all your fault, Alfonso; your fault for trusting in the authorities. They don't care about you. They don't care about any of us. They are only interested in their own skins, their own jobs. I warned you. I told you so many times. Now are you happy?'

She did not consider the distress he felt. She blamed him. How did he not see this coming? How could he have allowed Olivia to go?

'Maria, please. Don't shout at me. What more can I do? What more do you want from me?'

'Nothing, Alfonso. Nothing. Only my Olivia home safely.'

With this insult thrown at him she pushed him from the room and slammed the door. Alfonso leant on the door outside and wept. He couldn't understand why she was so angry with him. Why did she resent his work so much? Why was she blaming him? He had only done what he thought was for the best.

They didn't talk for two days. Alfonso spent all his time trying to get news. He went to Glasgow to see if they had heard anything there. At night, air raids and black-outs built up a sense of fear. News from London was bad. They were evacuating more children from the city. They were expecting bombings.

Notices came for them all to report to the police station to confirm their addresses. Italy was not at war with Britain but the Italians were still classed as aliens.

A few of the young Italian boys who were born in Britain received their call-up papers. They were going to fight for Britain.

The shops were quiet. In the street a young man spat at Alfonso.

'Dirty Eyetie. Hitler's pal!'

Three days, four days, there was still no news from Italy. Alfonso stopped sleeping, sitting up at night praying for his daughter to be safe.

When Maria had questioned his involvement with the Fascio in the past he had thought carefully about her concerns but always come to the conclusion that it was for the best. When he was young, Tadon Michele had taught him to be strong. He had always said, if honest men don't take responsibility, it leaves the way for dishonest men to rise unchallenged.

He had had every faith in Mussolini. Who else could have pulled Italy together as he had done, from North to South, for the first time in its history? Harsh tactics had been used, but Alfonso remembered during the last war having to kill the enemy to prevent slaughter of his own soldiers. Women had never had to fight to the death in war. They didn't know the depths a man could fall to.

Even Mussolini entering Abyssinia had seemed reasonable to Alfonso. He had fought in Africa when he was still a teenager. He had seen at first hand the poverty and deprivation. If Fascism could chase starvation from the mouths of Italian babies, then why should it not also help the poor black babies in Africa? Surely the end justifies the means when the futures of so many can be improved.

The collapse of the bank had shaken Alfonso. He had never suspected anything bad of Olivieri. He had misjudged him completely. Now war had broken out, and Mussolini had made a pact with Hitler. Could it be that Il Duce himself was a conman, an evil man disguised as good. Had Alfonso misjudged again? Could it be that he had risked his daughter's life by placing his loyalty in an evil man? Alfonso lost trust in himself.

When it seemed the only thing to do now was to go to Italy and look for Olivia himself, a wire arrived, short and to the point:

'Crossing arranged. Arrive Friday pm.'

When Maria read it she felt a flood of relief. She fell into Alfonso's arms and wept.

'I'm sorry. Alfonso, I'm sorry.'

He stroked her hair.

'*Non ti preoccupare*. You know I love you all. I'm sorry too. I just tried my best.'

Standing on the dock waiting to board the ferry at Calais, Olivia felt very frightened. This ship looked much bigger than the one on which they had crossed on the way out. It was dark and threatening. The dock was full of soldiers, French and British, with packs and knapsacks jammed with supplies.

Long queues of families wound their way back up the road, with carts laden with everything they owned: pots, pans, blankets, suitcases, bicycles strapped at the side. Olivia noticed many groups of

271

children on their own, labels hanging round their necks. Italian, Polish, Belgian. There were many children, both ragged and well dressed, standing forlorn, hand in hand, reassuring each other.

In Rome a few of the older boys had been told to keep their guns, just in case they needed them. This had frightened the girls more than anything. Why would a fifteen-year-old boy need a gun? How would he even know how to use it?

They had travelled a different way back on the train, through Genoa and Nice, nearer to the coast. They were so glad to be going home that they had tried not to pay attention to the long columns of soldiers marching inland, the ugly grey tanks with gun barrels pointing out aggressively, and the aeroplanes criss-crossing the sky like an orderly, ominous flock of birds.

The camp leader showed the guards and customs officers his communal passport for the 384 children. The guards were not happy. They wanted identification as proof that the children that they were taking out were the same ones that they had brought in. But there was no solution to this as there was no detailed list. Three ships sailed without them before the Italian Consul from London finally contacted the French border police to gain permission.

It was almost dark when they left the shores of France. The girls stood at the railing on deck, innocent little Fascist holiday-makers, desperate to return home to an uncertain fate. Alert, they heard some adults talking.

'We'll be lucky to get off this ship alive.'

'The soldiers said there's a real risk of us getting scuppered by a U-boat.'

Mines and submarines could blow them into the sky. Planes overhead could bomb them and blow them into the sea.

The crossing terrified Olivia more than anything in her life. As the sky darkened and the ship lurched in the swell, she was overcome with a premonition of danger. The noises around her – whispering, seagulls, fog horns, sirens – faded into a dull background buzz. The crippling knot in her stomach was the only sensation she felt.

In the event they crossed safely, with no sign of the dangers that had haunted her. After an overnight wait on the dock at Dover and a slow train journey up to Edinburgh, she arrived home.

She felt traumatised and exhausted. She hadn't closed her eyes for forty-eight hours, fearful of slipping into unconsciousness and never waking up again.

When eventually she stepped down onto the platform she looked around her, dazed and confused. She stretched her back and neck to ease the aching from sitting huddled on the floor of the packed train.

'Olivia? Olivia? *Carissima.*'

She looked up. There was her father. She was safe.

She fell forward into his arms and burst into tears.

26

Cockenzie
1939

Cesidio was sitting on the rocks. His eyes were drawn to a small fishing vessel off to the east. It was probably the *Day Spring*. He had seen John Dickson sail this morning when he had been at the harbour at Port Seton looking for fish. He said he was going to the Isle of May and would be back by the afternoon. Cesidio would go along and see the catch. He needed four stone of haddock at least.

It was a lovely autumn afternoon; the sea was like glass and the coast of Fife was clearly visible in the distance.

He reached for his rosary beads in the pocket of his white apron. He sat quietly, thoughtful in prayer. He often came down here to think. It was very peaceful, with an ever-changing horizon depending on the weather and the time of year. Sometimes he thought it was even more beautiful than home in Italy.

The war had arrived on their doorstep. Yesterday German planes had flown overhead, dropping bombs near the Forth Railway Bridge. A locomotive had been crossing the bridge at the time but the bomb had luckily missed.

Last night news came through that a battleship had been sunk off the west coast. This afternoon the *Evening News* ran photographs of missing seamen, long lists of names of men lost at sea. Marietta had shown him a picture of one of the fishermen from Port Seton. They had both been shocked.

'Those poor boys; they look no older than nineteen or twenty, no older than Johnny. How unbearable for their families: imagine having to look down a list to see if your son's name is on it. Please God we never have to face that.'

They had heard about it first on the news at nine o'clock last night.

'HMS *Royal Oak* sunk in Scapa Flow, eight hundred lost.'

Everyone in the shop had stood still. Many of the young men had already been called up, most into the Navy because of their experience at sea. Some of their boys could have been on the ship and might be lost. It was barely six weeks since the war had started and already the losses were mounting up.

Most of the fishermen in the shop had fought or lost friends in the last war. They'd been down this road before.

'Bloody wars!' One of the fishermen kicked the side of the counter in frustration.

Usually Marietta operated a no-swearing policy, almost impossible among these men used to a harsh life at sea. Offshore almost every other word was an expletive. But this time she had let it go. She had felt exactly the same herself.

Reports this morning said that a German U-boat had slipped through the defences in Scapa Flow and blown the *Royal Oak* out of the water. The older fishermen were angry. The Admiralty should have had better defences set out before they left ships in anchor.

Anna came down to the rocks looking for her father. She sat beside him, quietly looking over the water.

'I can't believe so many men drowned last night. The sea looks so calm and safe today but it has taken so many lives.'

Cesidio looked at his daughter. She was just the age Marietta had been when he had proposed to her. Anna looked very like her mother, very beautiful. It was such a joy to see her blossom into a young woman.

'The sea doesn't take life, Anna. God takes life. When a soul is ready for God, he chooses the time.'

'I don't believe that. I can't love a God who destroys so many families.'

'Don't forget, God is your father. He always knows what is best.'

Anna was silent. Sometimes she didn't understand her father's faith.

Lena came down and stood at the shore. She called to them to come in for tea.

Cesidio heard her but didn't turn round. He was looking intently into the distance. Far away towards the right, high in the sky, he could just see a large dark shape. He put his hand over his eyes. Faintly above the wash of the waves he could just pick up the drone of an engine. He stood up. A second black shape appeared and then a third.

They weren't birds. They were aeroplanes. It was another air raid.

The larger plane swooped up higher than the other two. They were moving fast. When they were parallel to him out in the Firth he heard the rattle of machine-gun fire.

Aware of Anna behind him, he turned quickly, 'Anna, get back. Get back. They're German planes!' As he shouted, the three planes swooped noisily overhead, travelling at great speed back out towards the sea.

'Oh, my God.' The war *had* arrived.

The noise of more gunfire echoed against the wall of the house. The larger four-engine black plane had a swastika visible on its wing. The two Royal Air Force planes chasing it were lighter and faster and could swoop round it, dive underneath and pull up behind, firing again into its tail. There had been no warning siren, no air raid, but the firing itself was enough to bring everyone down on to the rocks.

Out in the Firth, the *Day Spring* looked vulnerable. A stray bullet could easily sink it. The German plane flew higher, trying to escape its attackers but, just as it looked as if it would get away, the British planes fired a further round of ammunition.

The German plane's engine spluttered, it keeled over and dropped, screeching, into the sea, left wing first. The RAF planes circled around for two or three minutes examining the wreckage.

Relieved that the danger had passed, everyone at the water's edge clapped. The plane must have been heading for Edinburgh or Rosyth.

'There's a man in the water. Two!'

They watched as the *Day Spring* made its way to the floating wreckage of the downed aircraft. Seeing the boat sailing towards the German pilots, the RAF planes circled once more. The pilots in the cockpit waved down to the cheering crowd before flying off.

Everyone rushed along the street to the harbour at Port Seton, lining up along the pier to wait for the boat to come in. Someone called the police station at Prestonpans. Marietta sent Alex to get Dr Black but he was already on his way.

'Fetch Nurse Swan. They may be injured.'

John Dickson chugged the heavily laden *Day Spring* into harbour. As well as a hefty catch of fish he had lifted three German fighter pilots from the sea.

They were badly injured. One had a severe eye injury; the other two had bleeding wounds and cracked ribs. Constable Alex Craig and Dr Black were waiting, each keen to get hold of the Germans first.

As the boat tied up, Alex Craig jumped down and the injured Germans were hauled ashore on stretchers.

Anna was shocked.

'Papà, they're just young men. They look nice.'

One of the Germans could speak quite good English. He was a tall, fair-haired man wearing a dark high-necked sweater and thick fur-lined leather jacket; he had blood pouring from his face. He was anxious to explain that they had not been attacking. 'We were taking photographs. We had no bombs.'

The German pulled a thick gold ring from his pinkie finger.

'Here,' he pushed it into the skipper's hand. 'Thank you for saving us.'

The pilots had been in trouble out at sea, barely hanging on to the broken wing of the plane. If the *Day Spring* had not come to the rescue they would probably have drowned.

The story reached the newspapers, even the national press. This was the first German plane of the war to be shot down, a twin-engine Heinkel bomber: the first of thousands.

Constable Craig took the men to the police station on Links Road. Their clothes were ripped, soaking wet and covered in blood. One of the men had terrible injuries to his arm. Dr Black cut his clothes from him and did what he could to stem the flow of blood.

Alex Craig, a tall, strong gentle man, had recently been transferred to Port Seton from Dunbar, further along the coast. His young wife was the daughter of the Tognieri family who had the ice cream shop in Dunbar.

Sorry to see the airman in such a bad state, Alex Craig fetched one of his suits for the German boy. Weeks later a brown paper parcel arrived from Edinburgh Castle where the Germans had been sent. It was addressed to Constable Craig and contained his suit, neatly folded with a German war medal tucked in one of its pockets.

From then on, the black-out restrictions were enforced with even more severity. The war was real and, as news of evacuation and impending rationing filtered through, they went into the dark, cold winter with trepidation.

1940

The winter trundled on. The bench in the Cockenzie café was less full now, as more and more of the young lads were called up. The older men and soldiers home on leave took up the spare places. Every night at nine they sat listening to the wireless, keeping abreast of the news. Through winter and into spring, things changed in fits and starts. News was good one day, bad the next.

At night Alex Craig and Harry Stevenson, the other local policeman, got into the habit of popping in to see that all was well. Often they would sit with Cesidio and Marietta over a glass of wine and a fish supper and chat about the day's events.

Rationing was introduced and, in the shop, ration books had to be stamped to share out chocolates, ice cream, sweets. The fish and chip shop did brisk business. Fish was still plentiful; the older fishermen went out and landed their catch on the Boat Shore, just as they had always done.

Marietta kept chickens at the back of the house. She had fresh eggs every day, a luxury now in town.

Petrol rationing had curtailed Alfonso's journeys down to Cockenzie. He had only visited once since December. Now, if they needed provisions, Cesidio went to the shop in Elm Row by tram. Marietta made their pasta by hand most days, just with flour and eggs.

The news was mixed, some good, some bad. The initial reaction to the declaration of war had eased. The 'phoney' war seemed to be a mixture of sporadic bombings, accidents caused by car crashes in the black-outs and news of minor battles in Europe, nothing as drastic or as frightening as had been anticipated. Children had been evacuated all over the country. Some started to make their way home. The feeling was that, after the first alarming skirmishes, the war might pass them all by.

This feeling of complacency began to change when gradually success swung in favour of the Germans. The British army had gone in aid of Norway but with little success. Things were starting to look ominous

It was not until towards the end of May that Alfonso visited Cockenzie again. He had telephoned Cesidio to warn him he was coming and had the car loaded with the order. When he arrived, Cesidio was shocked at his appearance. He looked smart and clean-shaven as always but, instead of the lively, optimistic Alfonso they were used to, here was a worried, anxious man.

'Alfonso,' Cesidio embraced him, happy to see him. 'Come through, my friend, come through.'

Marietta came forward to embrace her *compare*. The men sat down. Marietta poured Alfonso a glass of wine and put some bread on the table.

'*Grazie, compare*. I smelled the smoke-house when I came into the High Street, Cesidio. Are they smoking fish?'

'Yes, they'll be smoking salmon or maybe haddock. Alex!' He called his youngest son through from the front shop. 'Alex, go along and ask James for a smoked salmon for Zio Alfonso. Tell him I'll square it with him later.

'*Come stai?* How are things in Edinburgh?'

'Not too bad. Everyone is well.'

'How is the new bride? I can't believe it's so long since the wedding. What a lovely day we had.'

'Margherita is in Glasgow now, so we don't see her very often. 'Marietta,' Alfonso called through to the back kitchen, 'Great news. Margherita's expecting! My first grandchild is on its way!'

'*Auguri!* Congratulations!' Marietta heard the news as she came through with two plates of thick minestrone soup made with chunks of cabbage, carrots, onions, celery and some broken pasta. She added some chunks of dry bread and grated the crust of some cheese on top. 'What lovely news. That's just what we need to hear.' She showed Alfonso the crust of cheese. 'I hope you brought me some cheese. This is my last piece and it won't last much longer. I've cooked a bit of skin in the soup for you.'

'Don't worry. I have kept some for you. There are no deliveries. But there are still some ships coming into Leith Docks. There is always something on board I can get my hands on.'

Marietta went back through to the front shop. As soon as she was out of earshot Cesidio leaned towards Alfonso and lowered his voice.

Alfonso, I've heard that Germans living here have been called up for tribunals. A chap from Musselburgh has been interned. He's been living here for forty years. Have you heard anything? Will they come for us?'

'We have to realise that we are vulnerable. They already see us as aliens. The thing is, if they call you for a tribunal, at least they'll allow you to explain your position. It's obvious your allegiances are to Britain. You've done so much good down here, even in this little community.'

'But, Alfonso, my friend, what about you? Are you not in a vulnerable position; with your involvement with the Fascio and everything?'

Alfonso Crolla, alien no. 686356, 11 September 1939

I'm sure the Italian Government will support us if things get tricky. I've known all the officials in the council in Edinburgh for years. They know me. They know we believe in co-operation between our two countries.'

'It is a worrying time. So many lads here are already at war. We're lucky in a way, our sons are on the sidelines.'

Alfonso looked behind to see if anyone was listening. He spoke in dialect.

'*Cesidio, attenzione!* I need to warn you. Keep your head down.'

'What do you mean?'

280

'I've had a letter from London. There's a lot of bad feeling building up against us. The newspapers are firing up anti-Italian feeling.'

'Why are they doing that? What good will it do?'

'There is talk of a "Fifth Column". They're saying that we Italians are all over the country and that some of us are potential spies, subversives, enemies.'

'Do you think that's true? You know the Italians better than I do? Have you seen anything? Tell me, Alfonso.'

'It's nonsense. Utter garbage. Do you and I look like spies? We're just patriots. We love our country. What's wrong with that? It's the same love that made us fight in the war: isn't it, Cesidio? What's wrong with that?' Alfonso was losing faith in his own judgement.

'What's going to happen?'

Alfonso had been avoiding the question. He was very concerned. 'The news is bad, Cesidio. The Germans are pushing the British army back towards the coast. I have heard that Mussolini is thinking of siding with the Germans.'

'Yes, but he is still neutral, isn't he? Italy is not going to war against Britain surely?'

'It could go either way. I am afraid that if he does declare war we'll all be in the firing line.'

'What do you mean?' Cesidio sensed Alfonso was hiding something.

'Well, put it like this. I've heard rumours that a ship is leaving from Glasgow in a few weeks.'

'So?'

'So it will be full of Italian diplomats and nominated friends of Italy who want to return home.'

'How do you know that?'

'I don't. Not officially. That, Cesidio, is what's worrying me. I haven't been officially told anything. I haven't been advised to leave. Even if I had, I wouldn't choose to go. This is our home after all.'

'It's a bad business. Johnny is upset about the whole thing. Most of his local friends have been called up. He's still here and he feels uncomfortable.'

'My boys feel the same. But would Johnny fight for Britain? He was born in Italy wasn't he?'

'Yes, I presume he'd be called up to fight for Italy. But how can he fight against his own home? And look at Alex. He was born here. Thank God he's only sixteen. He won't be touched.'

Marietta came back through and heard what they were saying. 'Is there news of the boys being called up, Alfonso?'

'I haven't heard anything. That's the problem, Marietta. Mind you, some of the Edinburgh boys who were born here have already been called up for the British forces. We're all in no-man's-land. In Italy we are strangers, here we're aliens.'

'Domenico was born in Italy, Vittorio was born here. Whose side can they be on, either of them? We're in the hands of God. Like the deal of the cards, we've no control of the outcome.'

'*Non c'è niente da fare!* You're right, Alfonso. There's nothing to be done.'

He waved goodbye to Alfonso, smoked salmon, two dozen eggs, *baccalà* and a big box of fresh vegetables in the back of the car, Cesidio crossed himself and said a prayer.

He felt anxious for Alfonso. The poor man was worried sick about his involvement with the Fascist Party. Here in Cockenzie they had had nothing to do with it. Only the boys had been to the holiday camps, but that was when they were still children. It had nothing to do with the situation now.

He thought about the local Cockenzie boys who were away fighting. A sick feeling filled his stomach as he remembered his own experiences in the last war. He knew some of these brave lads would not be coming home.

Why were their lives controlled by a few powerful men, men whose decisions could change the course of history?

As he went into the shop to light the fryer for the evening, he shook his head sadly. *C'è niente da fare.*

27

10 June 1940

In Cockenzie, Mrs Donaldson came rushing out into the street. She shouted at Alex, who was pushing the ice cream cart up Harlaw Hill.

'Alex! Alex!'

Alex stopped and looked round. He must have given her the wrong change.

'Alex, you'd better go hame, son. That's Mussolini declared war!' Mrs Donaldson still held the three cones she had just bought from him. She'd gone into the house and heard the news flash on the wireless.

'Away hame, son. Yer Ma'll be worried sick.'

This June it had been warm and sunny every day. Alex and Johnny had been really busy, selling as much ice cream as their father could make. Even with sugar and milk in short supply, somehow there was always enough to make a fresh batch.

Alex turned his tricycle round and pushed it back down the road. He ignored the kids that ran up to him shouting for a penny cone. As he walked past, they stood still and looked. Something must be wrong if Alex wasn't selling his ice cream.

Margaret had been sent to find him. 'There you are, Alex. You've to come home.'

They pushed the trike home together, not exchanging a word.

The shop was full. Mr Osborne, the minister, and Dr Black were in the back shop with Cesidio and Marietta. Police Constable Alex Craig was standing outside the shop. Most of the locals were standing around, hands deep in their pockets, shirt sleeves rolled up in the heat.

'Ye're OK, lad. Not to worry.' Bobby Dates called after Alex as he went in.

His mother was sitting at the table crying. Anna and Lena were trying to console her.

Jeannie Heriot came through with a cup of tea. 'Here, Mary, take that. I've put a wee nip of whisky in it for you.'

Cesidio was talking to the men. 'I can't believe it. I saw it coming but still I can't believe it. After all we've been through getting our poor men out of Dunkirk, Mussolini has to stab us in the back. I'm ashamed. I'm ashamed. I can't imagine Italy fighting against us.'

'He's a treacherous monster, as bad as Hitler.'

Alex went over to his father. 'What'll happen, dad? Will we have to go to Italy?'

'I really don't know. We'll just have to wait and see, son, but you've not to worry. You're only sixteen. Whatever happens, you'll be here to look after your mother and your sisters.' Cesidio put his arm round his youngest son.

Since the middle of May the fate of the northern armies had hung in the balance. The rout at Dunkirk had had them all on tenterhooks over the last ten days. The café had been packed night after night; everyone's attention focused on the wireless when Sis switched it on to hear the nine o'clock news.

When Churchill, now Prime Minister, rallied the country saying that 'we will fight them on the beaches . . . we will never surrender' there was a special significance to these fisherfolk. They well understood their vulnerability here on the Firth of Forth.

They had watched the huge concrete blocks being laid down all along the coast, as a defence against the invasion. Every day now they were reminded of how much of a threat an invasion was. They understood the North Sea. They knew only too well the sea routes to Holland and France. It was no coincidence that the first German war plane of the war had come down on their doorstep.

But they were fighting men. Their livelihoods made them strong, fearless men. They would fight on the beaches if necessary. Churchill had no worries there. They were behind him to a man.

After the speech the radio presenter said, 'Now we'll broadcast something to lift your spirits.' Over the airwaves they were thrilled when they heard the roar of the Hampden football crowd. They all stood up and cheered, clenched fists stabbing the air.

When the troops had been rescued so heroically from Dunkirk

the mood had been almost victorious, huge pride at the success over almost impossible odds; they had been buoyed up with relief.

Since then they had been waiting. Day after day they listened to see what Mussolini would do. Now the die was cast. Italy was at war with Britain.

Cesidio kept the shop open as usual. After the initial news, nothing had happened. They waited; they could do nothing else. They didn't feel an immediate danger. Everyone here knew them. The whole village knew they were not a threat, not an enemy.

Nevertheless the shop was strangely quiet. Perhaps the locals would stay away for a few days till they got used to the idea. Those who did come in talked about the cowardice and double dealing of Mussolini.

Johnny, Lena and Anna sat talking. 'Will you be called up by the Italian army, Johnny? What will happen?'

'They can try if they like. I'm not fighting against Britain. I've only been in Italy for three weeks in my whole my life, for God's sake. I suspect we'll get internment papers. Or we might get deported. We're still classed as aliens. They have already interned a lot of Germans so I suppose we'll be classed as enemies.'

Cesidio came over and put his arm round his son. His face was drawn.

'Dad, are you all right?'

Cesidio rubbed his forehead with his hand and shook his head. He took a deep breath. 'Oh, Johnny, I'm so sorry.'

Anna saw tears in her father's eyes.

'I'm so sorry. Mussolini has betrayed us all. Not just us, but every Italian man, woman and child in the country. He's such a fool, looking after his own skin instead of his people. He has sided with the Devil; he has sold us all down the river. Poor Italy. My poor Italy.'

Anna was shocked to see her father so distressed.

'What about the family in Picinisco and I Ciacca? Will they be in the fighting?'

'God knows what is ahead of them. Nobody is safe from today on.'

He looked at Johnny, 'Son, we'll have to be strong for your mother. She's going to find it hard. You know they'll probably ask us to the police station. We will have to be interviewed by the authorities, face a tribunal to state our case.'

'Do you think we'll be interned, Dad, do you think they'll lock us up?'

'I don't know. We've not done anything to make them think we're a threat. We'll wait and see.'

Anna was determined. 'Don't worry, Daddy. Lena and I will look after Mum.'

'And, Anna, whatever happens, look after Alex. He's just a lad. He'll be the most vulnerable. Watch out for him.'

They closed early. It was ten o'clock but it was still reassuringly light outside. Cesidio was not surprised when the policemen didn't come in for their usual drink. They must be busy somewhere.

Marietta felt calmer. Before they went to bed she called them all together.

'Let's say the rosary together. Just one decade. You're all tired. Nothing drastic has happened so it looks like things are going to be all right.'

Cesidio was relieved. 'It could have gone either way. There could have been some trouble. Thank God our friends here have supported us. I feel better. I'm sure things will be fine. We'll have a good night's rest, and tomorrow, Johnny, you and I will go to see Alex Craig at the police station and see what they want us to do. I'd have asked them tonight if they'd come in. They'll look after us, you'll see.'

When eventually they were alone, Cesidio and Marietta lay in each other's arms and wept. *Povera Italia!* Poor people who have been betrayed, sacrificed. Being Hitler's ally was no more than surrender. They had been afraid of this since Mussolini's Abyssinian affair. They had seen this coming.

'Marietta, you've not to worry. We're lucky. We've not been involved with the Fascio. We've kept ourselves away from Edinburgh and we're well known here. Thank God our home is in Scotland. Look how good the people are to us.'

'What about everyone in Italy? And my family in London? We're scattered all over the place. If only we were all together.'

'Thank God, our own family here is together. That's all we can look after at the moment.'

They lay quietly, holding each other. Cesidio stroked her hair. She was still his sweetheart, always would be. Never a day passed that he didn't thank God for her love.

'How long is it since I've told you how much I love you?' He kissed her and moved closer to her, pulling her to him. 'I can't imagine life without you. We are one, you and I. We are so blessed.'

'Do you know, Cesidio,' Marietta laughed, 'do you remember when you told me you loved me and I agreed to wait for you?'

'I just knew it was to be.'

'I've never told you. I had been watching you in the piazza when you were with the boys. You were standing apart, thinking. I noticed you. You were different, quieter than the others, who were making such a racket. I think I fell in love with you then, even before you spoke to me.'

'Marietta, I asked you then to wait for me. No matter what happens, will you still wait for me?

Marietta's heart lurched. She moved her body towards him and kissed him tenderly. Wait for him? She couldn't live without him.

In Edinburgh earlier in the afternoon, the boss of the McVitie's bakery had come out of his office. There were forty or so workers on the shift, packing biscuits. He called for quiet. 'Quiet! Listen please! Italy has declared war.'

He walked over to Addolorata, who had been working for him for nearly seven years.

'I'm sorry, Dora.' He handed her an envelope. 'There's no job here for the enemy.'

'What do you mean?'

'You're fired.'

She sat on the bus going home, shocked. She had been sacked. Out of the blue, she had lost her job. What had she done wrong? She looked in the envelope. It had her cards and her wages; just the right amount for up to three o'clock today.

She looked in the envelope again. No reference. Nothing.

What would she do now? If she was an enemy as he said, how on earth would she get another job?

As the bus passed Di Ciacca's shop in Morrison Street she noticed the window was smashed. The Di Ciacca boys were standing outside in the street with their father. She craned her neck to see what was happening but the bus moved round the corner.

As the news broke, a crowd had gathered outside the Italian Consul's offices at Picardy Place. There were already a lot of police around, as if they were expecting trouble. Four special constables on horseback were approaching from Queen Street.

At about five o'clock a black car drew up. Two uniformed constables and two officials in dark suits and hats, incongruous in the summer heat, pushed through the crowd and banged on the locked door of the Fascio hall.

The two officials stepped aside. The constables broke the door open.

Inside some Italians were hastily tearing down the photograph of Mussolini. Others were setting light to some documents. In the confusion a fire broke out. When they were unable to douse the flames, fire engines were called. Everyone was evacuated from the building. Within minutes, fire engines pulled up outside the Fascio hall and several fire officers tackled the blaze.

Whether this was a trigger for what followed, who knows. The crowd outside now amounted to over a thousand. They stood watching, gauging the mood. They sang patriotic songs and intermittently shouted abuse at Italy and its citizens.

A commotion broke out in the street. A core element of youngsters, egged on by some older men in the crowd, started to move forward in a menacing group.

One of the mounted police shouted over the heads of the crowd.

'Now come on, lads. Let's not have any trouble. Make your way back to your homes. There's to be no trouble.'

A stone flew past the policeman's helmet, knocking it off. His horse reared in fright.

The youths split up and, from the top of Picardy Place, one group moved down Broughton Street, the others went down Leith Street, some spread down Union Place, the others marched down towards Elm Row.

The jeering and shouting began. They picked up sticks and bricks, anything lying around. Some produced knives. Some had guns.

Others joined them, coming from adjoining streets, converging on the trouble-makers. A terrifying aggression built up.

Giovanni Crolla's shop on Union Place was the first to get hit. Inside the shop, getting ready for the night's business, he heard the uproar. He sensed trouble. This is it. This is what he had been afraid of.

He chased his family upstairs. His staff ran out the back door. Not a word was exchanged. He switched off the gas under the fryer, locked the till and pulled the cigarettes off the shelves, hiding them under the counter.

He went to the door and stood with his two sons, all in their clean white overalls, sleeves rolled up, hair smoothed back with Brylcreem, ready for business.

The crowd of youths approached him. It was still light. He could see their faces clearly; at least a handful of them were regular customers.

'Come on, lads. Come on now. What good's this going to do?'

He was really lucky he wasn't hurt. The ringleader yelled at him with unbridled fury and knocked him away from the door.

'Get out of the way, you Italian bastard!'

He fell to the ground, hitting his head. Giovanni's sons went to help their father up. Their mother and sisters were upstairs, barricaded in, hiding away from the windows. The noise outside was terrifying.

The crowd pushed past them into the shop. They smashed the front window, breaking through with metal bars, tore the door from the hinges, kicking it in fury with thick steel-capped boots. They threw the chairs through the engraved glass partitions and wooden frames, demolishing them.

One lad picked up the wooden paddle that Giovanni used to make the batter for the fish. He waved it along the shelves sweeping all the polished sweet jars and sauce bottles from the shelves, smashing them on the tiled floor.

Giovanni's sons pulled their father away from the shop. They stood and watched helplessly as the looting began. Cigarettes, chocolates, a tray of filleted fish, everything was taken. When the men couldn't get the money from the cigarette machine on the wall they battered it with an iron bar until eventually it broke open. They threw the till against the wall, cracking the tiles. As the drawer sprang open they crammed the coins into their pockets.

Seeing more crowds of youths move down Leith Walk, Giovanni thought of his brother.

He called to his son, 'Michael, run down to Alfonso's. Quick. Warn him.'

By the time Michael reached Elm Row it was too late.

The tall Georgian windows of the shop were completely destroyed; the bottles that had been so proudly displayed lay smashed on the ground. Red wine, like a river of blood, flowed down Leith Walk.

The familiar smell of coffee was overpowered by alcohol fumes.

Inside it looked like a slow-motion movie. The coffee dust had risen like a fog. The vandals were climbing up the stout shelves sweeping everything onto the ground.

The looters were selective. They stole bottles of whisky, sherry and brandy. They left the salami, cheese and pasta. No one wanted filthy Italian food.

They disappeared as quickly as they had come, shouting and screaming abuse. They threw bottles as they left, moving on down Leith Walk, to get Costa's, Gasparini's, Capaldi's, Coppola's, Paolozzi's. They knew exactly where all the Italian bastards were. 'The Tallies are in yer face.'

Nearly every Italian business was attacked. Not a scrap of glass remained unbroken, not a stick of furniture undamaged, not a family's livelihood left intact.

At the height of the rioting, the police charged and tried to control the crowds with batons. Mounted police attempted to break up the crowd but it was almost impossible.

Arrests were made, but each patriotic rioter was applauded by the crowd with the National Anthem and patriotic war songs. The hatred manifested against the foreigners was stripped to its ugly core.

Trapped in the back shop at Elm Row, Alfonso and his sons could only watch the carnage outside. Alfonso's lifetime work and ambition were destroyed in minutes. He sat down on the floor, his jacket torn and his white handkerchief smudged with blood dripping from a cut on his face. He put his head in his hands and wept.

'*Ragazzi, mi dispiace.* I'm sorry.'

Vittorio and Domenico put their arms round their father.

'Papà, don't say sorry. It's not your fault. This is nothing to do with you.' Vittorio kissed his father. 'Papà, I saw some pals I know from the football, they're good lads. This is just because of war, Papà. They're terrified. They don't know what's going to happen. We're all cannon fodder. Scots, Germans, French. Italians, we're all in the same boat now.'

Looking up at his son, Alfonso saw a look that reminded him of Olivia. With a start he realised Maria and the girls would not be safe. '*Oh Dio!* The girls! Maria!' The crowd could have gone along to Easter Road.

They ran out of the door, leaving everything. As fast as they could, the three men ran along Montgomery Street, pushing their way through the crowds, gasping for breath.

Vittorio reached the corner first. Maria, Olivia, Gloria and Filomena stood outside the shop in the middle of the road. Mrs Glen, Mary Praties and Lilly Rough stood beside them, crying. A small group of neighbours and customers stood behind them, a few paces apart.

'Papà!' Olivia shouted and ran to her father, her face smeared with black streaks of tears.

'Papà, they broke up the shop! They broke up the shop!'

'Are you all right? Are you all all right? Did they hurt you?'

'No, Mamma made us come outside. She said to let them do what they needed to, we weren't to stop them.'

'Your Mamma's right.'

His other two daughters came to him. He pulled them to himself and held them close. 'Thank God you're safe.'

Domenico came running up from their second shop near the football ground.

'It's too late. Everything's destroyed, Papà. They've smashed everything. It's all over.'

Alfonso looked at his wife. She wasn't crying. It was as if she had been expecting this and it hadn't come as a shock.

'Maria, take the girls home. We'll lock up the shops and come home as soon as we can.'

'Mr Crolla.' It was Jimmy, one of the men that helped in the shop. 'Mr Crolla, you go home. I'll help the boys board up the shops.'

291

In the back of the café the gramophone record-player was stuck. The eerie sound of Gigli singing an aria from La Bohème repeated itself over and over again.

By the time the boys got home, it was dark. The black-out was enforced. It had taken them four hours to go round everything with Jimmy. Lastly they had gone to the warehouse. Thankfully it hadn't been touched. The mob probably didn't know where it was, tucked away in St John's Hill.

On the way round, they saw all their uncles' and friends' shops broken and destroyed. A fire had broken out in a fish and chip shop. The looters had thrown a bottle of lemonade into the hot fat, causing an explosion. People had been taken to hospital.

Vittorio and Domenico found their family in the front room, huddled round the fire. Olivia was sitting by her father, Filomena was on his knee. Gloria sat beside her mother. She had been crying.

Vittorio looked at his father. He was a broken man.

'Thank God you're home. Are you OK?'

'Yes. We're fine. Have you heard from Margherita? Have you managed to get a call through.'

'No, I've been trying all night.'

Domenico sat down, exhausted. 'They've been nearly everywhere, Papà. Up the Royal Mile, down Broughton Street.'

'Surely not? Why? Why? We've never done anything but good here. Nothing but good.'

'Papà, that's what they're afraid of. They are people who don't want good. They are most likely not even Edinburgh people. They are probably organised gangsters, like the ones who rioted the last time. They're trouble-makers.'

Vittorio had seen some familiar faces.

'There were some youngsters I recognised but they were not the ring leaders. Food's been rationed for months. They were just grabbing what they could.'

'I saw quite a few women shouting at them, telling them to stop and leave well alone!'

Alfonoso was worried about his staff.

'What about Miss Dennison? And the staff?'

'They're all fine. They're really worried about us. Miss Dennison said she'll do anything to help.'

Alfonso nodded, relieved. He was broken-hearted. How could Italy be at war with Britain? It had never happened before. He couldn't understand it.

'And Il Duce? Who has double-crossed him? Who has made him lead us into the abyss? Who has betrayed him?'

Maria had no sympathy for him. She was angry at Il Duce. '*He* has betrayed us, Alfonso. He has betrayed you.'

They were all exhausted. It was quieter outside now because of the black-out. They felt safer. At least they were in a top-floor flat. Tomorrow they would decide what to do. They had friends all over Scotland: Italian friends and Scottish friends. Tomorrow they would decide.

'Girls, come and kiss your Papà. Say your prayers with me then kiss your old father.'

After their prayers the girls hugged their father, tenderly kissing him.

Olivia patted his face. 'Don't worry, Papà. We're all together. We can clean up the shops. I'll help. As long as we're all together, nothing can hurt us.'

Alfonso hugged his daughter. Her words tore at his heart. He knew they were not over the worst. But he didn't want her to be afraid. He scrunched her hair with his hand.

'*Capa Nera. Capa Nera.*' he whispered.

28

Maria couldn't sleep. She was waiting. Lying beside her husband, she could do nothing but wait.

She thought she heard the footsteps on the stair.

She waited.

She heard the punch on the door.

Alfonso was asleep beside her. She looked at him. She gently put her cheek beside his. She took a deep breath and smelled his cologne. She gingerly put her hand out and touched him.

He woke at her touch. He moved towards her, reaching out.

The banging on the door was louder this time, hostile.

Alfonso heard it. 'They're here. This is it.'

Vittorio came into his father's bedroom. He didn't knock as normal. Everything had changed. 'Papà, the door.'

Alfonso cupped his hands round his wife's face and kissed her tenderly on the lips.

'*Mi dispiace, cara. Mi dispiace.* Be strong for the girls. *Ti voglio tanto tanto bene.*'

He got out of bed and pulled his trousers over his pyjamas. Maria put a coat over her nightdress.

Alfonso opened the door, keeping the chain on the latch.

A voice came from the other side of the door and a card was pushed through the space. 'Alfonso Crolla?'

'Yes.'

'MI5. Please open the door.'

Alfonso removed the chain and pulled the door open. Three men in dark suits and the local constable from Easter Road pushed past him into the house.

'That's him, sir. That's Alfonso Crolla.'

The four men stood in front of Alfonso's family.

The saw a woman of fifty-two, tired, her greying hair dishevelled, holding her coat protectively over her chest; two, strong, striking young men, in their mid twenties, unshaven, bare-footed and untidy in striped pyjamas; three beautiful young girls, sixteen, fourteen and thirteen, dark hair, sultry skin, big brown eyes, lovely young girls wearing matching, long fine nightdresses with anxious looks on their faces.

'Who is Domenico Crolla?'

'I am.'

'Who is Vittorio Fortunato Crolla?'

'Me.'

'I have a warrant to search the premises.'

'What, at eleven o'clock at night? We've all been in bed. We're hardly going to have anything hidden if we're all asleep.'

'I'm sorry, Mr Crolla.' The constable felt uncomfortable. He knew Mr Crolla. Over the years he'd watched him lay many a peace wreath at the war memorial on Armistice Day.

The senior official in the suit wanted nothing personal to creep into the proceedings. There was a job to be done. This chap's luck was up. He'd played the wrong card.

'Under the authority of the War Office, Alfonso Crolla, I have a warrant for your arrest.

'Domenico Crolla, under the authority of the War Office, I have a warrant for your arrest.

'Vittorio Fortunato Crolla, under the Emergency Powers Defence Act, 1939, section 18b, I have a warrant for your arrest.'

'Mrs Crolla, please stand aside. Right men! Search the place!'

While the girls sat terrified with their mother on the settee, four men turned their home upside down. They tore open cupboards, pulled out clothes and threw them aside, opened boxes, tipped letters and papers on to the floor. Any papers they found were in Italian, the men didn't know what they were. They didn't say what they were looking for. They found nothing.

In the girls' bedroom Olivia's picture of Mussolini was beside her bed, next to the holy picture of the Sacred Heart of Jesus. They took them both. They put her black shirt and Fascio uniform from her holiday into a bag.

In their thoroughness they pulled the sheets and mattresses off the beds, throwing them aside.

Vittorio was furious. 'Why are you doing this? What are you looking for?'

'What's this?' the senior official picked up the Il Duce Silver Cup that was on the mantelpiece.

This was a farce. Vittorio shouted 'For heaven's sake, man. It's a sport's cup. We won it at the tug-of-war!'

The policeman looked at him sympathetically. 'Don't be angry, son. We're at war.'

Vittorio shook his fist in anger. 'I'm not at war! I'm not at war! I'm just a bloody grocer!'

'There's nothing here. Mr Crolla, I'll have to take you and your sons down to the station to ask you a few questions. Please get dressed. You won't need anything. Maybe a change of clothes.'

'Where are you taking them?'

Maria was starting to panic. She had expected they would come for Alfonso. She never dreamt they would take her sons as well.

The policeman saw her shock. 'Now don't worry, Mrs Crolla. They're only coming for questioning.'

Maria went through to the bedroom after Alfonso. She went to close the door but the policeman barred her.

'If you don't mind.' He stood, arms folded, looking straight ahead.

She ignored him and went over to Alfonso who was sitting on the bed, dressed in his suit, struggling to put his socks on. He had a small suitcase at his feet. She sat beside him and put her arms round him. He tried to reassure her.

'*Non ti preoccupare, carissima*. I've done nothing wrong. Everyone in the town council and the police knows me. I've been working with them for years. They know us. Once they see us and ask a few questions we'll be allowed home.'

'And if not?'

'Maria, don't think like that. You must be strong. Trust in God. Say your prayers for me, for us all. I'll be fine. We'll all be fine.'

The girls came through the open door to kiss their father. By now they were distressed and crying: a hideous, gulping crying that tore at Alfonso's heart.

Olivia looked at her father as her sisters held on to him. Clinging to normality she noticed he had forgotten his handkerchief. She

looked around. His drawers were all emptied out. She lifted a handkerchief from the floor. She found his cologne spilt out under the
chest of drawers. She sprinkled some on the linen and tucked it into
his jacket pocket. She patted him reassuringly.

'Here, Papà. You have to look smart.'

The boys dressed quickly. This would be just a formality. It was
too ridiculous. Maybe after the riots the authorities just wanted to
make sure they were all right.

The boys hugged their sisters and their mother.

At the door, Alfonso embraced each of his sons. He whispered
to them in the dialect of the shepherds of Fontitune, '*Figlio mio,
attenzione. Non dire una parola a questi Scozzezi. Chi sa quello
che succede.*'

He followed his sons through the door. He turned round and
looked at his loyal wife and his three beautiful daughters looking
on with disbelief at what was happening.

'Now, girls,' he said, 'be good to your mother, or I won't come
back!'

He turned and walked down the stairs.

When Alfonso came out into the street he found a huddle of
other Italians, all pulled from their beds like him. Alfonso was
outraged. What in hell's name was going on! Like criminals they
were marched up Montgomery Street, the stragglers from the earlier
rioting standing by, jeering and yelled insults.

'Italian traitors. Tally bastards. Papes!'

The vitriol and fury spewed at them were hideous. It was as if
years of frustration and anger had come to a head and exploded.

Not everyone was against them. Many, mostly women, shouted
in anger at the protesters, mortified at their display of hatred and
xenophobia.

'You should be ashamed! They've done nothing wrong. It's
Mussolini that's to blame. Not them.'

Gayfield Square Police Station was pandemonium. There were
about a hundred Italians jammed into cells and interview rooms,
each becoming more distressed as they spotted a relative or friend.
Emidio and Giovanni were there, Achille Crolla, Donato and
Ferdinando, the Paolozzis, the Pias, the D'Agostinos, the Coppolas.

Practically all the chip shop owners and ice cream makers of

Edinburgh were now in Gayfield Police Station, indiscriminately branded as desperate enemy aliens, dangerous characters, a threat to public safety.

All of them had the same thought. What the hell was going on?

At about the same time as Maria had heard the thump on the door, a Black Maria police van drew up outside the Cockenzie Café.

Three men got out. They were dressed in dark suits, their hats pulled down, shielding their eyes. One man stayed at the open car door, the other two climbed the outside stair to the front door.

Anna had not been able to sleep, anxious about the news. When she heard the loud knock on the door she ran to it and opened it, almost relieved. Who would come round at this time of night?

'What's wrong? Has something happened?'

The oldest man showed her an identity card and asked to be allowed in.

Confused, Anna nodded.

The man nodded to the bottom of the stair, where Anna saw the black car. In the dim moonlight of the summer night she saw the shadows of some people, a few more silent figures coming down School Lane. What were they doing out at this time of night?

Johnny came to the door, alerted by the noise.

'What's this? What's happened at this time of night?'

The men shepherded him back into the house.

Anna went to get her father. Johnny led the men into the living room. It was dark. He fumbled to find the light switch.

Cesidio and Marietta came through, dressed in their night clothes. Alex followed, still sleepy, rubbing his eyes.

The older man in the dark suit spoke.

'Mr Kes . . .' He hesitated, he was annoyed with himself. These foreign names put you at a disadvantage to start with.

The second man took the paper from him.

'Mr Cesidio Di Ciacca. I have a warrant for your arrest. And,' he looked across at Marietta who was standing with her hand over her mouth, '. . . for Alessandro Di Ciacca.'

Alex looked at his mother. What was the man talking about?

Why were they saying his name? He had been born here. He was British. He was only sixteen.

'Dad?'

'There must be some mistake. Alex is only sixteen. What do you want him for?'

Alex was horrified. Terrified. Why did they want to take him? Who were they anyway?

'Dad! It's a mistake. It's Johnny you want. My brother. It'll be him you want.' Alex didn't understand. He had never experienced cold-blooded fear before. Not until now. He broke out in a cold sweat. He felt dizzy. He almost vomited.

'Dad! Help me, dad! They can't take me.'

Johnny put his arm round his younger brother.

'Alex, it's a mistake. Calm down. It'll be all right.' He spoke to the older man. 'You're making a big mistake. Alex is only a boy. If they want anyone it will be me. I'm twenty. I'm the one born in Italy, not him.'

Marietta, seeing the terror on her youngest, agreed.

'It's a mistake. Take Johnny. He'll be able to stick up for himself. This has nothing to do with Alex.'

The official sensed there must be a mistake but there was nothing he could do. These instructions were directly from the War Office in London. He had no power at all. They were on a war footing. He had no option but to obey instructions to the letter.

The second detective took over. 'I'm sorry. There is no discussion on the matter. Please get dressed, bring a change of clothes and a toothbrush, that's all you'll need. Hurry please, we have more work to do tonight.'

Marietta followed Alex into his room and helped him get his things together. She gave him some money, two ten-pound notes. 'Alex, hide this, in different places in your clothes. Don't tell anybody. We'll go to the police tomorrow and the Consul in Picardy Place and get you released.'

She went through to her bedroom and found Cesidio on his knees. She knelt with him and finished his last prayer with him. They embraced. She kissed him as if she would never see him again, passionately and with all her love. Through her tears she tried to laugh. 'Now, remember, when you come back I'll finish off that kiss.'

299

He held her close and kissed her again.

'*Amore mio*, it will be fine. They've nothing on me. We'll get out of this.'

'Look after Alex.'

'Don't worry. They can't keep a sixteen-year-old boy who was born in Scotland and whose mother was born in London. We're in Britain, not Nazi Germany. And at least Johnny is still here so you'll have him to help you get this sorted out. Go and see Alex Craig in the morning. He'll help us.'

The whole situation was ridiculous. They couldn't believe it.

'Can you hurry up, please.' The detective was becoming agitated.

When they came into the sitting room again, Anna and Lena were crying, Alex was hugging his sisters, visibly shocked. Johnny went over to his father.

'Dad, I'll come and find you tomorrow. Don't worry. I'll come and get you.'

Cesidio had fought in the First World War. He knew that tomorrow was no longer a guarantee for any of them. He held his oldest son close and kissed him.

'*Ci vediamo domani, figlio mio*. I'll see you tomorrow, son. Tomorrow.'

After he had kissed his daughters and his wife, Cesidio's courage almost deserted him: 'God bless you all.'

He put his arm around Alex's shoulder. They went together out of the door. He stopped at the top of the stair. Down below was a silent crowd of about two hundred, all his friends.

One of them shouted up, 'We'll look after the women, Sis. Don't you worry about them.'

Cesidio's eyes filled up with tears. He started to walk down the stairs behind his young son. Half-way down he stopped and looked back at his wife and three children: 'God Bless you.'

Then he looked at his customers and friends of the last twenty years. He shivered: 'God Bless you all! God Bless the King!'

In the back of the car, Alex wept. He sat close to his father, who whispered constantly to him to give him courage. He knew he would be all right. They drove to Edinburgh. In the dark, with only slits of light from the headlamps, it took over an hour. When they passed along the sea road at the winding bends on the way into Musselburgh, Alex was terrified that the car would fall into the sea.

The car swept past Arthur's Seat and up the Royal Mile. Cesidio started to have a sense of foreboding.

'Alex, remember, whatever happens, your mother and I love you. You know that don't you?'

Before Alex could answer, the car drew to a halt. The detective in the front got out and opened the door on Alex's side. He looked inside.

'Get out lad. Bring your case.'

Alex got out. He was in the middle of the square in front of St Giles' Cathedral. He recognised the Mercat Cross; he had laid a wreath there once with Zio Alfonso.

A policeman put his hand on his shoulder.

Alex looked round at the car, waiting for his father to get out.

The detective slammed the door shut and, banging the roof of the car twice, signalled for it to drive away.

Back in Cockenzie, after crying inconsolably, Marietta and the girls had fallen asleep all huddled together in Marietta's bed. Johnny had convinced them it was all a terrible mistake. The best thing to do was to get some rest. It was pitch black outside; it was impossible to do anything until it was light.

They would get up very early and get to Edinburgh first thing. Zio Alfonso would know what was going on. He would be able to help them.

Of course, Johnny couldn't get to sleep. His mind was racing. What really was going on? Why had they taken Alex and not him? Why had they come through the night? He walked up and down, up and down.

When he eventually sat down on the settee, he fell into an exhausted sleep.

Loud shouting outside in the street woke him. He hurried to the window at the front and looked out. It was barely light. Below he could see the Black Maria. The officials were back again.

Some locals were shouting.

'Leave the laddie alane. For God's sake, man. They've done nothing wrong.'

Johnny saw the men climb the stairs to his house.

So, they'd come back for him. He got dressed. By the time they were all awakened again by the knock on the door, the second time that evening, he was ready to go.

Before he let them in, he went to the kitchen, to his mother's cupboard, and took a bar of Cadbury's chocolate, hiding it in his trouser pocket. He grabbed a handful of notes from the sugar bowl in which Marietta hid her housekeeping money.

Anna had opened the door and was crying, shouting at the men.

'Anna, don't worry. I'm glad they've come. I'll find Dad and Alex quicker. We'll get them released. Mum, go in to Edinburgh tomorrow. Go to Picardy Place and see the Consul and go to see Zio Alfonso. He'll be able to help.'

Marietta was distraught. '*Madonna mia*! My husband and both my sons! I'm a British citizen. I've only lived four years in Italy all my life! Look, I'll get my passport.'

She couldn't understand. She collapsed again in tears, all her courage deserting her. The men were waiting at the door, embarrassed that they had had to come back. They didn't want to look incompetent. They wanted to get away as soon as possible.

Johnny kissed his mother and reassured her. 'Mum, this is better. I'll be fine. I'll find Dad and Alex. I've got some money. When I see them, I'll give it to them. We'll be home by lunch time.'

'Give this to Cesidio, he forgot it.' She pushed a one-inch metal container into his hands. He didn't need to look. He knew what it was, his father's figurine of St Francis carrying the baby Jesus.

'Give it to your father when you see him.'

He embraced his sisters. Then Johnny, the handsome, carefree charismatic boy that everyone loved was taken from his home, branded as an enemy alien.

It was dawn as he walked down the stairs. The crowd were still at the bottom of the stairs; they had been standing guard, protecting their friends all night.

Alex Craig, out of uniform, was standing apart from the crowd. He shouted across:

'Don't worry, lad.'

Others in the crowd called out:

'Johnny, come back soon, lad.'

'Good luck, find yer dad and yer brother!'

'Good luck, lad!'

Someone started to sing . . . 'Will ye no come back again . . .'
Others joined in.

Marietta stood at the top of the stairs with her two daughters,
in their night clothes, and wept. In the space of a few hours her
world had been ripped apart. The country she had left years ago
had imposed its power and ruined her life, from thousands of miles
away.

29

The next morning, after a sleepless night, when Marietta heard a knock again she rushed to the door. That must be Cesidio and the boys home. Thank God. She knew it had all been a mistake.

She was devastated when she saw Constable Craig standing with his helmet under his arm.

'Mary, Can I come in?'

They hadn't opened the shop. The milk delivery was still lying at the back door. Margaret, Jeannie and Tommy Dougal were all in the front room, just as distraught as Anna and Lena at the night's developments.

'Come in, Alex. Come in please. I'm so glad to see you. Where are they? Do you know where they've been taken? Why have they been taken?'

'I am not at liberty to say. I don't know where they are. Honestly, Mary, I don't know. It's Mussolini. It's him declaring war. You've all been classed as enemy aliens.'

Anna was incensed. Anger was taking over from fear. It was Italy that had declared war, not them.

'What do you mean "enemy aliens"? Mum was born in London. Alex and I were born here. You know us. We're no more enemy aliens than you are!'

'I am only doing my job, Anna. I know this is not right but I have my instructions.'

'What do you mean instructions? What instructions?' Lena was listening to all this and was beginning to get really frightened. Of the three of them left, Lena was the only one who had been born in Italy. The policeman hadn't come to see if they were all right. He'd come to take her away. She sat down shocked, deadly white with dread. What was going to happen next?

'Mary, I have instructions from the War Office. I am sorry but you have to go. You have to leave the coast, to move at least thirty miles away.'

Marietta didn't understand. What did he mean? What did leave the coast mean?

'Is that where they are? Away from the coast?'

'I don't know where they are. I just know that you and the girls have to leave. You have fourteen days to get organised and then you have to report to the police station to tell me where you're going. Meanwhile I have to confiscate the wireless from the shop, and any maps you might have.'

Now Anna was confused.

'If we have to leave the coast, why can my dad not come with us?'

'Anna, I'm not allowed to say anything.'

'Please, tell us what's going on. Why are we enemy aliens? What does it mean?'

'Anna, there's a war on. The forces have just crawled back from Dunkirk. The Germans are on the coast of France getting ready to invade. Your country has just declared war. What do you expect? The government doesn't have time to talk to every person.'

He lost his temper. He couldn't believe he was doing this to his friends. He was caught up in this whole mess as well.

'We're at war! At war! Don't you understand?' He calmed down a bit. He lowered his voice.

'Mary, I shouldn't be telling you this but my wife, Ines, her uncle, Tognieri in Dunbar. He's been lifted as well.'

Anna was stunned. She started to cry. She looked at her mother, incredulous.

'But, Mum, don't they know? *This* is our country.'

In Brunton Place the same scenario was played out. Two detectives called on Maria and issued her with an instruction to leave the city within fourteen days. They confiscated her wireless and refused to give her any information about her husband and sons. Her English was so poor her daughters had to translate every word.

The shops were lying empty with smashed windows and broken doors. Most of the stock had been looted. Miss Dennison had come along in the morning asking for instructions. Maria didn't know what to do. She was left with three young daughters, three wrecked shops and an instruction to leave her home.

They tried to telephone the Consul, Gayfield Square Police Station, then Margherita in Glasgow, all to no avail.

Miss Dennison asked permission to employ a carpenter to board up the shops. She asked Maria if she had any cash to pay the man. Maria had a little money but was reluctant to hand it over. She refused and told Miss Dennison to write a cheque.

'Mrs Crolla, there's no money. I've been warning Mr Crolla over the last year. Most of the Italians owe him money. Their shops have all been destroyed. He's not going to get any of it now, is he?'

Maria looked at Miss Dennison. The two women did not really get on with each other but they both knew Alfonso. His heart ruled his actions, not his brain.

The carpenter refused to take a cheque and Maria had to give the man a quarter of her cash.

Olivia went with Miss Dennison to watch the front of the shop in Elm Row get boarded up. Olivia was shocked when she saw the shop. Everything was ruined. Between them they swept up and tried to clear the broken debris from the shop. As the man nailed secure boarding at the front, Olivia couldn't understand how Mussolini had betrayed them all. Someone must have betrayed him. The banging of each nail made her shudder. She felt the man was striking her with every stroke.

Maria spent most of the day outside the police station in Gayfield Square, with Gloria and Filomena. There were at least thirty other Italian women there, all in various states of distress: Giovanni's wife, Preziosa, now over sixty years old, Emidio's wife, Carolina, Achille's wife, all of them. When Olivia came across she was devastated to see her friend Vera standing forlornly with her mother. She embraced her friend.

'Olivia, they've taken my father.'

Olivia didn't have the courage to say the same words out loud.

When Marietta got off the tram with Anna and Lena at Picardy Place, they were relieved to see Maria. Marietta rushed across the street.

'Oh! Maria. Thank God. Where's Alfonso? I need to talk to him. They've taken the men.'

Maria looked at Marietta and burst into tears. She couldn't get a word out. Olivia was forced to speak up. She took a deep breath to stop herself from crying. 'Zia Marietta, they've taken Papà as well, and my brothers. We don't know where they are. We don't know anything.'

Anna put her arms round Olivia. They clung to each other and wept.

'I thought Zio Alfonso could help us. Now he has gone, who will look after us?'

Some of the women whispered to Maria that one of their sons, or their father or husband, had not been picked up. Each had gone into hiding. Tonight they would sleep in the park or go into the country to avoid being caught.

They noticed a few of the women were absent. Rumours flew around that some had been arrested as well. This added a further wave of fear. What if they took the women next? What if they were separated from their daughters and younger children?

The Archbishop and two of the priests came to the police station to object to what was going on and to protest at the treatment of the women and their families. They were told in no uncertain terms to keep out of it.

The Consul had kept out of it. He and his officials were nowhere to be seen. Perhaps he had been arrested as well.

Many women had babies or young children; a few were pregnant. Most of them had very little cash and no means of getting money from their husbands' bank accounts, assuming their husbands had money in bank accounts. It had happened so quickly. No one was prepared. Every family was affected. Every family was shattered.

Maria realised there was nothing to be done.

'Come back to the house, Marietta. There's no good staying here.'

That night, the rioting broke out again, though thankfully on a lesser scale. In Brunton Place, they prayed incessantly, rosary after rosary. Maria's faith was stretched to the limit. Had her God deserted her? Every hour that passed, her despair increased. She was desperate not to leave her home in case Alfonso came back or tried to get in touch.

On the third night, they barricaded themselves in again. There was nothing to do but pray.

There was another loud knock on the door. The girls and their mother screamed in terror. What now?

Olivia opened it, her mother standing behind her. Two policemen stood on the landing.

'Mrs Crolla, may I come in. I have a warrant to search the house.'

Olivia spoke up. It was the local policeman. She recognised him from the shop.

'My mother doesn't speak English very well. What are you looking for? They searched the house on Monday night; turned it upside down. They didn't find anything.'

The policeman felt uncomfortable.

'Olive, I'm sorry, my dear, I've to look for a wireless.'

'Why? They took it away. We don't have one.'

'Well, there have been reports that you,' he lowered his voice, aware that the walls had ears, 'that you are sending radio messages to Italy. That you are spies.'

Olivia shook her head, incredulously. What was he talking about?

He continued, 'There are reports of mumbling in Italian every night at exactly six o'clock for at least an hour.'

The other policeman nodded.

'You can't deny what three people have reported, Miss Crolla. There are witnesses. And we heard something just now, before we knocked.'

Olivia was no older than his own daughter. Her eyes were large and shocked in her pale, beautiful face. He felt very sorry for her.

'It's our rosary!' She shouted at him, furious that three people had reported them. 'We are not spies. We pray our rosary every night at six o'clock. Listen, listen.'

Terrified, she started to pray, nodding at her sisters to join in.

'*Madre di Dio, prega per noi, peccatori, adesso e nell'ora della nostra morte, Amen.*'

They chanted the words in Italian, over and over again, just as they had been doing, non-stop.

Gloria's voice was shaking. Filomena burst into tears.

'Please,' Olivia was distraught, 'please, just leave us alone.'

*

After being separated from his father, Alex had been driven to the west end of town. He noticed high-security gates of a large compound. They drove through.

In a stark room, two officials behind a desk asked him questions, looking down all the time at forms and lists in front of them.

'Name?'

'Alessandro Di Ciacca.'

'Date of birth.'

'19 September 1923.'

'What age are you?'

'Sixteen.'

The two men looked at each other, not saying a word.

Alex was petrified. They'd taken him from his father. He was completely alone. He was afraid to say anything unless he antagonised them. It was two in the morning. They were not exactly in a good mood.

The questioning went on. Who was his father? Who was his mother? Where was he born? Where were they born?

Was he a member of the Italian Fascist Party?

Alex's stomach lurched. He'd been on holiday to Italy two years ago but that was all.

He didn't answer. He didn't know what the answer was.

They took him to a shower room and told him to strip and scrub himself. They searched him and shaved his hair. He was issued with two sets of prison underwear, shirts and a pair of trousers. On top, one man piled a set of bed linen. He was marched along a stark, concrete corridor with one electric light bulb dangling from the ceiling and pushed into a cell.

The door was slammed shut. He heard the key turn in the door.

The light was switched off and he was left alone.

On the fourth day, Margherita managed to get through to Olivia from Glasgow on the telephone. She was panic-stricken.

'Olivia, Olivia, get Papà. The police have taken Tony and his father and all his brothers. I've been trying to call. Tell Dad to come. I'm here with my mother-in-law and my sister-in-law. They've wrecked the shops. Get Papà. Please. Let me talk to him.'

After that, Maria and the girls decided the best thing was to go through to Glasgow. They would stay with Margherita until they found out what was going on. They started to prepare.

Rumours spread. A picture of what had happened gradually began to emerge. Newspapers reported riots in other cities, all over the country, London, Manchester, Liverpool, Ayr. Reports said Churchill had given the instruction to 'collar the lot!' and that the 'enemy Italians' had been 'combed out'. Internment of all Italian males between the ages of 17 and 60, or 16 and 70 (the reports were confusing), internment without trial, without a lawyer, without a tribunal, without rights.

The War Cabinet were expecting an invasion by Germany any day. They were obsessed with the thought of a Fifth Column, a group of dangerous enemies living within their midst. They saw no alternative but to ensure that all possible sympathisers were off the streets.

The locals in Cockenzie were also devastated and were trying all they could to break through the official silence. It was easier for then to get formation. After three days Anna got a hint from Alex Craig.

'There are Italians in Donaldson's Hospital in Edinburgh. Your dad and brothers might be there.'

A glimmer of hope like this was such a relief. At last she could do something. Immediately Anna made her way up to Edinburgh by bus. Marietta wasn't fit to travel. Lena stayed with her mother and waited anxiously for Anna to return.

Anna got to the gates of the hospital, a large imposing Victorian building set in extensive grounds, early in the afternoon. She was barred from entering by two soldiers with rifles.

'Stop. No civilian entry, miss.'

'Where can I go to find out if my father is here?'

'Ask over there at the sentry box.'

Anna went across, nervous. Even if he was locked up, at least they would know where he was, that he was safe. Just to know something would be better than this agony of knowing nothing.

'Excuse me, Sergeant; I am looking for my father and my brothers.'

'What's their names, miss?'

'Cesidio Di Ciacca, from Cockenzie. And Johnny, Giovanni Di

310

Ciacca, he's my brother. Alex Di Ciacca, he's my brother too.'

She pulled out the family picture that they had had taken at the dance last August. It seemed like a lifetime away.

'That's them, there, there.' She pointed to the images staring back at her.

The soldier looked down long lists of papers he had in front of him.

'I'm sorry, miss. No Cesidio here.'

'Are you sure? Have you seen him?'

'Here he is. He's on this list. He's gone. You've missed him. He was transported out early this morning.'

'Transported? What does that mean? Transported where?'

Anna slumped forward almost unconscious with shock. The soldier was embarrassed. This had been going on all week.

She shook herself.

'What about my brothers?'

'Nothing. I'm sorry, miss.'

'Please. Check the lists again. Look.' She pushed the photograph in front of him again.

'They're not on my lists. Now, move along. You shouldn't wait here. Move along please.'

'Where have you taken him? Where has he gone? Please. Please.'

The soldier lifted his gun. He pointed it over her head. His instructions were to avoid any scenes. Discourage any histrionics from the women. He shouted so loud that Anna jumped.

'Move along!'

Anna's lead had been correct but it was too late.

After more than fourteen days of waiting, crying, phoning, praying, a small card, marked with the censor's blue cross, dropped through Maria's letterbox. It read: 'Mamma. In Saughton Prison. Am OK. No sign Papà or Dom. Girls, keep your heads. Love, Vittorio.'

The same day Marietta got a note from Alex.

'Mum, frightened. In jail. On my own. Can't see Dad. Ask Johnny to help me. Alex.'

The word 'frightened' was crossed through with a blue crayon.

Both mothers were grief-stricken. Each now knew they had one son in prison. But they had no clue as to where their husband or older sons were. What could be worse than prison? Why were the authorities not telling them anything? Were would this end?

When he had been arrested, Johnny had been taken to Donaldson's Hospital very early in the morning. His name was on a list, another list of many lists.

After three or four days he still hadn't seen his father, or his brother. Either of them might have been in the next cell, the next hall, the next building, but he never saw them. The chocolate had been confiscated when he arrived, along with his money and the gold chain he had round his neck. He hid the small figurine in his pocket. They didn't find that.

At the same time as the War Office was detaining Italians without trial, the court rooms of Edinburgh were full of youths arrested for rioting and looting, being fined and imprisoned for stealing from the 'enemy'. The newspapers were full of such reports. Everyone was on edge, in a state of near panic. It felt as if the evil of the European War was on their front doorsteps.

Nicol Bruce, Alfonso's friend, bravely wrote to newspapers to decry the hooliganism and cowardly attacks on the Italians. He still didn't know where any of his friends were or, if he did, he wasn't saying.

Miss Dennison agreed to manage the Elm Row business until the men were released. She knew there was stock locked safely in the warehouse. With food shortages and rationing, there would be a good market for the produce; she could keep her job and some income for the family. Mrs Glen and the girls moved to Elm Row to help. They boarded up the ice cream shops, instructed the lawyer to try to sell them and waited to see what would happen.

Maria was grateful and trusting of the women. She and the girls packed a few bags and prepared to travel to Glasgow, queuing up on the railway station platform, as many people did, coming and going in and out of their lives, during wartime.

In Glasgow, the desperate search for information continued. They went every day to the Consul's office, wrote letters to the police, Church and the authorities but still there was no news. They scanned the newspapers for information. The Brazilian Embassy was handling news for Italians in Britain so Olivia and Gloria took it

312

in turn to wait there every day to see if any news would come through.

A sense of hopelessness took over. Exhaustion and depression took hold.

In Cockenzie, Marietta had left for Peebles, leaving Jimmy Caulder in charge of the shop. The minister, Mr Osborne, eventually managed to prove that she was a British citizen, thankfully, and got her a withdrawal of the Evacuation Order. Soon, she and the girls were allowed home.

But there was no respite for the gnawing worry of not knowing. They counted the days. One became two, two became twelve and twelve became twenty. They started to give up hope. Not knowing anything about their husbands and their eldest sons was insufferable. They started to despair.

In Saughton prison, after a couple of weeks, the Commandant gradually realised that he was actually holding a bunch of harmless shopkeepers. There was nothing much he could do, but the regime did become slightly less strict. The men at least were allowed to have open cell doors, move around and talk to each other.

Vittorio and Alex were in Hall C with about a hundred other men, mostly young like themselves. They were all born in Britain, all with an Italian parent. They had been arrested under the 18b Regulation of the Emergency War Powers Act and were in limbo. They had no rights to lawyers or home visits, they just had to wait until they were told what was happening to them.

They were all afraid for their lives and worried about the fate of their mothers and sisters outside alone, and their fathers and older brothers, wherever they were.

Seven or eight boys were sixteen, like Alex. Olivia's classmate Eduardo and her friend Vera's brother Ernie were there. The older lads tried to look after them. They should not be in prison. They applied to the Commandant to try to get them released, but no one was going anywhere.

Gossip went around that some Italian girls had been arrested and were housed with the local female prisoners. This made some of the men angry; but there was nothing they could do.

Maria and the girls had been allowed to visit Vittorio before they left for Glasgow. He was thinner, but looked well enough, though slightly odd in his prison uniform and with a shaved head. He was still trying to reassure them.

'Mamma, I'm sure it's not so bad. I've heard that Domenico and Papà are in a different prison because they are classed as aliens, not under this 18b thing, like me. It's seems to be only those who were born in Britain that are in this group. There's about a hundred of us. The guards are OK. Now that they've realised we're not dangerous criminals, just shopkeepers, they're a bit more lenient.

'Olivia, you look after mum and the girls. You're the oldest in the family until Papà, Domenico and I get back. You can tell Vera that Ernie is all right.'

He went on to tell them who was in the prison, who looked well, who had escaped detention.

'Tell Miss Dennison to carry on as best she can. If she can, tell her to sell the cars. Even if we get out of prison we'll not be allowed to drive.'

When they left, embracing and kissing each other, they felt better. It was such a relief seeing him, knowing he was all right. If only they knew where Alfonso and Domenico were, they could cope better.

They would have been devastated if they had known the truth.

When they left, Vittorio broke down and wept. He was incarcerated and trapped; his freedom had been taken away and he felt angry that his father and brother were not accounted for. He was terrified he would never see them again. How could he let his mother know how he felt? They all had to hide their feelings now, or they would go mad.

30

15 June 1940

After four days incarcerated alone in a cell in Donaldson's Hospital, Alfonso found himself in a queue with several of his friends, climbing onto buses. It was very early in the morning, three o'clock. It seemed everything was done under cover of darkness.

He was shocked to see so many of them. He anxiously searched for a glimpse of his sons but could see no sign. He had heard nothing, seen no one for four days. His heart pounded. He caught sight of his brothers, Giovanni and Emidio. Poor Emidio. He'd barely been back in the country a year. If he'd known this would happen he'd have stayed in Italy. At least they were together. He hoped to God his sons were together as well.

He had been frantic with worry, especially about Maria and the girls. He struggled to push the images of the rioters from his mind. Having seen so many of the Italian men and boys arrested in the police station, torturous thoughts that all the women and girls were alone haunted him. In waves of despair, he implored the Holy Virgin to protect his girls.

Seeing his brothers gave him the illusion of ordinariness, though there was nothing ordinary about being driven in buses under armed guard from his home town. They were forbidden to talk or look at each other, but as the men recognised each other they gave terse nods of acknowledgement. Instinctively they knew it was safer to give their captors least cause to react, not to let them know what they were thinking.

After a couple of hours winding along country roads, the buses turned off the road into a barbed wire encampment at Woodhouselee, near Penicuik. Standing lined up at the sides of the buses with their suitcases and bags, Alfonso and his fellow captives noted the heavy military presence; armed soldiers were patrolling the grounds. They were under military control.

At the sight of the row upon row of canvas tents, Alfonso was struck by the thought of Olivia visiting the camps in Italy. How could he have taken such a risk? What if Italy had declared war while she was away? What if she had been stranded? He felt overwhelmed by his own stupidity, his gullibility.

After the roll call they took their allotted sleeping areas, ten to a tent on straw mattresses. Now they were free to walk around. It looked as though a lot of the older Italians had been transported together. First he found his brothers. They embraced, relieved that they were all safe.

Zio Benny from Newhaven was there. He was nearly seventy. What was he likely to do to harm anybody? There was Donato Crolla, Ferdinando, Pia, Paolozzi, De Marco . . . The authorities had done a good job; he'd give them that.

Then he saw other friends from around the country, customers that he visited in his van. Ferrari, Kirkcaldy; Fontana, Carlisle; Felloni, Aberdeen; Fusco, Dundee; Togneri, Dunbar! My God, not a town had been missed, not a family overlooked.

Alfonso was overwhelmed by the scale of the arrests. It appeared that they had lifted everyone.

When Alfonso saw Cesidio, he rushed towards him, embracing him warmly.

'So you're here as well, Cesidio? Did they come to your house in Cockenzie?'

'Yes, Alfonso, they lifted me and Alex. I don't understand. He's just a boy.' Cesidio broke down. 'Alfonso, I don't know where he is. They took him from the car in the centre of Edinburgh. That's the last time I saw him. He was crying, he was so frightened.'

Alfonso felt anger welling up. This was so very cruel.

'What about Johnny?'

'They left him behind with Marietta and the girls. I don't know what's going on.' Cesidio looked at his friend. 'Where are your sons?'

'They lifted Vittorio and Domenico with me, but I haven't seen them for four days.'

'Alfonso, can you not do something? We've had no chance to get

316

word to the women. Do you think they know we're all right? They'll be worried sick.'

'I've tried, Cesidio. I've tried. I keep demanding to talk to the camp commandant. They won't tell me anything. I don't know what's happening any more than you do. I've heard we're going to the Isle of Man. Someone said we're going to Liverpool.'

Achille Crolla came across. They embraced.

'Cesidio, I'm sorry. I heard they lifted your Alex? They took my Ernie as well.'

Cesidio and Achille held each other. Both their youngest sons were just sixteen.

'Please God they're together.'

They were all becoming more angry. Where in hell's name was the Italian Government now? Everyone demanded answers from Alfonso. He couldn't help them. He knew no more than they did. His contacts and friends in the Council and Consulate had disappeared into the ether. Most likely they had all been arrested as well.

They were all in the same boat.

Between bouts of fury, they held their own council, trying to be strong for each other. Sitting eating stale bread and jam, their first food for twelve hours, they were terrified of what was happening at home, and of what was ahead for them.

News that the rioting had been all over the country, not just in their own towns, was a bad sign. The whole of Britain had come out against Italy. They were all shocked that the anti-Italian feeling was so strong. There hadn't been rioting like this when Germany had declared war last September. Why was there so much fury against them?

The next day, more busloads of men arrived, this time from Glasgow. Cesidio's brother Louis showed up. He had his young son, Harry, with him, a boy the same age as Alex and Ernie.

'How did you get to keep Harry with you, Louis?'

'Just a stroke of luck, by the looks of things. They told him to come with me and that was that.'

They didn't understand. There appeared to be no rhyme nor reason for who was in the camp. Some people Alfonso knew had been in the Fascio with him, but there were just as many, like Cesidio, who had never joined. There were teachers, doctors and a few lawyers, men born in France, Britain and Italy.

There were hundreds of men already there when they arrived, and buses and cars were bringing more all the time. Not just immigrant Italians, also Italian merchant seamen, German internees and German prisoners of war. Cesidio thought he saw the three German airmen who had come down in the Forth last year. As the camp filled up, new groups of internees arriving were housed in separate areas, so no fresh news was passed on. Hunger was becoming a real issue as more men were arriving while the allocation of food remained unchanged.

They had nothing to do but walk around aimlessly and talk. Were the Germans going to invade? Maybe they already had? What a fool Mussolini was to side with Hitler.

It was ironic that Italy had been doing a roaring trade between the warring parties for the last ten months and would have done very well by staying neutral throughout the war. Some men had heard that Churchill had offered plenty of incentives to achieve this end and was now furious with Mussolini for rejecting all chances to avoid this horror that he had plunged Europe into.

Many of the men of Alfonso's age or older had sons fighting with the British forces. One of the men saw his son on guard duty at the gate. He ran shouting to alert him but was pulled crying from the barbed wire. He never saw his son again.

No newspapers, wireless or communication were allowed from the outside. The men weren't even allowed to send a card home to their wives. Sitting day after day incarcerated in the camps, they felt betrayed.

After about eight days, without warning, a group of them were called by their prisoner number and instructed to gather their belongings. They lined up at the gates, a motley crew of over two hundred. Alfonso looked around. They had been living and sleeping in their clothes, sharing a couple of latrines and a few cold-water taps to wash with. Their clothes were decidedly the worse for wear.

'Now we really look like "filthy Eyeties",' he thought wryly.

The camp commandant issued instructions.

'Married men to the left, single men and sailors to the right.'

Then he repeated the instruction in German, and in Italian.

Most of Alfonso's friends were married; the younger sons were not with them. They all stepped to the left. Families tried to stay

318

together, so they moved to the same side. A sense of apprehension settled over them. The cards were being dealt again.

The first group moved forward to take their places on the waiting buses. Cesidio and Alfonso climbed the steps.

'Stop!'

The sergeant put his gun forward, barring the way for Harry to climb the steps. A fresh-faced young boy, thin and lanky, the colour drained from Harry's face.

'You're in the wrong group, lad. You're not married. Move to the right.'

'No. No, please. I want to stay with my father.' Harry started to panic. He had to stay with his father. He couldn't go to the right.

'Move, lad, come on.'

Louis stepped forward. Without hesitation he pushed his hand forward and pushed something into the sergeant's hand.

'Let him be, man.'

Before the sergeant could stop him, Louis pushed his son up the stairs of the bus. The men behind moved faster, pushing their way on to the bus. It would be more hassle to get the young man off; Harry was lucky again.

As the buses pulled out of the camp and drove south, the men were subdued. God knew what was ahead of them.

Warth Mills, near Bury in Lancashire, was a decaying cotton factory, disused for over ten years. Two acres of uninhabitable wasteland became home for three thousand prisoners. There was no electricity or heating, filthy dug-out latrines for toilets and cold taps of running water for hundreds of men to use to wash or drink.

Issued with a straw mattress and a single blanket, the men made a bed wherever they could find a space. Oil, grease and old rusting equipment made an odious, dank environment. At night, rain dripped through the rotting roof and rats scurried around.

Seven-foot-high barbed wire fencing separated the men into groups; heavily armed guards punished the inmates severely if fights broke out over lack of food.

Alfonso and his relatives stuck together, terrified of being separated. Now they thanked God their sons were not with them. Poor Harry, he shouldn't see this squalor. Night after night passed, more

319

and more men arrived. Surely they weren't going to be kept here? It was inhuman.

The men gradually became weak; their food allocation was meagre. Illness broke out: dysentery and chest infections. Each day was spent queuing for food, for water, for use of the vile latrines. Each night was even worse, with men moaning and coughing, some crying, calling out their prayers to the Madonna, disoriented and distressed.

Surely this couldn't be where they were going to be kept? Surely this wasn't a British camp?

Alfonso still had fight in him. He spoke to the guards repeatedly.

'What's this all about? We have rights. At least to let our families know where we are? At least feed us enough food. Give the sick medication. Let us have a chance to wash, clean our clothes.'

'It's war, mate. Our soldiers have just crawled back from being slaughtered in France. Nobody cares about bloody Italians.'

Men turned up from other parts of the country, from London, from Manchester. The young Italian priest, Father Rossi, who had been in Glasgow last year, arrived. He had been on holiday in Manchester, and had been traced all the way from Glasgow. He had been arrested during the night at the church he was visiting.

Perhaps it was best that Alfonso didn't know that by now Domenico had also arrived in Warth Mills. He had been transported south two or three days after his father, and was in another part of the prison with other young men, enduring the same inhumane conditions.

It was now almost eighteen days since any news of their families, since they had been fed a decent meal, since they had been able to wash properly.

Father Rossi gathered all his strength. He was just twenty-four, but as one of only three priests in the camp he was looked on for leadership. The authorities also had more respect for him as a priest. He talked to the men and tried to communicate their concerns to their captors. He tried to find out what was going to happen. Were they staying in this dreadful place or were they to be transported out?

He organised the men to clean the kitchens and eating areas. Bizarrely the kitchens were manned by chefs from some of the top London hotels, the Savoy, the Piccadilly, all Italian immigrants who had also been arrested on 10 June. Now they cooked with basic ingredients to provide meagre food for their compatriots.

Most importantly, Father Rossi persuaded the authorities that he must be allowed to say Mass. After much discussion the commandant finally agreed. A makeshift altar was set up. An artist among the prisoners sketched a Holy Picture and pinned it above the altar. Father Rossi spoke to the men, thousands of them, bedraggled and destitute.

'Friends, we need to keep our faith. This is a test of our will. Our faith in God will give us strength. You'll see. This will pass. Tomorrow is 29 June, the feast of St Peter and St Paul. I have asked for permission to say Holy Mass. For those of you who would like to receive the Sacrament of Confession I will be available over in the corner.'

This was a great morale boost for them all. They hadn't heard Mass since being arrested. All gatherings were banned.

That evening, beneath the stairs in the corner of the decaying mill, with a rusty metal door separating him from the young priest, Alfonso confessed his sins.

'Bless me Father for I have sinned . . . Father, I have caused my family so much pain. I've let them down. I thought Mussolini would be the best for us all. Look at all these men here, suffering, hungry . . .' Alfonso started to weep, 'I encouraged so many of them to join the Fascio. It's my fault they are here, treated like criminals, like enemies of the country they have grown to love and respect.

'Father, my wife,' Alfonso gulped, 'my wife warned me. I was too proud to listen, too proud.'

Of the hundreds of confessions the priest had heard, here was a troubled soul, a spirit broken by self-doubt and despair. He felt compassion for the man. He remembered him from the Ferragusto picnic the year before. It was not right that this man should blame himself.

The priest paused, waiting for inspiration from the Holy Spirit, 'My son, you used the talents that God gave you. Do not blame yourself for the evil that drives men to war.

'You must take pride in the good that you have done. You must accept that God wanted you to lead and you did what you thought was right. Il Duce has betrayed your people, not you.

'*Coraggio, figlio mio*, you still have a job to do. You must have

321

courage and faith. Be strong for the other men. They will still need you in the trials to come. You are still their leader.

'I absolve you of all your sins . . .

'*Ego te absolvo ab omnibus peccatis vestris* . . .'

Alfonso walked away past the line of men waiting for confession, visibly moved. Looking at each of them, poor souls, abandoned, weakened and frightened, he felt his courage rise in his soul. The priest was right. The Holy Spirit would guide him. This was the true test of his leadership. He had to sacrifice his own pain and give his all to his friends.

He never did hear Mass the next day. In the morning, Alfonso and many of the men who had arrived with him were told to collect their belongings to prepare to leave. At roll-call as the guards called out their numbers each man stepped forward. Without regret, they marched away from the horror of the Mills.

Alfonso walked with Emidio.

'Where are we going now?'

'I've heard rumours we're being deported. That'll be a joke, Alfonso. I'm just back in the country and they're sending me away again.

'It can only be better than that place. I feel sorry for anyone left here, even for another day.'

Farther Rossi had volunteered to go with the men. He stood waiting with his own small suitcase but was not allowed to go. He watched more than two hundred men leave with a heavy heart, fearful for them all.

The spaces left behind were soon filled by more trainloads of prisoners, including one that had Johnny on board. He had spent the last ten days in the camp at Penicuik and was now to experience the Mills. He was distraught with worry about his father and brother. He too had had no news and was with a group of younger Italian men from all over Scotland. They had all been born in Italy.

The prisoners had to fend for themselves so he had taken a job in the kitchen, hoping he could find his family during meal times. When he was transported out, he had hidden a lump of cheese in his pocket, desperately thinking that he would be able to give it to his father when he saw him.

Arriving in Warth Mills, the soldiers stopped each man.

'Name?'

'Category?'

By now they all knew under which legislation they were being held.

'Category A.' Johnny, the twenty-year-old ice cream barrow pusher from Cockenzie, was classed as a 'dangerous enemy alien' and was to be interned for the duration of the war.

'Empty your pockets.'

Johnny pulled the lump of cheese from his pocket. Having had only bread and jam since the early morning, he had been starving on the journey. The cheese had sweated in his pocket, enticing him constantly to eat it. Thinking of his father, hoping the next place he was taken to he would see him, he resisted. His father would need it more than he did.

The soldier took the cheese, looked at it disgusted and without a thought threw it in a bucket.

Johnny burst into tears, ashamed at his reaction. He'd hidden that cheese for two days to give to his father. It was as if the soldier was throwing away his last chance of finding him.

Day after day he walked round the camp asking anyone he recognised for news. No one knew anything. No one had seen any of the Edinburgh Italians. Eventually he met up with the young priest he had seen at the picnic the year before. He asked him if he had seen his father.

Father Rossi recognised Johnny.

'Johnny, I can't tell you for sure. I don't know if your father was among them, but a lot of older men from Edinburgh and Glasgow left last Sunday. I know Alfonso Crolla was among them. Would your father have been with him?'

'Yes, that's Zio Alfonso. He must have been with him.' Johnny felt an enormous relief. Here at last was some evidence. 'Father, do you know where they were going?'

'God will give them strength. Anywhere's better than here, so don't worry.'

The young priest didn't realise how wrong he was.

The train had disembarked the men at Riverside Station. Alfonso, Cesidio, his brothers and his friends were marched out of the station straight to Liverpool Docks.

In front of them towered a 15,000-ton liner of the Blue Star Line, the magnificent *Arandora Star*. A luxury liner that had sailed the Mediterranean hosting luxury cruises for the rich and famous, its lavish fittings had been ripped out, its holds fitted out with crude metal bunks and its sparkling white paintwork hastily camouflaged in grey.

A 4.7-inch cannon and a 120-lb anti-aircraft gun decorated its decks along with barbed wire and a swastika menacingly painted on its funnel.

Directed by armed soldiers, the men climbed the gangplank, each calling out their name and prisoner number.

'My God! It's a sailing boat.' Giovanni had seen ships like this before. 'They're not taking us to the Isle of Man. They're deporting us.'

'What do you mean?' Emidio was confused.

'We're going to Canada. Look.' Giovanni pointed at a partially hidden sign on the wall, Canada Wharf.

They were directed to cabins on A deck, one of the lower decks of the ship. Their allocated cabins held four or six to a room. When the cabins were full, more Italians took mattresses that were laid out in the stunning mirrored ballroom nearer the top decks. There were 734 Italians in all.

There were toilets and shower rooms but when the men ran the water it dripped out brown and filthy.

It was sweltering. They made their way back on to the deck for air. They watched as more prisoners were embarking, Germans this time, some in uniform, some in civilian clothes. Some were rowdy, confident, happy to be leaving British shores. Others were bedraggled and despondent like the Italians. They made a sorry sight. Piles of discarded luggage lined the quayside; one light suitcase per person was the maximum baggage allowed.

Armed British soldiers aggressively kept the men in line. Any arguments were quickly subdued.

Further along the docks they saw rows of more men climbing the gangplank onto another similar ship. They tried to see if they could recognise any one but they were too far away. Little did they know that hundreds of their sons and nephews were boarding that ship, the *Ettrick*, including Alfonso's son Domenico.

Gradually Alfonso and his compatriots moved to the starboard side of the ship, away from the dock. The sight of the alighting passengers was too oppressive. It was a warm sunny evening. The sea was calm. If it wasn't for their circumstances this journey would be an adventure.

Alfonso saw the barriers on the deck.

'What's the barbed wire for? Do they think we're going to jump overboard?'

They looked down into the sea, a hundred feet down.

'None of us can swim. None of us is likely to try to escape!' Achille was sarcastic. They had been ground into submission, accepting the path that fate was taking them.

They all gathered together: Alfonso, Giovanni, Emidio, Achille, Cesidio, his brother Louis and his son Harry, Benny and Donato. They'd shared a lot together in these last few weeks. They looked around. Scores of their friends from Edinburgh and countless relatives and customers from all over Scotland were milling around. There were hundreds of them. They talked about their wives and families, all broken-hearted that they were being taken away from them like this. They bitterly regretted not having been given the chance to say goodbye. Their fierce independence and self-sufficiency had been stripped from them, leaving them for the first time in their lives out of control of their own fate. Their self-respect had been taken from them.

Cesidio was really distressed.

'Why will they not let us just contact our families? I can't bear to think of them still worrying about where we are. I can't bear to leave them.'

Giovanni tried to console him. He put his arm around the younger man.

They had heard that some men had been given a card to fill in to send a message home. None of them had been given that chance.

They stood quietly, thinking about what they were leaving behind. Alfonso shook his head in disbelief about what was happening to them.

The noise of the anchor being lifted roused him from his thoughts. The rattling, clanking noise sounded dangerous and sinister. The horn sounded twice. This was it. He breathed deeply, trying to control his fear.

A seagull called above their heads. He remembered the last time he stood on a deck with his brother, many years ago. He started to laugh.

'Boys, you won't believe this. The last time Emidio and I were on a ship was twenty-seven years ago, crossing from Calais to Dover. Do you remember, Emidio? We didn't have two pennies to rub together, we looked like tramps and we were feeling nervous about the British authorities, even then!'

Emidio laughed. He had almost forgotten.

'Lads, you should have seen him! He made a great fuss at the desk and the poor immigration officer didn't know what had hit him!'

'Yes, and you picked up that lovely young girl!' Alfonso slapped his brother's back. Emidio pushed his hair back from his brow and shrugged his shoulders.

'Well, you know, the girls have always had a thing for me. I can't help it.'

Giovanni wanted to hear more:

'So what happened?'

'Even though we had nothing, Alfonso insisted we travelled first class and we got a straight run through immigration!'

'Typical, Alfonso . . . always above himself.' Giovanni looked with affection on his brother. He'd always admired Alfonso's imagination, his desire to do things better, his drive to be the best.

Emidio was enjoying the story.

'Alfonso, do you remember you wanted to look like the fancy businessmen with their pin-striped suits and their umbrellas in the sunshine. You put a handkerchief in your top pocket so that you could look the part?'

'It's that why you always wear that handkerchief?' Giovanni laughed.

'Alfonso, I think you've cracked it!' Cesidio took a step back. The fresh air, blue skies and relief from knowing at last where they were going was lifting their spirits.

'Look at you, *guaglione*, poor boy.' He gestured to Alfonso. 'May I present Cavaliere Alfonso Crolla, businessman and entrepreneur!'

326

Alfonso puffed out his chest, removed his hat and bowed with a flourish.

'At your service, my friends.' The middle-aged man standing before them was dressed in torn, grease-stained trousers and a tattered jacket. His waistcoat hung loosely around his middle. He had lost about a stone in weight. His white shirt was dirty grey and his collar frayed and filthy. His hat was bashed and ripped but his top pocket still sported a not so fetching, not so white linen handkerchief.

He looked like a tramp.

'A first-class passenger if ever I saw one!' Cesidio bowed in return.

They all burst out laughing and in mock salute raised imaginary glasses.

'*Salute!* Cavaliere Alfonso Crolla!'

'Alfonso!' They all cheered.

The armed guards looked over and shook their heads. These Italians had no self-control. The guards were not looking forward to the journey. They'd soon wipe those smiles off their faces.

Just at that moment, young Harry ran forward looking for his father.

'Dad, come on. They're serving tea in the ballroom!'

'What's for dinner, Harry? Did you see?' Alfonso was starving.

'Two sausages on a tin plate and a cup of tea!'

'Well, what about that! *Salsiccie!* Couldn't be better!'

31

3 July 1940: It was now twenty-three days since Alfonso and Domenico had been arrested; endless agonising days without a word of where they were.

Not knowing was agony. Constantly worrying and hoping, jumping at every knock at the door, every ring of the telephone, scouring every newspaper, waiting for every delivery of post.

Twenty-three days and twenty-three nights.

Unable to sleep, Maria had lain awake night after night, weeping with despair. Her mind raced, her emotions ran from anger and fury to waves of panic and sheer terror.

For the third time in her life, Alfonso had left her. Three times she had watched him walk away and three times she had been overcome with despair. Again and again she traced the details in her mind.

She remembered when he had first left Fontitune that early spring morning. Now it seemed like a lifetime away. Domenico was just a baby. When she had called, Alfonso had turned from far away down the hill, had waved and called back.

She remembered when, handsome in his olive green uniform, he had marched past her at the war parade in Glasgow. He had looked at her with his beautiful eyes, happy and proud that he was going to defend his country. She had stood waving and crying, left alone with two children in a foreign country.

Now she wished she could forget the details of the night he was taken. Every tiny detail crowded her mind: the knock on the door, Alfonso sitting on the bed pulling on his socks, Olivia sorting his handkerchief.

She remembered that he had walked down the stairs without looking back. She so wished that he had, that he had looked round again and waved, that she had seen his precious face just one more time.

Sometimes she would fall into a deep sleep and awake as if in his arms. For a split second, suspended on the edge of consciousness, she was with him again. For a delicious moment he was holding her, whispering in her ear, stroking her hair. It was almost as if, wherever he was, he was willing himself to be with her, willing her to know that he was safe and alive.

Then, one morning, without warning, the morning of the 2nd of July, the dream had changed into a nightmare. In a cold sweat, choking and gasping for breath, she felt real terror gripping her. As clear as anything, she heard Alfonso call. She heard his voice; she heard him call her name. She awoke with a fright. She was sure she saw him. She stretched out her arms to him. She opened her eyes. There was no one there. He had gone.

Marietta and the girls had been allowed to visit Alex. Walking through the gates at Saughton, they felt confused. How could it be that he was in prison? Alex was overwhelmed by everything that had happened. He asked about his father all the time. What had they heard? Was there no news? He asked for Johnny. He wondered why his brother hadn't visited him. They had to tell him that his brother had been arrested as well and that they didn't know where he was Alex had heard rumours in the prison. Vittorio had told him that Domenico had been arrested. He had hoped his brother had been lucky.

The girls slept with their mother, trying to comfort her. The interminable waiting was wearing her down.

Anna was working in the shop. Lena rushed in waving the newspaper.

'A ship's gone down off the west coast of Ireland! It says it had Italians on board: a lot of Italians.'

Anna grabbed the newspaper. She read the report over and over again.

'The *Arandora Star* was torpedoed in the early hours of Tuesday morning. Enemy aliens are being transferred to Canada for internment; Italian males on board. Actual numbers missing not yet known.'

The report said hundreds had drowned. Lifeboats had been spotted by a Coastal Command Sunderland Flying boat in the early hours of the morning. The survivors had clung to scraps of wood for eight hours in the Atlantic.

Anna didn't want to believe any of it. This was a mistake. This could have nothing to do with her father. She began to cry. She looked at the Lena.

'It has nothing to do with Dad; they took him away in a car, not on a ship.'

'Anna, look at this.' At the bottom of the page Lena ran her finger along a sentence. Anna read it again and again. The report was from a survivor.

'I felt sorry for the poor Italians, whose average age must have been about 60. They did not know what to do, and many of them hung on to the ship for dear life.'

Anna fainted.

On Thursday evening the disaster was broadcast to the nation. In Glasgow Maria and her daughters listened to the BBC radio news bulletin at nine p.m. It confirmed the rumours that they had heard flying round the Italian community. The *Arandora Star* had been travelling to Canada to deport internees. It had sunk within half an hour of a torpedo strike, with a massive loss of life.

Rumours circulated that survivors had landed in Greenock on Wednesday. Newspaper reports showed a group of British survivors, some of the soldiers who had been on board guarding the prisoners. There must have been Italian survivors as well.

Maria was traumatised. Could Alfonso or Domenico have been on board? And Tony. Margherita still didn't know where her husband was. If they were on board could they have survived?

Olivia managed to get through on the telephone to Anna.

'What have you heard, Anna? Do you know anything?'

'Olivia, it says in the paper more than four hundred Italians are lost. I keep thinking my father couldn't swim. He couldn't swim.'

Olivia hadn't thought about that. She didn't want to think about that.

'We don't even know if they were on board. We don't know. We mustn't think the worst.'

'How can we think anything else?'

The report in the *Edinburgh Evening News* that night shocked them all. It said that the prisoners had panicked and fought among themselves, that the Germans had pushed the Italians aside. That they had caused increased fatalities because of their cowardice.

When the women heard about this they wept. Surely their husbands and sons couldn't have been on board. They would not have behaved like that.

Finally on Friday, the Brazilian Consul in Glasgow issued a list of survivors, a list of the eight hundred or so men brought ashore in Greenock. A phone number was listed for relatives looking for information.

Italian women all over Scotland were frantically trying to get through. After trying for what seemed like hundreds of times, Anna eventually got through. The woman on the end of the phone sounded distressed.

'Can you spell the name please.'

'D . . . i . . . C . . . iacca' Anna's voice shook.

'Yes Di Ciacca survived. I have a Di Ciacca on the list.'

Anna's heart was thumping. She took a deep breath to stop herself panicking.

'Do you . . . do you have the first name? The initial?' Was it her father or her brother? Anna knew Uncle Louis and his son Harry were missing as well, and many other Di Ciaccas, all her uncles and cousins.

'L . . .' The woman hesitated. 'Yes, Louis. Louis Di Ciacca. That's all just now.'

'What about C? C for Charlie? Or J for Johnny? Please check. How about G then, G for Giovanni. My brother is called Johnny and Giovanni.'

'No, sorry, my dear. Nothing on this list. This is the survivors' list. There's nothing else on it'

Anna phoned again the next day. The lists of those missing had been released.

Another voice answered the phone.

'Yes, I have two Di Ciaccas listed as missing.'

Anna held her breath. Was Johnny on the boat with his father? Is that where he was?

'Aristide Di Ciacca.'

That was Anna's young cousin, Harry, Uncle Louis's son. Harry had drowned. Anna drew in a sharp breath, shocked. He was just her age.

She didn't hear what the voice said next.

'Hello. Hello. Are you still there?'

Anna shivered. 'Sorry, sorry. I'm here. Can you repeat that, please.' She could hardly breathe.

'C. Di Ciacca. Yes I can confirm, C . . . e . . . s . . . i . . . d . . . i . . . o Di Ciacca is listed missing.'

Anna couldn't think. Tears rolled down her face.

'Yes. Yes. That's my father.' Irrational relief swept over her. At last she'd found her father. 'Is he all right? Is he safe?'

Her voice was trembling, odd.

'No, I am sorry, my dear.' The voice on the other end of the phone was full of compassion. 'He is reported missing, presumed drowned.'

Anna dropped the phone.

Marietta and Lena had been standing transfixed, listening. Neither said a word.

In Glasgow, Margherita and Olivia went to the Brazilian Consul to find out for themselves. They set off, leaving Gloria and Filomena with their mother.

'Gloria, stay by the telephone. Answer it for mother if it rings. Can you do that? Will you be all right?' Olivia didn't want to leave her younger sisters alone.

'Yes, we'll be fine.'

Later on the telephone did ring.

Gloria answered it and, hearing one of her cousins, passed it to her mother.

'Zia Maria. I've been to the Brazilian Consulate. My brothers and father are safe. I saw A. Crolla on the list. Zio Alfonso must be safe. Zio Alfonso is safe.'

This time Maria collapsed on the floor.

She gulped, trying to get the words to escape from her throat. She put her hand on her chest.

'He's safe. He's safe. Alfonso is safe.'

'What about Domenico? Did you see anything about Domenico?'

'No, Zia. I saw Emidio and Giovanni Crolla on the list.'

'Thank God. Who else? Can you remember? Who else?'

'I can't remember. There were about 250 names. Survivors. I can't remember.' The young girl started to cry. She was confused. It was all so confusing.

Maria sat all afternoon with Gloria and Filomena and waited for the girls to get back. She was worried about Domenico. Had he been with his father? Why had his name not been on the list? But at least she knew Alfonso was safe. And Giovanni and Emidio. My God, it was all their men who had been on that ship. The enormity of it started to dawn on her.

There was pandemonium in the Brazilian Consular Office. It seemed to Margherita as if every woman or girl who had been at her wedding a few months earlier was here in the room. The poor women were distraught. Some were screaming with grief, some collapsed on the floor, some had good news and left quietly, overwhelmed with guilt.

Eventually they got a chance to squeeze through the crowd and look at the list. There were so many names, so many names: pages and pages of names of Italians who had drowned. The newspaper reports had been right. There *were* over 450 Italians missing. It had been a disaster.

It was late when they left to go home. They were afraid that they wouldn't get back before the enforced curfew.

Anxiously Gloria watched at the window, pulling aside the blackout curtain, ears alert for any sound. Eventually she saw the girls at the end of the street. She opened the door and rushed excited to the end of the garden.

'We know, we know. Papà's all right. We know.' As she put her arms out to embrace her sister, she stopped. She looked at Olivia. Her face was red and swollen with crying. 'What? What?' Gloria knew something was wrong.

Maria was at the door. She looked at Margherita. Neither woman said a word.

Margherita walked forward and put her arms round her mother and held her tight. Very tight. Without a word between them, Maria understood.

The message from her niece had been wrong. It was Achille Crolla who had survived, not Alfonso.

Maria screamed. This was what she had been afraid of all her life.

Edinburgh

6 April 1947

The Easter Services were always Maria's favourite. The week-long celebrations of the Lord's Death and Resurrection acted as a balm for her tortured spirit. She gradually came to terms with the loss of her husband.

Her brothers-in-law, Giovanni and Emidio, were waiting for her and her family at the back of the church. They had been among the lucky ones. They had survived the sinking of the *Arandora Star*, hanging on for eight hours in the freezing water, hearing the voices around them, praying to the Madonna and calling for their mothers, gradually fading into oblivion. Of the 734 Italians on board, 486 had been lost.

After their rescue, the brothers, along with about 200 other survivors, had been indiscriminately transferred, without even a change of clothes, back to the dreaded Warth Mills. They had still not had any contact with their families since they had been arrested on 10 June, apart from a card on which they had been told to write their address and the words 'I am alive'. By now the frenzy of hatred against the Italians in Britain had reached fever pitch and, instead of being treated with compassion after their horrific ordeal, they had been punched and kicked and their remaining belongings stolen. They had then been deported yet again, this time on the *Dunera*, bound for Australia. The conditions on the journey had been unspeakable, fifty-five torturous days in which the men endured hunger, illness, beatings and suicides. After four years of forced internment in Australia, they had eventually been transported back to Edinburgh to take up their lives once more. After the war many soldiers had been court-martialled because of their maltreatment of the internees.

Coming out of the church the men greeted their relations. Giovanni handed Vittorio a parcel wrapped in jute sacking.

'*Buona Pasqua, Vittorio. Ecco.* Can you believe it? A *pacco* from Fontitune!'

'*Grazie, Zio Giovanni!*' Vittorio was excited. 'Who is it from? Is there any news? Is there a letter?'

Giovanni gave Vittorio an envelope.

'It's from Pietro. Read it to your mother later.' He shook his head. '*La guerra, la guerra!* All my life, Vittorio, I've seen war and destruction and, believe me, it's no answer to anything.'

Both Giovanni and Emidio had aged. They were thin, with greying hair, but still determined and strong. Only their eyes reflected the deep sadness they had lived through. They were aware of their responsibility for their poor brother's widow and her family.

Giovanni kissed his sister-in-law. She was an old woman now, her hair grey, her face wrinkled and lined, the strain of her loss etched on her face.

'*Maria, Tutt'a posto?* Is there anything you need?'

'*No, grazie, Giovanni. Grazie.*' She always felt comforted when she saw Giovanni. When he had first returned from Australia he had sat with her for a long time and talked to her about Alfonso.

Vittorio wanted to get home. He was itching to open the *pacco* and read the letter.

'*Iami!* Mamma. Come on. Let's get home. I'm starving!'

At home in Brunton Place, Olivia was in the kitchen, rolling out some fresh pasta. She had flour all over her apron. The table was set, some spring primroses decorating the centre. She had the radio on. The Italian station was broadcasting Gigli.

Olivia could hear her youngest sister laughing from the bottom of the stair. She was such a tonic, Filomena, always full of fun; she swept into the kitchen followed by her mother and Gloria.

'Where are the boys? I don't want to cook the pasta until they arrive.'

'Olivia, my darling, here I am.' Vittorio came in behind his mother, kissing his sister. 'That smells good. Look!' He put the *pacco* on the table. 'Our first *pacco* from Fontitune in seven years!'

They stood and waited as Vittorio cut through the string with a sharp knife. The familiar pungent smell of pecorino and *salsiccie* filled the kitchen. They looked at each other incredulous. It

Gloria, Olivia, Domenico, Maria, Vittorio, Filomena c. 1947

was just the same. Exactly the same! Maria blessed herself.

'*Grazie a Dio!* Thank God. Smell the cheese, Filomena. Do you remember it? Do you remember when we opened the *pacco* like this with Papà?'

'Mamma, there's a letter from Pietro.'

Maria sat down at the kitchen table. She took a deep breath.

'Read it, please, Vittorio.'

The girls sat down as well, preparing themselves for the news. 'Read it.'

'*Carissima Maria, Carissima famiglia,*' Vittorio began.

Maria put her hand over her mouth. Gloria put her arms round her mother. Thinking about their family brought all the emotions of the last years rushing to the surface.

'I have heard the terrible news of the death of my brother. God Rest his Soul.' Vittorio's voice broke. Tears fell from his eyes, blotting the ink on the blue paper. Olivia took the letter gently from him. She continued.

'We too have suffered in this terrible war. In the beginning our young men were all called up to fight. They had no stomach for it. They had no desire to fight, least of all against our Allies in the

Italian men interned on the Isle of Man 1942

last war. But they went. They did their duty for their country, although many never returned.

'Picinisco was used as a *confine libero*; many enemies of the regime were confined here high in the mountains. Life was hard, but we are used to hard times, aren't we? We know how to cope.

'But from September 1943, when Italy surrendered and Il Duce fell, it was our turn to suffer. Overnight the Germans became our enemies.

'Fontitune and many small villages along the *tratturi* lay on their line of defence, the Gustav Line. We were right in the path of the battles to defend Rome from the advancing armies.

'The German soldiers descended on us. They confiscated everything: sheep, cattle, wine, cheese.

'Many poor people hid in the mountains, terrified. We helped them where we could.

'The winter was cold. Very cold. The war came closer and closer. For miles around the ground was ripped up with shells. We saw hidden anti-tank guns blow the bodies of the advancing soldiers apart. Unexploded mines and barbed wire littered our beautiful mountain, all the way from Cassino to Frosinone. Air bombardments shook the mountains. Night after night we heard the bombs. We witnessed evil in its death throes.

'Then, in February, just after the Feast of Sant'Antonio, the Gestapo came to Fontitune in ugly trucks and took us all away.'

'*Oh, Dio!*' Olivia stopped reading. She put the letter down on the table. She was shocked to the core. Filomena took the letter and scanned the words.

'My God!'

Vittorio was shocked.

'I hadn't realised they were so vulnerable. When I was in the camps I used to wish we had never left Italy. I thought it would have been safer for us all there.' He shrugged his shoulders. 'It's just war. Normality disappears and luck decides your fate.'

'What else does Zio Pietro say?' Gloria wanted to know what happened. 'Give me the letter.'

She took the letter from her sister and continued.

'*Non ti preoccupari,* my dear family. We have survived. Thank God, we have survived. By the end of the spring the Allies had taken Monte Cassino and had advanced along the mountains, eventually freeing us from our captors. Although many perished, we managed to build a false wall in a back room behind which we hid our men and saved them from capture.

'But cherish only this thought. The Italian Arditi fought with the British soldiers again, once more we were Allies.'

They all looked at each other with tears in their eyes. It was almost as if their father was talking to them through the voice of his brother.

Gloria continued.

'Believe me when I tell you, after the fighting was over, Picinisco was once again full of laughter and singing. The Allied soldiers were surprised and delighted that here, in the heart of the Italian mountains, in a remote village that their trucks took half an hour to climb up to, there were people who had lived and worked in Britain! The piazza was full of British and Americans and we all understood each other!'

At this they all burst out laughing. Maria took her daughter's hand and squeezed it.

Vittorio had some more news for the family.

'Mamma, the lawyer came to the shop yesterday. Papà's papers have finally been released. Everything can be sorted out once and for all.'

'Good, Vittorio. Good.' Maria was quiet, 'Thank God. I know your father would have been proud of you all.'

Olivia had worked with Filomena all through the war, trying to keep the shop in Elm Row trading while their brothers had been interned: Vittorio on the Isle of Man, Domenico in Canada.

During the war Miss Dennison had taken on the responsibility of running the company. Astutely she had recognised that all the Italian businesses that had been destroyed now had to be refurbished, so Valvona & Crolla became a supplier of manufacturing equipment for ice cream and fish fryers. As the Italians gradually returned to their shops, she was at hand to help them get set up in business again.

Vittorio never wanted to dwell on the past.

'Good. Enough of the past. Olivia, what's for lunch?'

'Home-made pasta with *sugo*. I've made it with *polpettini*.'

Rationing was still in force. Even now, three years after the war ended, food was scarce.

'Gloria, did you make the pudding?' In the camps they used to dream of Gloria's cakes.

'Yes. I've made my rhubarb pie, and Filomena is going to get ice cream from Easter Road.'

'The boys, the boys!' Vittorio was starving.

They heard a commotion in the stair.

'That'll be Domenico now.' Olivia went straight to the kitchen.

The door flew open and in burst Domenico, laughing and joking, followed by two young lads, complete strangers.

'Ma, I met these German boys outside the Cathedral. They're working on the roads, digging the drains. They don't have any family here. I've invited them for lunch.'

Vittorio looked at his mother; typical Domenico, mad as a hatter. Oh well, never mind. There was plenty of food to go round.

'Sit down, my friends. Sit down. You are welcome in our home.'

Olivia went into the kitchen with her mother.

'Trust Domenico, Mamma. He'll never change.'

In the afternoon, the mesmerised German boys left, bowing gratefully for the hospitality they had been shown and shaking Domenico's and Vittorio's hands as if they would never let them go.

Domenico came into the kitchen as Olivia and Filomena finished washing the dishes. Maria was sitting at the table, looking again at the parcel from Italy.

'Come on, everyone, it's such a lovely afternoon. Let's go for a drive down to Cockenzie.'

'That's a great idea, Domenico. I'll take some cheese and *salsiccie* to Marietta.'

It was well past five o'clock by the time the old black Ford drew up outside the Cockenzie Café. It was a beautiful spring evening, still bright, the sun reflecting red and orange on the clouds. The sea air was fresh and a little chilly.

Three ice cream tricycles were lined up outside the front of the shop. Johnny and Alex were standing outside, dressed in their white cotton coats, open necked, with their sleeves rolled up. They had had a very busy day, selling out to the hoards of day trippers that had taken advantage of the sunny weather.

Johnny had seen the car approaching and raised his hand in salute.

'Happy Easter! Happy Easter!' He called to his mother and sisters.

'Mum! Anna! Look who's here!'

The women came out from the shop. They had been busy making ice cream all through the day.

Marietta looked far older than her years. She was happy to see Maria. The two women embraced.

Italian internee football team Isle of Man c. 1943. Johnny back row, fourth from left

'*Buona Pasqua, compare*. Come in, I was just making a cup of tea.'

Arm in arm the two widows went through to the back shop.

Outside, the young ones greeted each other and chatted together animatedly. They were firm friends, their common hardships bringing them closer together. Only Lena had married; she was living in Glasgow like Margherita, whose husband, Tony, had spent the first four years of their marriage on the Isle of Man.

Alex stood a bit apart. After six months or so in Saughton he had been released along with Eduardo Paolozzi and Ernie Capaldi, all of whose fathers had also perished on the ship. As soon as he had come of age he had volunteered to join the RAF and spent the war in Burmah and India, driving trucks for the British. This courageous act of solidarity for his country of birth underlined his family's commitment to making a life in Scotland.

They all laughed and joked, planning to organise the next Alva Glen picnic, which had not taken place for almost ten years. Young and fit, they had all begun to look to the future and try to leave the past behind them.

Anna acted as hostess.

'Come on, what would you like? Tea or an iced drink.'

Johnny spoke enthusiastically, genuinely pleased to see his friends. 'As soon as the chip shop opens we'll all have a fish supper! You can't beat it!'

Olivia remembered the *pacco* in the car. She took it into the shop. Nothing in the shop had changed. It was just as she always remembered it. She kissed Margaret, who was working behind the counter. She had worked loyally with the family through all the troubles.

'Oh, Olivia, how lovely to see you. Things are fine, the boys are back home and Anna is here with me in the shop.'

'Zia Marietta, here is some pecorino and *salsiccie* from Fontitune.'

'How wonderful. Margaret, come and taste this cheese. You'll remember Alfonso used to bring it for us.'

As Olivia unwrapped the cheese she noticed a picture on one of the sheets of newspaper. She pushed the cheese aside and spread the newspaper on the table. The date on the newspaper was 28 April 1945.

Alex in RAF uniform c. 1942

Johnny, c. 1946, after release from the Isle of Man

Olivia smoothed out the crumpled stained paper. Half the page displayed a gruesome picture of six dead men tied by their feet from metal girders. A woman hung among them, her skirt tied at her knees. Their arms hung below their heads, loose and helpless.

Soldiers and armed men stood underneath the corpses, where a crowd was gathered. The people looked angry and jeering, throwing things at the bodies.

Olivia read out the headline: '*Il Duce è morto!*'

'What does that mean, Olivia?' Margaret didn't understand.

'It's a picture of Mussolini. They shot him and hung him up from a meat hook in a garage in Milan.

Olivia was silent. She thought of her father. Nothing made sense in her life. She started to cry.

Maria looked at Marietta. The older woman raised her eyebrows and, lifting her chin a little, skimmed her right hand under her chin. This man had been responsible for devastating both their families, with the loss of millions of lives in a wave of destruction he had created which had swept them all along in its path.

Neither woman had any pity.

'*Non c'è niente da fare! È finito!*'

The boys came through from the front shop.

'We're going to the Thorntree for a beer.' Johhny wanted to relax with his friends.

Vittorio saw his sister crying. He lifted the paper and, seeing the picture, screwed it up.

'Olivia, don't waste your time looking back. It's all over. Finished.' He tried to distract his sister. He pulled a piece of paper from his pocket. He had been writing an advert to put in the paper. The writing was scored through.

'Look. I'm going to put an advert in the *Scotsman*. Never mind all that old news. I'm going to create the news.'

Johnny was intrigued. 'Read it then.'

Vittorio cleared his throat.

'A Complaint!'

They all laughed. What was Vittorio up to now?

'Listen!. . . A Complaint. We often hear that it is too expensive to drink wine with food as is done abroad.' He looked up, making sure they were all paying attention. 'Our reply is to offer "Good

Bordeaux Wine, both Red (Dry) and White (Medium Sweet) at 6/6 per bottle. Valvona & Crolla Ltd., 19, Elm Row."'

'There! Between that and the *salsiccie* from Fontitune the Scots won't know what's hit them. The boys the boys! It couldn't be better!'

Olivia Crolla c. 1947

Acknowledgments

This book is inspired by oral history, some passed by word of mouth through generations, some recorded on tape or written in letters and articles. Over time, memories are blurred. Some reports highlight differing experiences. I have endeavoured to confirm and cross reference as many details as possible. I am aware that other versions of this story will be known in other families. Many official files of this time are still closed. At the time of the disaster it was officially recognised that mistakes were made, though no apology was ever issued.

Thank you and all my love to my family, Marietta Di Ciacca (deceased), Johnny Di Ciacca (deceased), Alex Di Ciacca, Anna Di Ciacca, Cesidio Di Ciacca, Gertrude Di Ciacca and Margaret Davidson. Also to Vittorio Crolla (deceased), Olivia Contini (née Crolla), Gloria Crolla, Domenico Crolla (deceased) and Pierina Crolla. They have all supported me and encouraged me in the telling of this story, bravely talking about a time that was so painful for them and affected all their lives.

My love and thanks to Joe Pia (deceased), Desiderio Coppola, Addolorata Harris (née Valente) and Ines Craig and to the memories of all the Italian immigrant families who made their lives in Scotland. This story is a celebration of their heritage.

Thanks to the inspiration from so many professionals who encourage me, advise me and allow me the luxury of writing this book, all of whom have known me and Valvona & Crolla for years. Special thanks to Jenny Brown, my agent, and Giles Gordon (deceased), to Jamie Byng, an inspirational publisher, Helen Bleck, Jenny Todd, Jenny Vass, Jo Hardacre, David Graham and all at Canongate, and especially for the careful and gentle advice from Mairi Sutherland, who edited my work with kid gloves! Thanks also to Ian Begg, who drew the maps and the family tree and Russell Walker, who meticulously proof-read the book. My love to Sophie Dow and Charlie Fletcher and to Pru Irvine and Fiona McIntyre who both pushed me to write a long time ago!

I have had a passion to record this story all my life. I have lived the dreams of Cesidio and Alfonso, working first in the shops in Cockenzie and then in Valvona & Crolla. It is a wonderful privilege to have worked with and known so many colleagues and customers who have helped create, enjoy and maintain the vision of those early immigrants.

And most importantly my true love to my husband and mentor, Philip, and my two daughters, dear Francesca and dear Olivia.

Mary Contini, Edinburgh, 2006

Further reading

Angus Calder, *The People's War Britain 1939–45*, Jonathan Cape, 1969

Michael Cant, *Edinburgh Shops Past and Present*, Malcolm Cant Publications, 2005

Winston Churchill, *Their Finest Hour*, Penguin, 2005 [Cassell, 1949]

Helen Clark and Elizabeth Carnegie, *She Was Aye Workin'*, White Cockade, 2003

Terri Colpi, *The Italian Factor*, Mainstream, 1991

Lt Edward H. Dalton, John Neale and Baron Dalton, *With British Guns in Italy*, Methuen & Co, 1919

David Forgacs (ed), *Rethinking Italian Fascism*, Lawrence and Wishart, 1986

Count Ciano Galeazzo, *Ciano's Diary 1937–1943*, William Heinemann, 1947

Peter and Leni Gillman, *Collar the Lot*, Quartet, 1980

Des Hickey and Gus Smith, *Star of Shame*, Madison, 1989

D. H. Lawrence, *The Lost Girl*, Thomas Seltzer, 1921 [Martin Secker, 1920]

Patrick McVeigh, *Look After the Bairns*, Tuckwell Press, 1999

Svetlana Palmer and Sarah Wallis, *A War in Words*, Pocket Books, 2003

Angelo Pirocchi, *Italian Arditi*, Osprey, 2004

Rev. Msgr Gaetano Rossi, *Memories of 1940*, University of Glasgow, 1991